W9-CNI-662

*Picasso and Company*

BOOKS BY BRASSAÏ

Fiction

*Histoire de Marie*

Non-fiction

*Graffiti*
*Picasso and Company* (*Conversations avec Picasso*)

Books of Photographs

*Paris de Nuit*
*Voluptés de Paris*
*Camera in Paris*
*Les Sculptures de Picasso* (Text by D.-H. Kahnweiler)
*Brassaï*
*Séville en Fête* (Text by Henry de Montherlant with Brassaï)
*Trente dessins* (With a poem by Jacques Prévert)

Pour mon ami Brassai
Paris 27/IIIII 47

Brassaï

# Picasso and Company

TRANSLATED FROM THE FRENCH
BY FRANCIS PRICE

Preface by Henry Miller

Introduction by Roland Penrose

With photographs by the author

*1966*
*Doubleday & Company, Inc., Garden City, New York*

*The days and dates as given in the text are the author's.*

This book was published in France
by Éditions Gallimard in 1964
as *Conversations avec Picasso*

Library of Congress Catalog Card Number 66–24331

Printed in the United States of America
First Edition

TO PICASSO
for his
eighty-third birthday
this bouquet
of remembered moments
from the rich harvest of his hours

# PREFACE

When I first met Brassaï, in 1930, he had not yet established himself as a photographer. He had been a painter and was eking out a living (in Paris) writing for Hungarian newspapers. It was his eyes which I first noticed upon being introduced to him by our mutual friend Alfred Perlès. ("The Eye of Paris" I dubbed him a little later.) His eyes were unusual, not only in a physical sense, but for the impression they conveyed of an uncanny ability to take in everything at once. There was another trait which I also sensed immediately, a sly humor which was at once critical and kindly. One might almost refer to it as malicious benevolence.

And then there was the story teller. One felt that he was compelled to relate, down to the last detail, the marvels which his eyes had just taken in. I say "marvels" because he was able to read into the humblest object, person, or incident things which no one else would have noticed. He did not go out of his way to choose striking or exotic subjects; he could talk about pebbles on the beach with the same fascination as he could discourse on his beloved Goethe or St. Thomas Aquinas.

It came as no great surprise to me therefore when recently he announced his intention to try his hand at writing. One of the first texts he showed me was a tribute to the late Hans Reichel, a mutual friend, who died not long ago virtually unknown except to the few. Reichel was a painter (mostly of aquarelles) whose life and career could be said to have been the exact opposite of Picasso's. Having just written a tribute to Reichel myself, I was surprised and delighted to see how superior was Brassaï's text to my own.

I have long held the opinion that Van Gogh's *Letters to Theo* is a far greater work of art than all his canvases put together.

The paintings will die, are dying already, but the spirit which animates the *Letters* is undying and will give courage and inspiration to countless artists in the years to come.

I say this because in some inexplicable way it seems to me that the spirit which animates Picasso can never be fully accounted for by his work, no matter how prodigious it may be. Not that I deny the greatness of his work, but that the man himself is and will remain far greater than anything or everything which he accomplishes with his hands. He is so much more than the painter, sculptor, or whatever he may choose to be while breath is in him. He is outsized, a human phenomenon.

Throughout this book, which is like a mosaic, there are abundant passages attesting to Picasso's extraordinary awareness. Nothing seems to escape his attention. He has trenchant comments on everything, from hieroglyphs to star dust. His curiosity is matched only by his memory, which is fantastic. As for his productivity, it is exceeded only by his powers of ingestion. He not only sees and understands what is going on in this mad world, but he *foresees*. He not only gives the shape of things to come, but the feel as well. Without his presence in our midst one feels that the world would be rudderless.

Brassaï has not only given us Picasso in all his varying moods, he has given us a picture of the world he inhabited, the world of artists, writers, actors, musicians who gave it direction. All this resurrected from scraps of paper Brassaï was in the habit of consigning to a huge vase each night after his talks with Picasso. He made these notes not with the thought of future publication but because Picasso's thoughts and observations, his way of life, seemed too precious to be left to vanish in thin air. It was not until some twenty or more years later that, riffling through these scattered notes, he decided to put them in form for the world to have. A difficult task for any writer, let alone a man who had not made writing his profession. And what a temptation! A temptation, I mean, to distort his subject through flattery, adulation, criticism, or envy. Instead, he permitted Picasso to reveal himself, to draw his own portrait. No wonder that Picasso, praised and maligned as he has been all his life, was pleased on reading the book.

What figures parade through these pages! What subjects expatiated on! Leafing through the book, which I have annotated heavily, it seems to me that nothing of true consequence has been omitted from this rich period in Picasso's life. We are given portraits and thumbnail sketches of such exciting figures as Paul Éluard, Pierre Reverdy, André Breton, Henri Michaux, Man Ray, Dali, Max Jacob, MacOrlan, Braque, André Malraux, Cocteau, Sartre, Prévert, Matisse, Raymond Queneau, and many, many others of the epoch. Along with discussions about Utamaro, Goethe, Balzac, Mallarmé, Jarry, Grock, the Cirque Médrano, archaeology, the dance, death, God knows what all. Even the world to come, if one but reads between the lines. We discover that Picasso is an omnivorous reader, au courant to everything taking place in the world of letters as well as the world of art, to say nothing of the everyday world which, through Picasso's eyes, seems crazier than ever. We see him as a story teller, discover that at heart he is a dandy, that by nature he is lazy(!), that he is an inordinate collector, one who finds treasures even in the trash can. (*"Le Roi des Chiffoniers,"* Cocteau once called him.) We also discover, and most happily, that when he puts pencil to paper, or brush to canvas, Picasso himself never knows what will come of it.

And on page 236 there is this admission by the master himself which I think every aspiring artist, every one who thirsts for fame and success, should read—not once but a dozen times. "I no longer want to see new faces. Why should I? But I am always here to my friends . . . And their visits are that much more precious to me because I live in seclusion, like a prisoner. I would not wish my celebrity on anyone, not even my worst enemies. I suffer from it, physically. I protect myself as best I can. I barricade myself behind doors that are kept double locked night and day . . ."

Now a word about the photograph of Picasso opposite page 50. As Brassaï relates it, he had decided on this particular day to take but one shot of Picasso and no more. This was in the year 1932; Picasso was only fifty years old. One is tempted to say he was in his prime, but then Picasso is always in his prime, it seems. To me it is the most striking photo of the man I have ever seen, and I have seen a good many. He seems to be looking square at us, Picasso. Eye to eye. He seems even more massive than he is, what with the sweater, vest, and large double-breasted jacket. The gaze is steady, piercing, fixed. He is looking clean through the lens, through his photographer, through the very world itself. He stands there like the Rock of Gibraltar, "the master of reality" which he has always been. A man who deals with angels and demons alike, a man who has no need to talk of God, for is he not himself some sort of god, albeit human to the core? He looks us through and through, us and the crazy, miserable world we have put together. To me that look says: "Life is good and I am the living proof of it. I have nothing but my genius to sustain me. Away with your illusions and delusions! I offer you grandeur, nobility, courage, daring. I ask for no better, no higher life. I am what I do, and vice versa. Take it or leave it. Offer me a throne and I will accept. But don't ask me to say 'Thank you!' I do what I must. Not what I ought to do, not even what I would like to do. I do, that is all."

So I hear him talking to himself as he stands there facing the camera—not defiant, as he may appear to be, but just himself, the man he is, the creator he is. God be praised, say I, that such a one is still in our midst. He has made his world; we haven't even begun to make ours. One might say that the gods were good to him. But that isn't the half of it. He was good to himself. He appreciates himself. He knows who he is and what he is. *Banzai!*

If tomorrow we were to bring about that "One World" which our benighted politicians dread so much, my choice of the leader to guide it would be Picasso. I would vote for him even if he were in his dotage. Certainly, at his worst Picasso could not make more of a mess of it than the humbugs who today regard themselves as the leaders of the world. Thus far we have never had an artist at the helm. Until we do, this sad and weary world of ours will never be anything more than the ass-hole of creation, Plato to the contrary.

. . . Long live Picasso!

*Henry Miller*

## INTRODUCTION

Brassaï came to live in Paris in 1923. He was born in the small Transylvanian town of Brasov on the borders of Hungary and Roumania in 1899. The name of his birthplace appealed to him mysteriously and he adopted the Hungarian version of it as his own. After a conventional education in Budapest and the Berlin Academy of Arts he made the acquaintance of Kandinsky, Ivan Pougny, and the avant-grade "Sturm" group before attempting to make a living for himself as a journalist in France and settling finally in Montparnasse. Paris has been his home ever since and it is there that he has found the nourishment he needs to become a poet, an artist whose drawings have delighted many, including Picasso, and a keen observer of people and the strange signs by which they give clues to their most secret thoughts. But it was not till he was thirty that he began to use a medium, photography, which suited particularly well his desire to capture the subconscious sources of human behavior. It was not so much the freezing of movement in a fraction of a second that attracted him, but rather the camera's ability to record faithfully the spoor, the scent, the sign left unsuspected, the private signal, the token, the omen which lies embodied in all forms of human creation, in clothes and graffiti as well as in painting and sculpture.

He realized very early that poetry knows no frontiers and he discovered treasures in unlikely, even absurd, places. The crumbling walls of backyards in Paris have given Brassaï the opportunity to watch the growth and disappearance of graffiti left by unseen wanderers. He has discovered that they are not only drawings of peculiar merit but also "the writing on the wall," or the cryptic language closely related to the scraps of anonymous conversation overheard and patiently noted by him in the back rooms of cafés.

Henry Miller, who has known Brassaï for years and explored with him the unself-conscious eloquence of the streets, tells us that Brassaï "was always sniffing the air, always ferreting things out . . . Everything, literally everything, was interesting to him. He never criticized, never made a judgment on things or events. He related simply what he had seen or heard. 'The prototype of the photographer!'—you might say."* It was in fact the great sensitivity with which he used his camera that placed Brassaï in a very favorable position when the editors of the *Minotaure* asked him in 1932 to make an extensive photographic study of the sculpture of Picasso, and from this beginning a friendship developed which allowed him to record his observations not only photographically but as a book which carries with it his own illustrations, or one can describe it equally well as a series of plates greatly enhanced by his illuminating commentary.

Characteristically Brassaï invented his own technique. In the early days he made notes after conversations and bundled them into a box with no particular thought about their future. It was not in fact until 1960, nearly thirty years after its beginning, that he showed Picasso the box labeled "Conversations avec Picasso," and at the suggestion of Picasso himself the box became a book.

Former successful experiments had given Brassaï the courage to realize his new ambition. His unfailing interest in the humble as well as the great had led him to publish a small book, *Histoire de Marie,* which contains the vitality and originality of a collection of poems. It is in fact no more nor less than the authentic sayings and richly colored gossip of that eternal partner in the household, his charwoman. A counterpart to this is the extraordinary collection of photos of graffiti which has now become well known throughout the world as an exhibition or in the form of a book.

Brassaï knows from his own experience that in photography you don't invent. You observe, select, and above all remain objective, and for this we are particularly indebted to him. The natural talent he possesses as a draftsman could have led him

* *Histoire de Marie,* Brassaï, with introduction by Henry Miller, Éd. du Point de Jour, Paris, 1949, p. 9 (translation).

into the extravagances of his own fantasy but his respect for life and for the infinite variety it presents makes him prefer the role of the man who sees and transmits objectively what he sees. Added to this is the way he listens, using exactly the same method. He has managed to listen and select, to string together detached images and edit his jottings objectively. "Bravo," wrote Henry Miller, "your ear has become as important as your eye!"

Before we open this book we know in fact that we have an author unusually qualified for this difficult task of probing deeper into the dazzling genius of Pablo Picasso. We can feel confident that he will not be blinded by its brilliance so that he neglects the things that are humble, trivial, and yet significant like the story he tells of the importance Picasso attaches to dust and how he forbids anyone to remove it in his studio, the simple reason being that he can see in it the traces of anyone who has been meddling with his affairs, and we hear Picasso's laughter as he adds: "And it's because I live constantly with dust, in the midst of dust, that I usually wear gray suits—they're the only ones that don't show any trace of it."

Brassaï had also the enviable position of working close to Picasso as an expert in an art which was complementary to his own and greatly appreciated by him. "When you see what you express through photography, you realize all the things that can no longer be the objective of painting. Why should the artist persist in treating subjects that can be established so clearly with the lens of a camera?" That he should be allowed the unusual privilege of having the free run of the studio is understandable. They could work together and exchange their views on every subject, including the mysteries of the arts and the evil background of the war and the Nazi occupation, for it was during the war that Brassaï worked most closely with Picasso, a time when friendship and confidence were the first and ultimate necessity: "We wear the same badge," Picasso told him when talking of the restrictions which had been imposed on them both.

The presence of Picasso during these demoralizing years without doubt gave courage to a wide circle of friends. With them he faced the dangers of bombardments and betrayal, but we see in Brassaï's account that he remained unshaken and that it was his continued preoccupation with his work and an Olympian sense of proportion which helped him and his friends to survive. "After all," he said when the destruction of all his work seemed probable, "the only thing that's important is the legend created by the picture, and not whether it continues to exist itself." In all this Brassaï allows us to appreciate the ever-present undercurrent of saturnine humor shared by Sabartés, Picasso's cynical and devoted friend, who had become immune after some forty years to the gibes leveled at him. Brassaï calls him Hermes and describes him performing his duties as intermediary between Picasso and the mixed crowd of devotees that poured in after the liberation of Paris. The comments of Sabartés on those who come into their sphere are like the relentless drift of the wind-blown dust that moves over the surface of the parched Spanish soil, the laugh that accompanies them is hidden, dry and deep, a good accompaniment to the ribald absurdities enjoyed by Picasso for whom nothing is immune to attack. He delights in making a piece of his own sculpture look absurd by dressing it up with a white coat and placing a palette in its hand, or mocking himself by playing the part of the old academician at work, for Brassaï to photograph, or again seeing himself as the painter become an ape. Such doubts about his own value are deeply ingrained. They are echoes from the early days of insecurity and disillusionment summed up in the words of Max Jacob: *"Le doute, voilà l'art!"* They reveal unexpectedly a fundamental humility in a man who has known fame for so many years that this quality in him could long ago have become extinct.

Thanks to Brassaï we live in the anteroom of inspiration and are given a taste of the stimulants needed for the fecundation of Picasso's genius; the delights of life, the women, the poets who come to visit him, and miseries, sometimes as trivial as the loss of a flashlight, sometimes as heart-rending as the death of a friend, that stir and ferment this fertile soil. We meet, in the intimacy of the family, Marcel the chauffeur deprived by the war of the splendid old Hispano-Suiza, and the infant prodigy who after being given sympathetic encouragement is told to come back in fifty years. We can enjoy the description of Picasso's friends who appear before us with the accuracy of a photographer who tells us that the technique he favors is slow and deliberate. "I felt—" he says, "rightly or wrongly—that by concentrating on a solitary portrait I could capture its essential character better than by making several dozen negatives . . ." We can judge of his success in the illustrations but when there are verbal descriptions such as those he gives us of Paul Éluard and André Breton, we are even more convinced of his veracity.

It is perhaps more than anything by his appreciation of poets and poetry, beginning with his early devotion to Goethe, that he has gained access to the intimacy of the great painter. Picasso has always been closer in his friendships with poets than with painters and the surrealist movement attracted him because of this fruitful combination between the two forms of expression. In spite of his reservations it is clear that Brassaï in a similar way is more in sympathy with the spirit of surrealism than with any other contemporary movement and that his friendship for Michaux or Prévert springs from the same understanding. He agrees readily with the surrealists "that poetry has no fixed domicile, that it does not necessarily inhabit the poem, that it may be encountered in the street, along a wall, no matter where," and by doing so he shows his acceptance of the fundamental importance of the transformation of meaning that Picasso, the master juggler, can bring about with such ease.

But there are dangerous consequences attached to the splendid joke of metamorphosis. A saddle and handlebars from an old bicycle become the head of a bull in Picasso's hands and by doing so they have gained an ambiguous identity or rather a suspicious lack of identity which could lead into the chaotic state where finally it would be impossible to recognize anything. No one questioned Picasso's right to play with reality in this way, but an awkward situation arose which to this day has not been forgotten by the master conjurer. Brassaï, tickled by the way in which the painting of a head set up on a chair above a pile of papers looked like a seated figure, took the liberty of arranging the master's carpet slippers so as to complete the illusion. But to Picasso who entered at that moment this photo was a poor joke not within the legitimate scope of the photographer. Brassaï gives us the artist's prompt reaction: "I like your photographs precisely because they are truthful," he said reproachfully and objected that this was not a true document because he never would have placed his slippers in that way himself. The photos Brassaï had made years before in his apartment were in fact like a "blood sample" from which an analysis could be made correctly. It follows from this that there is a law for the painter and a law for the photographer: both indeed are searching for the truth but on different levels and with disciplines that should not be relaxed.

The candor with which Brassaï recalls his conversations is an additional proof of his ability to look objectively at the world and to develop with great sensitivity the various techniques that he has mastered each within its own limits. By so doing he becomes a more imaginative poet, a more skillful draftsman, a more perceptive photographer, and one who can successfully capture and recount accurately the gist of paradoxical and elusive conversations.

*Roland Penrose*

## LIST OF PHOTOGRAPHS

*Picasso and Company*

*Early September, 1943*

Appointment with Picasso this morning. The Métro is always crowded, the buses few and far between; I prefer to walk. The weather is fine, and the trees—the only things still exempt from any form of rationing—are beginning to clothe themselves again in their most beautiful colors. The winter to come will be the fourth of this war, and I dread it; last year's was terrible. But in spite of the fact that their broadcasts are constantly jammed the BBC has brought us new hope: Anglo-American forces have landed in North Africa, and on the fourth of May they won the battle for Tunisia; last month the Allies completed the conquest of Sicily and began landing troops in Calabria and at Salerno; Mussolini has fallen and Italy has surrendered; on the fourth of February, Von Paulus' encircled army gave up and the battle of Stalingrad came to an end; the German army retreat has now reached the banks of the Dnieper; Allied bombers pound at the factories, the ports, the marshaling yards, almost daily . . . The invasion of the Atlantic coast seems imminent . . .

I am a little afraid of walking down the Boulevard Raspail. One night, about two weeks ago, as I was passing the Hôtel de la Paix with a friend I dropped my precious pack of cigarettes. We stooped over in the darkness, searching for them, and suddenly the glare of flashlight beams struck brutally at our faces. "*Hande hoch!*" We lifted our arms. German soldiers in front of us, pistols in hand, a stream of oaths in their mouths. The other passers-by crossed the boulevard hurriedly, terrified. "*Papiere!*" But how do you look for papers in your pockets, with your hands in the air? The soldiers examined our identity cards, took down our names, our addresses, questioned us, searched us . . . They released us at last, but not before warning us that we had not heard the end of this. For ten days I didn't dare remain at home. I learned later that there had been a bomb threat against the German-occupied hotel shortly before we passed, and when we crouched down in the gloom of the street we automatically became suspects . . .

On reaching Montparnasse, I glance furtively at the terraces of the cafés, thinking perhaps to see one of the friendly faces which are now so rare. I cross the Luxembourg garden, remembering the childhood year in Paris with my parents, and the many times I had sailed one of the little white boats across that pond. I come to the Boulevard Saint-Germain, so quiet now, almost like a street in some provincial town, since the automobiles and taxis of Paris have been left to rust in their garages. Then down through the rue Saint-André-des-Arts, home of all the cut-rate tailors, and I come at last to the rue des Grands-Augustins. Eleven years have passed since my first meeting with Picasso . . .

It was in 1932. The year that marked the end of the "post-war" period was also the beginning of the period that led us to the Second World War. At that time, after having squandered ten years, the foolish years, in Montparnasse, I was working on my first book, *Paris de Nuit*. Among my friends and acquaintances of the period was Maurice Raynal, a close friend of Picasso. He had taken part in the cubist movement with all the enthusiasm of the young poet he then was, devoting to it not only his pen but also his pocketbook. Having inherited a modest fortune, he was the only well-off member of this group of more or less starving and impoverished poets and artists. A quiet man with the face of a Roman patrician and a mind that was more lucid and methodical than intuitive or spontaneous, Raynal was entranced by everything that was opposed to his own intrinsic nature—the truculent verve of Alfred Jarry, the impetuosity of Alphonse Allais, the roguish pranks of Manolo, the fantastic stories of Max Jacob, the weather-vane changeability of Picasso, the impulsive spirit of Guillaume Apollinaire, the candor of the Douanier Rousseau. Gradually detaching himself from poetry,

Raynal directed his talent toward the writing of art criticism, thus following in the footsteps of André Salmon and Apollinaire. Over a period of many years, these three musketeers of modern art defended the "new spirit" with pens that were always sharp and often cutting. André Salmon had his regular column in *L'Intransigeant*, Leon Bailby's *très parisien* evening newspaper. The other two carried the battle to reviews of varying degrees of obscurity and longevity, primarily the *Soirées de Paris*.

In 1910 Salmon left *L'Intransigeant* for another newspaper and turned over his column to Apollinaire, who was delighted with the opportunity thus provided him to support Picasso, Matisse, Derain, Vlaminck, the Douanier Rousseau, and his great friend Marie Laurencin. Then came the famous affair of the Phoenician statues stolen from the Louvre, and the author of *Les Mamelles de Tirésias* was sent to the Santé prison and Picasso himself was questioned by the police. Personally shattered, and compromised in his position, Apollinaire was forced to abandon his post at *L'Intran.* It was at this time that Maurice Raynal succeeded him. A few years later he took on as an associate a young Greek art critic, E. Tériade, and thus was born the celebrated column of the "Two Blind Men," the humorous *nom de plume* with which they signed their work. Along with Fernand Léger, Le Corbusier, and a group of other artists, Raynal frequently invited me to dinner in their apartment on the rue Denfert-Rochereau, where the walls were covered with Picassos of the cubist period. It was on one such occasion that I first met Max Jacob, his monocle winking brightly beneath the gleaming ivory of his skull.

The second Blind Man was a frequenter of the Café du Dôme, as was I, and I met him quite often at this crossroads of Montparnasse. A plump, rounded silhouette, an unctuous manner, constantly shrouding himself in veils of mystery—that was the picture I had of Tériade. One day, having assured himself that no one was listening to us, he took me aside and, in oracular tones, confided to me the outlines of a project within a project . . . "Something was being planned . . ." "They were about to . . ." "It's possible that . . ." It was a question of a very important mission; he wanted only to tell me that he couldn't yet tell me anything; that I should hold myself in constant readiness, and above all that I must maintain absolute silence about everything he had just told me, and promise him not to mention it to anyone . . . With Tériade, I felt as if I had walked into Greek mythology, and could not help wondering on what strange journey this prudent Ulysses was leading me . . . The fog of mystery became steadily denser for the next several weeks, and then at last H hour arrived and the veil was torn away. I was snatched up on a cloud and deposited at No. 23, rue La Boétie, in the studio of Pablo Picasso.

When I crossed the threshold of his "studio" for the first time, Picasso had just passed his fiftieth birthday. His reputation, of course, was already well established, but it was this crucial year that saw the beginnings of his truly world-wide fame. The great retrospective exhibition of his work which opened on the fifteenth of June in the gilded salons of the Georges Petit gallery—the climactic event of the Parisian season—marked an important date in his existence. For the first time, a dazzling collection of two hundred and thirty-six of his canvases was gathered together in one place, and with a single glance around the room the viewer could witness the blue period and the rose, the cubist and the classic, the sum total of his creation.

Picasso, perhaps for the last time in his life, had grouped his works himself and personally surveyed the hanging of the canvases, which he saw—as he said to Tériade—returning from far-off collections "like prodigal children returning home, clothed in gold . . ." On the eve of the battle, which he knew would be decisive, he had wanted to pass all of his soldiers in review, one by one. An artist who had already arrived, he had all of the attributes of the position, all of the exterior symbols: a Hispano-Suiza driven by a liveried chauffeur, clothes made for him by the finest tailors, pedigreed dogs, an apartment like those of wealthy businessmen, a little château in Normandie—he had recently bought Boisgeloup—a safe-deposit box, and a beautiful companion. Nothing was lacking. In the salon of his apartment, "Squire" Picasso received such visitors as Count Étienne de Beaumont, Missia Sert, Erik Satie, Manuel de Falla, Artur Rubinstein, Jean Cocteau; all the celebrities of the day, the social world of Paris. He went out a great deal, attending the openings at the theater and the ballet, frequently accepting invitations to receptions and balls, and always in the company of his beautiful, elegant wife. He was at the height of his "worldly" period.

I was undoubtedly somewhat agitated at finding myself face to face with him, and there was a certain amount of apprehension mingled with my emotion. Didn't he have, at that time, the reputation of being an unapproachable man? In the confused moments of that first meeting, I attempted to study his face, wondering whether it would conform to the picture I had drawn from his work and his legend. His physical presence soon effaced both that image and my earlier apprehension. The man in front of me was simple and direct, without affectation, without arrogance, without sham. His frank and open manner and his kindness put me at ease at once. I began then to survey my strange surroundings. I had expected an artist's studio, and this was an apartment converted into a kind of warehouse. Certainly no characteristically middle-class dwelling was ever so uncharacteristically furnished. There were four or five rooms—each with a marble fireplace surmounted by a mirror—entirely emptied of any customary furniture and littered with stacks of paintings, cartons, wrapped packages, pails of all sizes, many of them containing the molds for his statues, piles of books, reams of paper, odds and ends of everything, placed wherever there was an inch of space, along the walls and even spread across the floors, all covered with a thick layer of dust. The doors between all the rooms were open—they might even have been taken off—transforming this large apartment into a single studio cut up into a multiple series of corners for the multiple activities of its owner. The floors were dull and lusterless, long since deprived of any polish, coated here and there with splotches of paint, and strewn with a carpet of cigarette butts. Picasso had stood his easel in the largest and best-lit room—what once had surely been the living room—and this was the only room that contained any furniture at all. The window faced south, and offered a beautiful view of the rooftops of Paris, bristling with a forest of red and black chimneys, with the slender, far-off silhouette of the Eiffel Tower rising between them. Madame Picasso never came up to this apartment. With the exception of a few friends, Picasso admitted no one to it. So the dust could fall where it would and remain there undisturbed, with no fear of the feather dusters of cleaning women. But, after the years in Montparnasse and Montmartre, how had it happened that the artist had come to live in the rue La Boétie?

The unexpected migration from the east to an unexplored far west of luxury shops and *haute couture,* of cafés, fashionable hotels and theaters, had drawn the art dealers in its wake. The rue Laffitte and its neighboring streets at the foot of Montmartre was the corner of Paris where Ambroise Vollard had his curious lair, Clovis Sagot his little boutique, and Durand-Ruel, the friend and first salesman of the Impressionists, his handsome showrooms; the Bernheim jeune gallery was there, and so were the sumptuous salons of Georges Petit. But there were already a few advance posts of the irresistible march toward the west, toward the Place de l'Étoile: the Rosenberg gallery, belonging to the father of Paul and Léonce Rosenberg, was on the Avenue de l'Opéra, the Druet gallery was on the rue Royale, and Kahnweiler's little gallery on the rue Vignon, near the Madeleine. John Hessel was the first to move to the rue La Boétie, followed by Paul Rosenberg, whose brother, Léonce, then chose a nearby street for his own gallery. Bernheim jeune, after an initial jump to the Boulevard de la Madeleine, settled on the rue du Faubourg St. Honoré, Kahnweiler on the rue d'Astorg, and Durand-Ruel on the Avenue Friedland. They, in turn, were followed by many other dealers, including "père Chéron" and the young Paul Guillaume, who was largely responsible for establishing the reputation of Chirico, Modigliani, and Soutine. Everyone had deserted the rue Laffitte. Only Vollard, by transferring his household gods to an old mansion on the rue Martignac, broke the ground for still another migration to the Left Bank. If the rue Laffitte was the stage for the Impressionists and the Fauves up until the turn of the century, the great period of the cubists and the surrealists was played out on the rue La Boétie.

In 1917, when Picasso made a trip to Spain to introduce his young fiancée, Olga Kochlova, to his family in Barcelona—he had met Olga shortly before, in Rome, while he was doing the sets and costumes for *Parade*—his studio in Montrouge was flooded. He then asked Paul Rosenberg, who had replaced Kahnweiler as his dealer after the outbreak of war in 1914, to find him a place to live and have his things moved into it. Rosenberg rented him an apartment in the building adjoining his gallery. It was thus as a result of his dealer's decision that Picasso was plunged into the geographic center of the commerce in paintings. As he had done before at Bateau-Lavoir, he first rented one apartment here and later a second, directly above the first and identical with it—one for living quarters and the other for his work. The lower floor became one of the focal points of the worldly life; the upper floor was his "studio." The contrast between them was striking: downstairs, there was an all-white living room, a large dining room with a round extension table at its center, a sideboard along one wall and small, occasional tables in each corner, and a bedroom with twin beds of copper. Not the slightest disorder, not a grain of dust. Floors and furniture shining, polished. Picasso had been living in this apartment for fifteen years when I met him. And the extraordinary thing about it was that, except for one mantelpiece on which there was some evidence of his fantasies, nothing whatever bore his stamp.[1] Even his own canvases of the cubist period—classics by this time—carefully framed and hanging on the walls beside Cézanne, Renoir, and Corot, seemed to belong in the apartment of some rich collector, instead of being at home with Picasso himself.* This bourgeois apartment was completely alien to his habitual way of life. None of those extraordinary pieces of furniture he is so fond of, none of the totally unexpected objects with which he loves to surround himself, no piles of anything, none of the confused jumble his fantasy usually created . . . Olga was jealous of the domain she considered hers alone, and she stood careful guard over it, lest Picasso mark it with the powerful imprint of his personality.

I learned then what my important mission was to be: to photograph the sculptures of Picasso, which were still entirely unknown. My photos were to occupy thirty or so pages of the first number of a new review: *Minotaure*. "The most beautiful art review in the world" was about to be born.

Tériade, its "artistic director," had gone into partnership with a young Swiss publisher, Albert Skira. Their tiny office—chance or premeditation?—was tucked away in No. 25, rue La Boétie, the building next door to the one in which Picasso lived. He was well surrounded: his dealer on one side of him, his publisher on the other . . . This young Swiss had the audacity to think that he could set himself up as a rival to Ambroise Vollard, and he wanted nothing less. Converting a promise from Picasso into

[1] (Throughout the text these numerals refer to the numbered photographs.)

* It was the beginning of a very beautiful collection. Picasso subsequently acquired numerous Cézannes (notably a view of l'Estaque and a Château Noir), a group of peasants by Le Nain, a Chardin, several small Courbets, some Vuillards (a portrait, and an interior with a woman lying on a couch), some very beautiful Renoirs, some Degas, and three or four Douanier Rousseaus. The majority of these paintings were obtained through exchanges for his own works, especially with Vollard. Picasso also possesses paintings of Braque, Modigliani, Matisse, Derain, Miró, and Max Ernst, as well as sculptures of Laurens and Adam, water colors of Max Jacob, and some works of young painters. He was one of the first to discover and collect the engravings of Bresdin. After having been stored in safe-deposit vaults for a long time, most of these are now at Vauvenargues.

promises of investment, and all of these promises into credit with printers and suppliers, was child's play to him. Through diplomacy, perseverance, and hard work, Skira had brought off one master stroke—he had published one of the most beautiful of Picasso's *de luxe* editions, *The Metamorphoses* of Ovid. After this success, it had been a relatively simple matter for him to obtain the collaboration of Matisse—in the amicable, but sometimes rough competition between the two painters, Matisse had no intention of allowing himself to be outdistanced by his friend and rival. A year later the *Poésies* of Stéphane Mallarmé appeared, illustrated by Matisse. *The Metamorphoses* had sold badly, although it was in Picasso's best classic vein. Skira, however, without concerning himself too greatly about reluctant bibliophiles, began to make plans for another publication, a work to which the unrestrained admiration of the surrealists had given a whole new luster—Lautréamont's *Les Chants de Maldoror.* It was René Crevel, the young poet who committed suicide shortly afterward, who suggested to Skira that he should entrust the illustration of Lautréamont's unique work to a young Spanish painter who had recently arrived from Cadaqués, burdened with complexes and obsessions—Salvador Dali. He had already been adopted as a new celebrity by some of the more snobbish and worldly circles in Paris, and his invasion of the surrealist group provided the movement with a much-needed stimulus. One of the most important books in the history of surrealism was now in the making.

When I saw Albert Skira for the first time in his little office, I was surprised to find him a young man; tall, slender, with blue eyes, a rosy complexion, and golden blond hair. He looked more like the hero of an operetta than a publisher of serious books on art; and never has physical appearance been more deceiving. Skira was a fanatic on the subject of work, a human packhorse, and he made no attempt to conceal his ambitions. They were spread out for everyone to see, on the enormous map that covered one wall of that tiny office. It was neither a map of Paris, nor of France or even Europe, but a planisphere of the world, with all of its oceans and all of its continents. Branching out from Paris, firmly drawn lines spread their network across the seas to the conquest of the world, and little flags marked the cities already conquered. Beneath his nonchalant, even somewhat Bohemian appearance, Skira dreamed of art; but of an industrialized form of art. Well before Malraux, he had imagined the museum without walls. He calculated his time to the minute, judged individuals and relationships from the angle of profit and results, weighed the value of every minute, of every smile, of every handshake. He never ceased repeating, "You have to be positive. Every day, you have to make positive moves." And late at night he would still be adding up the list of all of the "positive" events of the day.

*Minotaure!* Who proposed this title from among so many others? Georges Bataille? André Masson? In any case, it was adopted unanimously and joyfully. It placed the review under a sign that was dear to Picasso. The fabulous creature made its first appearance in his work in 1927, in *Le Minotaure et la femme endormie,* and had long been one of his major themes. Several years later it was the inspiration for a whole series of prints included in the *Suite Vollard,* and also for the beautiful etching *Minotauromachie.* And even after the distress of his marital difficulties Picasso maintained a predilection and fondness for this symbol, representing himself as a blind minotaur, or as the mythical beast harnessed to a chariot laden with household goods.

But this heavily symbolic name did not have the same significance for Picasso that it had for the surrealists. To the artist who painted *Guernica,* this ancient symbol, half-man, half-bull, was not far removed from the fighting *toro* of Spain, charged with obscure, potentially eruptive forces. Picasso sensed these somber forces at work within himself, and humanized them. His minotaur personified the "monster," scornful, dangerous certainly, but vividly alive, with smoke pouring from nostrils dilated by the lust which forces him to seek out sleeping, nude young girls and hurl himself furiously at their soft, provocative, and defenseless flesh. His minotaur would always be the monster with lowered head, pawing the ground and circling interminably around the sleeping woman.

For the surrealists, this name invoked dark and cruel myths: the monstrous union of Pasiphaë with the white bull, the labyrinth built by Daedalus, where the Minotaur devoured the young men and girls of Athens, myths which Freud reclaimed from legend and made part of the subconscious. The surrealists saw in the Minotaur the force which shatters the limits of the irrational, flooding across its frontiers, tearing down the laws and offending the gods. They identified him with their own aspirations: constant and universal violence, absolute revolt, total defiance, unbridled liberty. If Picasso loved the Minotaur for its "human, too human" side, the surrealists loved him for everything they detected in him that was counter to the natural order, that was super-human, super- or sur-real.

One afternoon, when I went to see Picasso at his studio, I found him at work on the composition of the first cover for *Minotaure*. He was making a montage of rare lightheartedness. On a wooden plank, he had thumbtacked a section of crushed and pleated pasteboard similar to those he often used for his sculptures. On top of this he placed one of his engravings, representing the monster, and then grouped around it some lengths of ribbon, bits of silver paper lace, and also some rather faded artificial flowers, which he confided to me had come from an outmoded and discarded hat of Olga's. When this montage was reproduced, he insisted strenuously that the thumbtacks must not be neglected. On the twenty-fifth of May 1933 the first issue of *Minotaure* appeared, with this handsome work as its cover. In succeeding issues, Derain, Matisse, Miró, André Masson, René Magritte, Salvador Dali each supplied his version of the monster for the cover of the review, measuring his strength against the fabled creature just as Theseus once had done.

At this particular time, the surrealist group had arrived at a turning point. The first *Surrealist Manifesto* was already nine years old. Scandals, excesses, riots were no longer the order of the day. The incurable despair, the condition of violence and premeditated sabotage were far behind. No one any longer talked about the memorable séances of "automatic writing, hypnotic sleep recitals of dreams," destined—or, at least, so André Breton hoped—to nourish all future poetry. In just a few years, this source, which had been held to be miraculous, inexhaustible, and "within the reach of everyone," had dried up. Although Breton still successfully drew from it the images of his own poetry, the majority of surrealist poets had turned away from the exercise of verbal delirium. As for the inherent contradiction which had split the movement for the past ten years, it was now at the point of a final rupture. Unable to choose between revolution and revelation, André Breton had constantly battled on the two fronts of political action and artistic creation. The social involvement which he considered "dishonorable" nonetheless held a certain fascination for him, and in spite of his denunciations of the "vanity" of all artistic or literary activity he was laying the groundwork—whether he knew it or not—for a new school of art. The incessant pulling and hauling between these two poles is the whole tormented history of surrealism. Compromised and divided as it was at every moment, only the powerful personality of Breton could have maintained a precarious equilibrium by expelling from the movement on one day the "agitators" who were determined to take part in the social revolution, and on the next the artists or poets who were too eager to "arrive," to make a name for themselves, sign contracts, and earn money. In the first decade of surrealism, the excommunications pronounced by Breton against deviations of the right or of the left, and the wave of expulsions, gradually thinned out its ranks. After first having been praised to the skies, the flower of the period's artists and poets were either eliminated or managed to escape from Breton's yoke.*

In 1933 surrealism was no longer a savage revolt, but a successful revolution whose promoters had acceded to power. Burdened with these new responsibilities, Breton and Paul Éluard had to try to strengthen the foundations of the movement. And that could not be done without making some concessions . . .

Although *Minotaure* offered them an opportunity to maintain the surrealist spirit, they were forced to renounce the combative-

* Pierre Naville was excluded because he was too "doctrinaire," Antonin Artaud and Philippe Soupault because of their literary activity. The largest purge took place in 1929. Robert Desnos, the movement's medium; Jacques Prévert, its *enfant terrible;* Roger Vitrac, its dramatist; Ribemont-Dessaignes, who had come to it as a fugitive from Dada; and several other members were included in this "tumbril to the guillotine." They published their resentment against Breton in a tract of unusual violence, entitled *Un Cadavre.* Other members were liquidated with the same cold resolution: Joseph Delteil, André Masson, Francis Picabia, Marcel Duchamp, Georges Bataille, Raymond Queneau, Marcel Duhamel, etc. And in 1931 Georges Sadoul and Louis Aragon, who deliberately went over to communism, were finally expelled. To Breton's way of thinking, surrealism was not only a manner of thought, but also a way of behavior. It was this attitude that resulted in the police-like investigations, the secret files, the intrusions into the private lives of his companions in the movement. Breton could not and would not admit that the surrealist poets must do some journalistic or other form of work, simply in order to subsist. But is it possible to judge his "inquisitorial decisions" without relating them to the lofty idea he had formed of both liberty and love? To ignore the norms of civilization, and re-establish the secret relationship of man with the cosmic forces; to rediscover all mystic, alchemic, esoteric knowledge—this is what he expected surrealism to accomplish, and it became for him a form of religion, resulting in his adoption of the attitude of a seer or chief of some secret society, in his references to occultism, the Orient, Buddha, the great innovators, the Dalai Lama . . . Like Robespierre, Breton employed "terror" in the name of the surrealist ethic.

ness which had characterized their earlier publications. And this sumptuous review, in an edition limited to three thousand copies and beyond the reach of proletarian pocketbooks, could only find an audience among the bourgeoisie it professed to scorn, and among the titled and wealthy snobs who were the first patrons and collectors of surrealist works. The question of whether acceptance of this collaboration, this collusion with capitalism, was not a betrayal of the movement's principles was debated for a long time before the offer of Skira and Tériade was finally accepted. Faced with the eternal alternatives of surrealism—"to go out in the streets with a revolver in your hand" or "to return home to art"—Breton and Éluard chose the latter path. Their participation in *Minotaure* brought an end to the "radical break with the world" and marked the formal entrance of surrealist art and poetry into the world.

One morning a man of about forty, tall of stature and proudly erect in bearing, came into the *Minotaure* office. His broad, high forehead sheltered eyes of a clear, almost liquid blue, reflecting a gentility and calm that was slightly feminine in the rose-tinted frame of a long, curiously asymmetrical face. He was wearing an extremely well-tailored suit, and his entire person seemed to breathe an air of easy well-being and indefinable delicacy. It was only later that one noticed the flicker of resignation that occasionally clouded the open smile of his face and eyes. We were introduced. His voice—gaunt, a trifle secret, and yet so direct, so immediately captivating—murmured a name: Paul Éluard. The hand he held out to me was trembling . . . I learned later, from his own mouth, that in spite of an appearance of health he had been gravely ill and had escaped death only as a result of his tenacious will to survive. At the age of seventeen he had been operated on for pulmonary pneumonia, and since that time he had been forced to think constantly of his health, living almost in a state of permanent convalescence.

It was in that same *Minotaure* office that I first met André Breton. I recognized him at once, even though he was no longer wearing a monocle or dark glasses, as he always had during the heroic period of the movement. The regular lines of his face, with its long, straight nose, clear eyes, and bohemian mane of hair brushed away from his forehead and falling in curls around the back of his neck, gave him the appearance of an Oscar Wilde rendered more energetic, more masculine, by some abrupt glandular transformation. His whole bearing, the proud carriage of his head, his impassive expression, grave, almost severe, his movements, calm and measured, extremely slow, stamped him as a leader of men, born to fascinate and to reign, but also to condemn and strike down. While Éluard had called up a picture of Apollo in my mind, Breton appeared to me as Jupiter personified. It was not until some time later, when our relationship had become a friendly one, that I recognized clearly that this serenely quiet man was not insensible to humor. I remember an afternoon I spent with him in the extraordinary atmosphere of his home at No. 42, rue Fontaine, a kind of den filled with African fetishes, masks from Oceania, surrealist paintings and sculpture, rare and curious objects of every kind. Over a period of hours he read me the stories of Alphonse Allais, who had only shortly before been enthroned among the patron saints of surrealism. Each of these little melodramas—so droll, so wicked, and occasionally so incredibly cruel—has remained in my memory. Breton mimed the roles, imitated the voices of the characters, gave a special accent to each phrase, to each word. I can still see the conspiratorial gleam in his eye, the look of contentment on his face, as he thus introduced me to the mysteries of black humor . . . He was entirely in his element. But although he was a master of the cutting remark, of irony and sarcasm, those vengeful weapons directed at others, I do not think that real humor, the sparkling, smiling humor which embraces everything in order to rid the world of some of its gravity and darkness, was within his province. He took his doctrines, his work, each of his actions, too seriously to leave room for the form of humor which—like charity—begins at home. In no circumstance of his life was Breton capable of not taking himself seriously . . .

Under the terms of the *modus vivendi* agreed to with the directors of *Minotaure,* the surrealists were not in complete control of everything that was done. While they were free to include in it whatever texts, subject matter, or imagery they might wish, they did not have any right of veto to reject things of which they did not approve. I remember an article by Maurice Raynal —a discussion of the work of several sculptors entitled *Dieu-Table-Cuvette*—which caused bitter discussion. Laurens, Lipchitz, and Despiau pleased the surrealists as little as Maillol or

Brancusi. They detested the cubists and the *fauves.* They also argued against certain textual inclusions. Pierre Reverdy encountered no opposition.* But Paul Valéry, Ramuz, Léon-Paul Fargue, and other writers often provoked their resistance.

One day when I was in the little *Minotaure* office, I was surprised by the sudden appearance of the massive silhouette of Léon-Paul Fargue, wearing his usual mask of some debonair Nero, the eyelids half-closed, and the stub of a cigarette glued between the lips. I knew him already, since I had met him at the Grand Écart, the fashionable night spot of that moment, where he held court every night. Even though he was not among the surrealists' hierarchy of saints, he had brought a manuscript for the review, and wanted me to illustrate it with a photograph of his hand clasping a woman's hand.

"Woman's hand," Fargue had written, "unique trance, extremity of my life, ravishing arm of the sea in which the affluents of blood are merged, round and perfumed hand rising airily to the head but seeking its place in the hollow, like a body surprised in a transitory bed into which one slips for the first time; pursued, imprisoned, frightened hand, struggling like a bird that is firmly held and is afraid . . ."

In spite of the discord, the rivalries, the disagreements, even the antagonism of its varying tendencies, *Minotaure*'s novelty and variety, coupled with the diversity of its material, made of it a review which became the most vital and the most representative organ of the developments of the period. It contained, in germinal form or already in full bloom, everything that was to manifest itself in art, poetry, or literature twenty or thirty years later. Although there was always an element of other schools of thought, it was the strong spice of surrealism which gave its real taste to a review whose more classical aspects, far from clashing with it, provided it with a solid base . . .

Until that time, I had had only individual contacts with numerous surrealist poets and painters, and of these the majority

* He was, in fact, *persona grata.* Aragon, Éulard, Soupault had always revered him as a pioneer, and recognized his beneficial influence on their own poetry. They had collaborated with him in his review, *Nord-Sud,* and had published in *Littérature* some poems of his which had an occasional surrealist glint. Maurice Nadeau, in his history of surrealism, quotes them as saying in 1924 that, "Our literature is greatly inferior to that of Reverdy. We are not in the least afraid of saying that Reverdy is actually the greatest living poet. Next to him, we are only children . . ."

were no longer a part of the group proper. Suddenly I had been plunged into the midst of the movement. I liked this fever of discovery away from the beaten paths of art and science, this curiosity to prospect for new veins of ore, this mental electricity which constantly charged through the little office at *Minotaure*, where André Breton flicked his whip at the mind. I agree with the surrealists that poetry has no fixed domicile, that it does not necessarily inhabit the poem, that it may be encountered in the street, along a wall, no matter where. And I will go at least a part of the way with the "brain trust" of the irrational. Either in the course of a conversation or in a letter written in that precise and tiny hand of his, with green ink on blue paper, Breton often asked me to come and see him at the rue Fontaine or at the Café Cyrano on the Place Blanche, where the surrealists normally gathered. In spite of my great esteem for him, our relationship, though always friendly, remained somehow distant. Too many things in this movement ran counter to my own feelings.*

The first pieces of Picasso's sculpture I photographed were a dozen or so extremely elongated figurines, some nude, some draped, roughly hewn with a knife in pieces of hard wood, and all done during the preceding year. He took them out of a hamper to show them to me, one by one, explaining to me that he had not wanted to carry the work on them too far, so that the wood itself—its structure, its knots, its fibers—would remain alive. I also photographed several sculptures in iron wire, done in the period

* The thing that especially irritated me was surrealism's attitude with regard to painting. Its purely pictorial quality was totally neglected. Nothing counted for the surrealists but the intentions, the sentimental content—be it erotic or poetic—the subject, the anecdote. Once the appearance of "surreality" is admitted as the unique criterion of art, works of blatant mediocrity can be elevated to the rank of masterpieces, and even good painting may be admired only for bad reasons. These reservations had already been expressed by Baudelaire, who was perhaps the only poet to love painting for itself, rather than for those ideas in it which might stir the poet in himself. Among other things, he wrote:

"I suffer when I see (the artist) seeking to capture the imagination through sources located at the very limits of, if not even beyond, his art."

"Looking for the poetry of purpose in the conception of a picture is the surest means of not finding it."

"Painting is not interesting only because of its color and its form; it resembles poetry only to the extent that the latter may awaken in the reader the ideas of painting."

"The importation of poetry, of the spirit, and of sentiment, into painting—all these modern miseries are vices peculiar to dilettantes."

1930–1931: linear, geometric constructions in a three-dimensional space—most of them triangular. In a way, they formed a sort of sculptural replica of his painted series on *L'Atelier* of 1927–1928, the human form reduced to pure schema. In these works Picasso had carried abstraction to its extreme limits, as if he had wanted to cut himself off from any contact with the real. They might have been taken for the work of some "constructivist," if it were not for the fact that the presence of the human body could be felt in each of them. Perhaps it was just that the tripods still evoked the legs, a disk the abdomen, a ball the head . . . For lack of time, I was only able to photograph four or five of these little metallic constructions, but there were others, covered with dust, standing on shelves beside bottles of linseed oil, turpentine, and hydrochloric acid.

On one of the mantels in Olga's apartment, next to a small bronze sculpture of the blue period, *La Femme à Genoux,* there stood a strange wrought-iron piece, tall and skeletal, a sort of scarecrow wearing a fur cap and topped with a little figure of Punch; a long, pointed iron foot, of a type still used by bootmakers, formed its base. Picasso had laden his "Christmas tree" with all kinds of souvenirs: a miniature airplane, a flag, tiny monkeys, all dangling from wires like silver balls on the branches of a pine tree. Just beside the "tree" there was a pot from which emerged the tormented roots of a philodendron whose stalk, shorn of all its leaves, carried a ram's horn and a red plume at its summit. But the majority of Picasso's sculptures were at Boisgeloup, and he proposed that we should all go there in his car. When I left him, he advised me to bring plenty of photographic plates . . .

I already knew some of his bronzes of the blue period, and the cubist wood carvings. But sculpture was sleeping now, like a disembodied potentiality at the very heart of his painting, betraying his nostalgia for the round relief. In his paintings, a period of flat areas and a bright and varied palette is regularly succeeded by a sculptural period, scarcely colored, almost monochrome, as if the pictures had been painted from some imagined sculpture. Leaning heavily on the example of Ingres and Cézanne, cubism—a reaction to the impressionist practice of dissolving volume and the solidity of form into areas of color and vibration—was born under the aegis of an *aggravated plasticity.* It is the work of a man naturally drawn to the fullness of forms.

Cubism gave the viewer the impression of looking at a sculpture that revolves, offering all of its different aspects *simultaneously.**

This inclination toward plasticity, toward a rigorous modeling of form, reasserts itself periodically in his later, postcubist, work. But curiously enough, in spite of this inner penchant, Picasso had almost completely abandoned sculpture after the *Verre d'Absinthe* of 1914. He had only taken it up again in 1929, and then in the utmost secrecy . . . We were among the first to see his new works.

At about noon of the following day, under a gray December sky, I joined him, Tériade, Olga, and Picasso's son Paulo, who was then eleven years old, and we all climbed into the monumental Hispano-Suiza, still new and gleaming. This enormous black car, with its elegant interior adorned with mirrors and little crystal vases of flowers, did not go unnoticed. The chauffeur, white-gloved and formal, closed the door behind us as a group of curious bystanders stood around and gaped. We left Paris and started out in the direction of Beauvais.

Picasso confided to us during the trip that he had bought this property because he was a trifle weary of carrying back to Paris every year, from Dinard, from Cannes, from Juan-les-Pins, the cumbersome harvest of his summer; of packing and unpacking canvases, paints, brushes, sketchbooks, all the paraphernalia of his traveling studio. At Boisgeloup, he could leave everything.

Just before we reached Gisors, the Hispano-Suiza turned off the main highway, following a little regional road that branched to the left. A roadside marker said: Hamlet of Boisgeloup. A few minutes later I saw the houses of a little village straggling up the side of a hill, and then the gate of the château, beside an old chapel. We had arrived. Picasso immediately assumed the role of proprietor, and led us on a fast-paced tour. It was an odd sort of château—most of the rooms were completely unfurnished, with just a few large Picassos scattered here and there on the naked walls. He and Olga and Paulo occupied two small rooms beneath the mansard roof. We also made a whirlwind tour of the dilapi-

* In 1908 Picasso told his friend González that if the planes of his paintings were to be cut apart and reassembled they would form a sculpture. And three years later, he stated that a painting should show objects with such a degree of plasticity that an engineer would be able to execute them in three dimensions.

dated little chapel, which was entirely covered with ivy. Picasso told us that it dated from the thirteenth century, and mass was still celebrated there on some occasions.[2] But we were pressed for time. "There are too many sculptures to photograph, and it will be dark very early," he said, and led us off toward a row of barns, stables, and sheds that lined one side of the courtyard, across from the house. I imagine that when he visited the property for the first time it was not so much the little château which had intrigued him as the sight of these vast, empty dependencies, waiting to be filled. He would at last be able to gratify a long-repressed desire: to sculpt really large statues. He opened the door of one of the great boxlike structures, revealing its multitude of sculptures, dazzling in their whiteness.

I was surprised by the roundness of all these forms. It was the influence of a new woman who had come into Picasso's life: Marie-Thérèse Walter. He had met her by chance at the rue La Boétie, and painted her for the first time just a year before, December 16, 1931, in the picture called *Le Fauteuil Rouge*. Her youth, her gaiety, her laughter, her lively nature all had charmed him. He loved the blond sheen of her hair, her luminous complexion, the sculptural lines of her body . . . Ever since that day, all of his painting had begun to take on a new and rhythmical movement. As with the flat periods and the sculptural periods in his work, there are often cases in which straight, angular lines are interrupted by curving lines; gentleness taking the place of harshness, tenderness succeeding violence. At no other period in his life did his painting become so undulatory, so filled with sinuous curves, the arms intertwined, the hair a mass of scrolls. The majority of the statues I saw before me now bore the stamp of this "new look," beginning with the large bust of Marie-Thérèse leaning slightly forward—an almost classic head, with the straight line of the forehead flowing unbroken into the line of the nose, a line that was beginning to usurp all of his work. In the series on the *Atelier de sculpteur* that Picasso was engraving for Vollard at the time—he had shown me some of the proofs at the rue La Boétie: a silent dialogue between the artist and his model, charged with sensuality and carnal pleasure—there were monumental, almost spherical heads in the backgrounds. So they were not imaginary! I was greatly surprised to rediscover them here in the flesh, by which, of course, I mean in the round; all curving lines, the nose becoming more and more prominent, the eyes like globes, resembling some barbarian goddess.[3]

I went to work photographing the sculptures, and worked without interruption all through the afternoon. In addition to the large heads there were a thousand other things; notably a magnificent cock with the head inclined toward the bristling plumage of the tail, and a cow with dilated nostrils and twisted horns . . . I reached a point where I had only one printing frame left. At that time I still used photographic plates. They were loaded into the printing frames, and they were heavy; I had enough of them for twenty-four photographs. If I wanted to make any more I would have to unload and reload them on the spot, in a kind of sack of opaque black material provided with two long sleeves, somewhat resembling a vampire. I was forced to go through all of this in order to continue. I had scarcely finished when night fell, and it was impossible to see anything in the shed any longer. Picasso lit a big kerosene lamp. It seemed that there was no electricity in these outbuildings. He told us then that when he was surprised at work by the dusk he often went on by the light from this unsteady source. He was accustomed to it. As a young man, he had often drawn by the light of a candle stuck in the neck of a bottle. The kerosene lamp, which he had set on the hard-packed earth that formed the floor of the shed, threw fantastic shadows on and around all of these white statues.[4] As a concluding effort, I took a photograph of the "group" in this light.

We had not finished. In the darkness of the night that was gathering over Boisgeloup, Picasso insisted on leading us across the park to the edge of the woods, where he had set up two of his wrought-iron statues—the larger one was called *Le Cerf*. They dated from the preceding year. Intrigued, as always, by every branch of art and craft that was foreign to him, Picasso had watched with curiosity as his friend Julio González, an expert ironworker, hammered and twisted the incandescent metal, and then had asked him to initiate him into the mysteries of iron and fire. And the apprentice surpassed his master. From this brief collaboration, however, González also emerged enriched; having learned the audacity of new forms from the genius who was his pupil, he moved on himself to cubism.

We were about to leave Boisgeloup. The headlights on the Hispano-Suiza were lit. And it was by that stabbing light that I took one last photograph: the illuminated façade of Picasso's little château.[5]

As we parted company that night, very late, and after an exhausting day, Picasso said, "We should all go out together some night . . . What could we go to see? Do you have any ideas? The Moulin Rouge? The Bal Tabarin?" Then, after a moment's thought, "Do you like the circus? Suppose we went to the Médrano? It's been an eternity since I was there . . . and we could take Paulo . . ."

The next evening we met again, this time on the Boulevard Rochechouart, at the entrance to the circus. Picasso took a box. I knew how strongly he had always been attracted to the circus, to the world of acrobats and bareback riders, and I thought of all the Pierrots, the Harlequins, the Saltimbanques, the Clowns in musician's masks that had been inspired by this building and this arena. The performance that night was very much like all the others—aerialists, acrobats, wild animals, girls in ballet skirts somersaulting on the ample rumps of percherons. Nothing startling. Picasso was in a joyful mood, delighted to be able to steep himself again in the atmosphere of the circus, to inhale the earthy odor of the stables, the damp straw, and the acrid scent of the animals. He laughed heartily at the clowns, seeming far more amused by their buffoonery than his son, who scarcely smiled all evening, or his wife, who remained taciturn and distant.

We went down to the stables during the intermission. And Picasso talked to us about the circus. Whenever he had a little money, he had dinner with friends and brought them here. The Médrano was almost next door to his studio then. Max Jacob, Pierre MacOrlan, André Salmon, and occasionally Kahnweiler or Braque had been his companions. The theater bored them. They almost never went to it.

PICASSO: I was really under the spell of the circus! Sometimes I came three or four nights in one week. It was here that I saw Grock for the first time. He was just beginning, with Antonet. It was incredible . . . I liked the clowns best of all. Sometimes we stayed out in the wings at the bar and talked to them through the whole performance. And did you know that it was here at the Médrano that clowns first began to abandon their classic costumes and adopted the burlesque type of clothing? It was a real revolution. They could invent their own costumes, their own characters, do anything they fancied . . .

I asked him if his first art dealer was really a clown from the Médrano.

PICASSO: Art dealer—that's saying a bit too much . . . Clovis Sagot was really a junk dealer who also sold paintings. But he was a real clown before he set himself up as an "art dealer" and rented a shop in the rue Laffitte, near the church of Notre-Dame-de-Lorette. His brother was an art book publisher, as a matter of fact, and that may be why he chose that particular profession. He was a hard man, Clovis Sagot, very hard—almost a usurer. But sometimes, when I was broke, I put a few canvases under my arm and sold them to him. It was because of that that Gertrude Stein's brother saw one of my paintings in his place one day. Père Soulier was another junk dealer in the neighborhood—just across from the Médrano, in the rue des Martyrs—and he used to sell paintings sometimes, too. It was in his shop that I unearthed the big Douanier Rousseau you saw in my studio.

The second part of the program that night featured a group of acrobats: three nude and muscular bodies forming daring compositions, balancing one upon another. A few days later, when I went to see Picasso, he gestured toward a group of canvases turned to face the wall, and said, "I'm going to show you something . . . look here . . ." It was our acrobats of the other night! I had caught Picasso in the throes of inspiration. I was all the more surprised because I myself, either that very night at the Médrano or on a return trip the next day, had photographed these same acrobats, without suspecting that they would also fascinate Picasso. The slow evolution of those athletic forms in the glare of multicolored lights, their fragile and audacious architecture, collapsing at almost the moment it formed itself in space, had impressed him so strongly that he had painted a whole series of them. Perfectly recognizable on the first canvases, the acrobats gradually disappeared as the composition became tauter, stripped of detail. It was the first time I had had an opportunity to see how Picasso peels a subject down to its essential descriptive traits, in search of a deeper, more profound resemblance. The last canvas in this series was almost abstract. A bold transposition had taken place. And yet the canvas still breathed that atmosphere which is so peculiar to the circus, with the luminous oval of the ring, the brilliant stars in the sky of the roofing, the public gathered in the shadows. As for the group of acrobats, it had been reduced to an ideogram vibrating in the spotlight of the projectors.*

Some time after our trip to Boisgeloup and the evening at the Cirque Médrano, I went back to the rue La Boétie. Madame Picasso took me aside: "We have no photographs of Paulo," she told me. "Cameras frighten him, and he bursts into tears. Now that he knows you and is used to watching you work, perhaps we can get him to pose." I was able to grant her wish. The same day, I also made a portrait of Picasso. At that time, when I photographed someone, I was satisfied with a single take. I felt—rightly or wrongly—that by concentrating on a solitary portrait I could capture its essential character better than by making several dozen negatives, as is customarily done today. We were in one of the rooms at the rear of the studio, dominated by the monumental canvas of *Jadwiga*, standing on the floor, unframed, just leaning against the mantelpiece. Rousseau had painted her in a dark colored robe, framed against the window, with a heavy curtain behind her, and the landscape of border fortifications serving as background. It was through this painting, unearthed in the junk dealer's shop around 1908, that Picasso discovered the Douanier Rousseau. Jadwiga, the beautiful Polish schoolteacher, was, in a sense, the muse of this ingenuous artist; the only woman devoted enough to pose nude for him. He painted her as Eve, full-length and in profile, taking the apple held out to her by the tempter serpent. He painted her reclining on a red couch, dreaming, transplanted to a virgin forest of gigantic leaves, pale foliage, dark vines, and tall reeds, surrounded by panthers, monkeys, and birds, bathed in a silvery moonlight as a mysterious personage played to her on the flute . . . *Le Rêve,* one of the strangest works of the Douanier Rousseau, who was a poet, too, upon occasion:

*Having slipped gently into night,*
*Jadwiga, in a beautiful dream,*
*Heard the music of a pipe*
*Played by a gentle charmer,*
*And while the moon shed its light*
*On the blooms of greening trees,*
*The wild serpents gave ear*
*To the gay sounds he made . . .*

* This series on the Cirque Médrano was later reproduced, under the title *Variations sur le Cirque,* in the study of Picasso's work from 1930 to 1935 published by the review *Cahiers d'Art.*

I wanted Jadwiga, who had presided over the banquet given in honor of the Douanier Rousseau at the Bateau-Lavoir, to be present in this portrait, too.

Picasso was wearing a blue pull-over sweater, and also a cardigan, beneath a well-worn gray double-breasted jacket with sagging pockets and lapels liberally sprinkled with stains. The collar of his shirt turned up at the ends, rolling over on itself like the petals of a flower. But I had no time for details of clothing, fascinated as I was by the eyes intently focused on me . . . "Black diamonds . . ." "Eyes of living coal . . ." "Eyes of jet . . ." Contrary to everything that has been said, and to the things that are generally believed, I realized then that they are neither abnormally large nor abnormally dark. If they seem enormous, it is because they have the curious faculty of opening very wide, uncovering the white sclerotic ring—sometimes even above the iris—in which light can be reflected and throw off sparks. It is the flaring line of the eyelids which causes his gaze to seem fixed, mad, haunted . . . And it is also this that makes the iris—a deep brown normally—appear so black against the widely dilated pupils. It is the eye of a visionary, prepared for perpetual astonishment. Schopenhauer was struck by a similar conformation of the eye of Goethe.

I have made many other protraits of Picasso since that day, but my preference is still for this one and only portrait of 1932. Picasso looms up in it like a monolith, in all the compact, distilled strength of his full maturity. And everything is centered on the flashing intensity of that gaze, piercing you, subduing you, devouring you . . .[6]

Since Picasso had given me "carte blanche," I photographed his reçent paintings, just as he had assembled them for the "presentation"; his mantelpiece, with some vases he had repainted himself—the first sign of his interest in ceramics—and the towers of empty cigarette boxes, which he piled one on top of another every day, never having the heart to throw them out[7]; a paper cap with a long visor—he wore it at that time to protect his eyes at night—sitting on a chair in the middle of the room. I also took a photo of the landscape he viewed from his studio: the roofs, the chimneys, and the Eiffel Tower; and some of the order and disorder in the other rooms: stacks of paintings, mysterious bundles revealing glimpses of other canvases by the Douanier Rousseau, and a group of African statuettes.[8]

The controversy aroused by *Les Demoiselles d'Avignon* is

well known: had or had not the influence of Negro art played a part in it? Picasso has always asserted that the birth of cubism owed nothing to Negro fetishes, and that he himself had not seen African sculpture until after the painting was completed. If the period of his work which is falsely labeled "Negro" occurred at the same time as the discovery of African masks and statues, it is pure coincidence.

However that may be, Picasso, like Matisse, Derain, Braque, and Vlaminck, had what amounted to a passion for all forms of Negro totemism. At about 1910 he was already filling his apartment on the Boulevard de Clichy with them, as Fernande Olivier has testified: "Picasso was becoming a fanatic on the subject of Negro works, and statues, masks, and fetishes from every country in Africa were accumulating in his apartment . . ." I imagine, therefore, that all of the Negro statues I photographed on the rue La Boétie came originally from the Boulevard de Clichy.

One morning, when I arrived at his studio, I found paints and brushes scattered across the floor, the tubes squeezed and twisted, left there strangled, with the feverish imprint of Picasso's fingers on their contorted forms.[9] The canvas he had painted during the night was still there, leaning against the wall. Without a thought to comfort, he worked in any corner he pleased, far from the easel, his body bent double, sometimes sitting on the floor, with the canvas placed anywhere at all, in any impromptu fashion. Discomfort did not bother him—it might even be said that it stimulated him.

One day Picasso showed me a series of drawings that I was to photograph for *Minotaure*. He had just done them, at Boisgeloup.

PICASSO: Do you know the *Crucifixion* of Matthias Grünewald, the central panel of the Isenheim altarpiece? I love that painting, and I tried to interpret it. But as soon as I began to draw, it became something else entirely . . .

Of course I knew this most moving of all altar screens. But only a few elements of that shattering scene of Calvary were identifiable here; some suggestions of the cross, of the body convulsed in agony, of the other protagonists in the drama . . . The mouth of Mary Magdalen had become a sort of gaping funnel; the clenched fingers of her folded hands, a starfish . . . In some areas the drawing was reduced to the almost abstract main lines of the composition, and in others it seemed as if Picasso had amused himself by using the legs and claws of shellfish in his reconstruction of the panel. There was little trace of religious emotion. Rather, a kind of humor: for example, that safety pin holding the folds of the loincloth in place—a new attribute of the *Crucifixion*.

I mention this series for a specific purpose, since it was the first time, to my knowledge, that a great painting had touched off the creative spark in him and he had concentrated his energies on a masterpiece, in order to extort its secret. Before Delacroix, before Manet, Cranach, Poussin, or Velázquez, Picasso chose Grünewald as his target. It was no longer a matter of being subjected to an influence, as it had been earlier when he came under the spell of Lautrec, of Cézanne, of El Greco, of Ingres. At that time, it was Picasso who had, in a sense, become Lautrec, Cézanne, El Greco, Ingres. But from this point on, it was the masters from whom he drew inspiration who became Picasso. With the *Crucifixion* he inaugurated a kind of pictorial critique, executed with his brush, and similar to an exhaustive literary critique, seeking to extricate the quintessence of a work. In the one case, as in the other, the problem is to enter into the skin of the creator, to penetrate to the hard core of his personality, to shed light on the quality that makes him unique, on the mystery of his language. Picasso's excesses in his lovingly irreverent imitations, his verve, his humor, his cruelty—taken together, they form the magnifying glass which unveils "the style beneath the brush."

That same day I had to don my black sack to change my negatives in his studio, and I left an unexposed plate lying on a table. Any objects placed on such a plate, any kind of matter, even the simplest forms, are like so many time bombs: they will explode at the desired hour. Picasso found my little plate, felt it, sniffed it, examined it, and was first intrigued and then fascinated by it. I do not know whether or not he was familiar with the engravings Corot had done on glass plates coated with gelatin. In any case, he could not long resist the urge to attack a surface as smooth and sleek as the ice on a frozen lake. When I returned to the studio the next day or the day after, he held out the little forgotten plate, holding it carefully between his thumb and his index finger, so that I could see it in transparence, and smiling mischievously.

"Look at what I have done with your plate," he said.

And, in fact, it was no longer a virgin surface. His infinitely patient fingers, using an etching needle, had transformed it into a tiny, two and a half by three and a half inch "Picasso." I remember it very well. It depicted a woman's profile, similar to those of his painting and sculpture of that period, inspired by Marie-Thérèse Walter—a miniature variation of his masterpiece, painted in the month of March of that same year, 1932, reproduced in color in *Minotaure,* and now belonging to the Museum of Modern Art in New York: *Femme devant le miroir.*

I suggested that I take the plate with me, and pull a "first proof" of it.

"No, no," he answered. "Leave it with me. I still have some work to do on it. I'll give it to you the next time."

"The next time!" All too often now, I have had occasion to discover that in his language the next time almost always means never. What became of that little plate? I have never seen it reproduced. Is it lying somewhere at the bottom of a trunk? Broken? Disappeared? However that may be, the idea of making original engravings on photographic plate, and even the first experiment in it, dates back to five years before the series of photo-engravings done in 1937 in collaboration with Dora Maar . . .

The text that accompanied my photographs of Picasso's sculptures in *Minotaure* was written by André Breton. He had met the artist some time before publication of the first *Surrealist Manifesto.* Later, on the occasion of Picasso's eightieth birthday, Breton wrote: "The surrealist attitude toward Picasso has always been one of great deference, on the artistic plane, and many times, his new propositions and discoveries have stimulated the attraction that drew us to him. To us, the thing that excluded him from the category of artists known as cubists—who were of little interest to us—is the lyricism which, almost from the beginning, caused him to take great liberties with the strict hypotheses he and his companions at the time had imposed on themselves!" (*Combat,* November 6, 1961). Breton also praised Picasso for having had the knowledge to transcend cubism through the "violent pulse of passion," as if the severe discipline of the school had been "haunted and shaken by a great wind." Breton was doubtless thinking of the "stupefying guitars"; of the glued constructions of 1913, with bits of yellowing newspaper; and especially of the *Femme en chemise dans un fauteuil* of the

1. Picasso in his rue La Boétie apartment, 1932

*. . . except for one mantelpiece on which there was some evidence of his fantasies, nothing whatever bore his stamp.*

2. A thirteenth-century chapel on the grounds of Picasso's country home at Boisgeloup, December 1932

*. . . mass was still celebrated there on some occasions.*

3. Picasso's sculpture workshop at Boisgeloup, December 1932

*... all curving lines, the nose becoming prominent, the eyes like globes, resembling some barbarian goddess.*

4. Picasso's sculpture workshop at Boisgeloup, December 1932

*The kerosene lamp, which he had set on the hard-packed earth that formed the floor of the shed, threw fantastic shadows on and around all of these white statues.*

5. Picasso's country home at Boisgeloup, December 1932

*It was by that stabbing light that I took one last photograph: the illuminated façade of Picasso's little château.*

same year, in which, against the background of a mauve armchair, Picasso had painted a delicate rose-beige composition of flesh and breasts emerging from an embroidered blouse. The surrealists considered this picture the forerunner of surrealist painting, and already in conformity with the esthetic laid down by André Breton: "Beauty will be convulsive . . ."

But is it possible to speak of surrealist influences? In 1924, far from surrealism, Picasso was painting his women as giants, drawing like Ingres, and composing synthetic still lifes. If he took part in one of their expositions, in 1925, it was without his knowledge—his paintings were loaned by collectors. Even his 1933 *Anatomie,* perhaps the closest to surrealism of his works—variations on the female body done, apparently, with everyday objects of carpentry—would find a perfectly legitimate ancestry in Arcimboldo and in many French engravings which represent one or another of the guilds by figures composed entirely of their respective tools. Unquestionably the surrealist concept of the mind liberated from all restraint, the audacity of the movement, and its admiration for him stimulated Picasso to "confront everything that exists with everything that can exist." Certain of his statements of the time bear witness to this: "One does not set limits on nature, and neither does one copy it; one allows imagined objects to clothe themselves in real appearances . . ." And in the same way, his painting, imbued with rejection, with reduction to the essential, with ellipses and the shattering of forms, often seems the product of a free invention. But even when he appears to be a thousand leagues from reality, to be taking every liberty he pleases with appearance, even when his work is bathed in an atmosphere of the fantastic or the surreal, a solid realism is at its base. In the basic fiber of the work, the model, mysteriously enough, is present. It was an error to see a surrealist painter in Picasso. But Breton believed it, and occasionally admitted it. He even fixed the date of his "adhesion" as the year 1926. And in 1928 he wrote: "It is for multiple reasons that we claim him as one of ours." He was forced, however, to recognize that what he had taken for "surrealism" was often just an unexpected depiction of the real, its reduction to symbols. Thirty years later, Breton had to admit that, "What has constantly created an obstacle to a more complete unification of his views and ours is his unswerving attachment to the exterior world (to the 'object') and the blindness which this disposition entails on the organic and imaginative plane" (*Combat,* November 6, 1961).* As for Picasso, he put the dots on his i's. "I attempt to observe nature, always. I am intent on resemblance, a resemblance more profound, more real than the real, attaining the surreal. It was in this way that I thought of surrealism, but the word was used in an entirely different fashion . . ." Picasso has said the same sort of thing to me, but I preferred in this case to cite the statement above, which he made to André Warnod in 1945.**

In *Picasso dans son Élément,* André Breton treated exclusively of his extrapictorial productions. Although written from a flagrantly surrealist point of view, it is an extraordinary text, leading Breton to say that Picasso the painter does not have the "presumption" of color, and Picasso the sculptor does not have the "presumption" of matter; that he is searching, for their own sake, into "the perishable and the ephemeral" . . . "I like the thought," he wrote, "that when certain of Picasso's paintings take their place in the museums of the world, he might contribute a share—and it would be enormously generous—of everything he has done that is not likely to become the object of a buyer's admiration or of any speculation other than intellectual." Then Breton speaks of the little canvas in which, between two figures —one in matchsticks and the other in twists of grass—the lacework of a butterfly and a dead leaf are limned into the white; of the plant with the tortured roots, transformed into a piece of sculpture by the horn and the red plume with which it is crowned; then of the character built on a bootmaker's form and nicknamed "The Christmas Tree."

* It was undoubtedly the bitter deception caused by Picasso's "nonadhesion" to surrealism that induced Breton to denounce as blindness what he had always previously praised as clear-sightedness. This disillusionment was only surpassed by the one he experienced from Freud's ferocious resistance to the establishment of any connection whatever between psychoanalysis and surrealism, in spite of all of Breton's efforts and his visit to Freud in Vienna. In a letter to Stefan Zweig in 1938, regarding a visit from Dali, Freud actually wrote: "Until this time, I was inclined to consider the surrealists—who seem to have adopted me as their patron saint—as one hundred percent madmen (or let us say, as we would for alcohol, ninety-five percent)."

** On the other hand, it is indisputable that Picasso's literary works, including *Desire Caught by the Tail,* have their origin in surrealist poetry. Without the example of automatic writing and free association, Picasso might never have thought of releasing the truculent verbal flow of his imagination. A curious point in connection with this is that he did it at a time when he was closely linked with Paul Éluard, who had, at the same time, renounced automatic writing forever.

At the end of his text Breton mentions a strange canvas, still in preparation: "Among a quantity of pictures and objects Picasso showed me the other day—each one more brilliant than the last, from the point of view of freshness, intelligence, and life—there was a little unfinished canvas, in the shape of a butterfly, and of which only the center was occupied by a large impasto. Even as he assured himself that it was dry, he explained to me that the subject of this canvas was to be an excrement, as would be readily apparent when he had arranged the flies on it. His only regret was that he had been forced to use color to make up for the lack of a genuine dried excrement, and more particularly one of the *inimitable* kind he had occasionally noticed in the country, at the time of year when children swallow cherries without bothering to spit out the pit."

Since he asked no more of painting than pretexts for "intellectual speculation," it was entirely natural that André Breton's attention should focus on this unfinished excrement more clearly than on any other work of Picasso's—it was undoubtedly the most "surrealist" because of its scatological subject, and the most "ephemeral and perishable" because of its basic matter. The mere idea of this extrapictorial picture aroused in him, in spite of his "slight repugnance," an access of lyric exaltation:

"I surprised myself," he wrote, "by imagining those gleaming flies, bright and new, as Picasso would know how to make them. Everything became gay; not only did my eyes no longer remember having been drawn to something disagreeable, but I was *somewhere else,* where the sun was shining, where it was pleasant to live, among the wild flowers and the dew: I plunged freely into the woods."

One day in that same year of 1932, I met a strange couple in Picasso's studio: the man was handsome—a thin, almost emaciated face and pale, olive-hued skin, with a tiny moustache; great, sparkling, hallucinatory eyes; the jet-black hair of a gypsy, gleaming with brilliantine.[10] A blue-striped celluloid shirt collar and a tie of red string betrayed his propensity to set himself apart. The woman was slender, small, built like a boy, very dark and of uncertain age. Her intense, chestnut-brown eyes gave her face a singular attraction. Picasso made the introductions.

"Brassaï, do you know Gala and Salvador Dali?"

I did not know this couple, but they were already famous, and I had heard a great deal of talk about them . . . They had met two years before, when several surrealist friends had made a trip to Cadaqués. Elena Dimitrovna Diakonova had been Paul Éluard's wife since 1917 and was known as the "surrealist muse"; a reserved and masterful woman who exercised an occult, yet considerable influence over the entire group and had contributed largely to the success of Max Ernst. Éluard and Gala had gone to Switzerland first, to see René Crevel, who was ill at the time, but when they arrived in Cadaqués lightning struck. As Dali said later, "We fell in love with each other instantly." The superior intelligence, the mysterious Slavic charm, the slender, boyish body won an immediate victory. When the surrealist group—Buñuel, Éluard, René Magritte and his wife—returned to Paris, Gala stayed with Dali in that whitewashed house ("a lump of sugar afloat in honey") where he had spent his childhood. It was the beginning of a fierce attachment, an idolatry without parallel. Dali had found "the Beatrice of his life." And as for Gala—mistress, teacher, guide, source of inspiration and manager, all at the same time—she took the phenomenon that was Dali firmly in hand; his dazzling success is in large part her work.

I spent about an hour with Gala and Dali, looking at Picasso's most recent drawings and prints. Picasso himself had seen Dali's work for the first time in an avant-garde gallery in Barcelona six years before, when Dali was only twenty-two. Since he thought that it was very promising—one of the canvases, *Dos de la Fille,* had particularly impressed him—he had mentioned it to Paul Rosenberg and Pierre Loeb, who then made a trip to Catalonia to meet the young artist. This initial prospecting, however, came to nothing. It was not until 1929, at Miró's instigation, that Dali came to Paris, and then he stayed only a week. He visited Versailles, the Musée Grevin, and Picasso, whom he preferred—so he said, thinking he was being flattering—to the Louvre. He bore public witness to a veneration for Picasso, an immoderate adulation which was only surpassed by his jealousy and unbridled hatred. It was intolerable that any artist other than himself could be considered "the greatest Spanish painter." Picasso received him warmly, and always demonstrated a great deal of interest in both his work and Dali himself. When Dali came to live in Paris, shortly afterward, he continued to help patronize him, introducing him to Gertrude Stein and to many of his other friends.

At the time I met him in Picasso's studio, Dali was at the

height of his "surrealist activity," and was already scandalously famous as the author (with Luis Buñuel) of *Un Chien Andalou* and *L'Age d'Or.* The *Jeu Lugubre,* with its minutely painted bits of excrement in the half-open drawers of a chest, the *Grand Masturbateur,* and other famous obscenities of the same kind, had found impassioned collectors such as the Vicomte Charles de Noailles, the Englishman Edward James, and several others. Dali's painted anatomical organs, his erotic, phallic forms suspended on pitchforks, his embryos, his bats, his crutches, his limp watches and flexible telephones, his lobsters and ants, his grasshoppers marching across the jagged rocks and deserted sands of Cape Creus, had opened the doors of the "world" to him. The "Dali phenomenon" was the star whose advent Breton had long awaited, calculating its trajectory, plotting its appearance in the skies. Chirico was respected, of course, but he was still an individualist who both antedated the movement and remained outside it, evidencing for it nothing but scorn and hostility. Picasso had constantly resisted the surrealists' determination to gather him into the fold; André Masson, Miró, and even Max Ernst were already distinguishing themselves more for their pictorial qualities than for their obedience to surrealist doctrines. And even though Yves Tanguy's deserted beaches on dead planets cast a phantasmagoric, ghostly spell, they did not startle the viewer with the convulsive beauty of which Éluard and André Breton dreamed. Dali fulfilled, surpassed all of their hopes: he was the imagined artist of the dream, of the ecstasy, the erotic fury; a man possessed of demons, a complex-laden neurotic, an explorer of "the irrational" as daring as he was lucid. Dali's authority, his influence, the extent of his audience, were extraordinary. And not only in the circle of snobs and wealthy celebrities to whom Dali and Gala paid court day and night—and who bought his paintings for ten or twelve thousand francs apiece —but also in the very heart of the surrealist movement. As Breton was to say of him, before qualifying his painting as "ultra-retrograde" and the man himself with the anagram he made of his name, "Avida Dollars," there was a period of three or four years when "Dali was the incarnation of the surrealist spirit, bringing to it a brilliance that could only have come from someone who had taken no part in the often unpleasant episodes of its early years."

Like all the rest of the surrealists, Dali was nurtured on Freud, and he told me later that the Viennese psychiatrist's *The In-*

*terpretation of Dreams* had been the greatest discovery of his life. He brought to the surrealist group, which by this time had lost some of its finest elements as a result of Breton's expulsions, not only a savage imagery that seemed wrested forcibly from a dream, captured with the scrupulous objectivity of photography, and translated into a kind of trancelike *trompe-l'oeil,* but also the key to his method, which he defined as *paranoiac-critique.* It was in 1930, shortly after their meeting, that Gala, having discovered Dali's gifts as a writer, set to work deciphering the secret, almost illegible scribblings he had hidden away in drawers. Dali wrote only in French, but it was a French without any notion of spelling or punctuation; almost entirely phonetic. She brought some order into the chaos of his notes, and it was her work that resulted in the text *La Femme Visible.* Dali here defined his method in the following manner: "Spontaneous knowledge, irrational knowledge, based on the critical and systematic objectivation of hallucinatory associations and interpretations."

The fact that Éluard and Breton could have lent so complacent an ear to the gospel as preached by Dali might have been surprising if it were not that—conquered, subjugated as they were by his assurance and his diabolical powers of persuasion—they saw in him a promise of renewal for surrealism, a still-untapped, unexploited mine, a perfect substitute for automatic writing, whose underground riches were fast being exhausted. But it marked a break with the pure automatism of Breton, which had always been the intangible base of orthodox surrealism. To the surprises and disorders of the spontaneous acts which had heretofore issued from the common, anonymous, and impersonal source of the irrational, Dali substituted a "systematization" of disorder, thereby restoring to the creative artist his right to a personal vision, to his own complexes and obsessions. Dali never ceased proclaiming his mistrust of "spontaneity," likening it to "the conventional, stereotyped taste of a restaurant lobster." He preferred "systematization inspired by paranoiac frenzy." Such a change involved nothing less than the establishment of an absolute monarchy—the reign of a fiercely imperialist individualism—on the ruins of an equalitarian, anarchical democracy. "Imperialist," in fact, was a word Dali was to use over and over again. "Paranoia," he stated, in *La Femme Visible,* "makes use of the exterior world to demonstrate the obsessive idea in such a manner that the reality of that idea is made disturbingly real to others. The reality of the exterior world serves as both illustration and proof, and is placed in the service of our mental and spiritual reality."

There was nothing very new or scandalous in this "intrusion of man's desires into the world." All art worthy of the name is obsessional; it interprets, dominates, reshapes reality. Paranoiac frenzy, with its accompanying exaggerated egocentrism, represents only an extreme, a pathological case of the creative mind and vision. It was not until much later that Breton, freed at last of the ascendancy Dali had exercised over him and the entire group, would deny any form of originality in his paranoiac-critique, and define it as a method inspired by "the lesson of Piero di Cosimo and Leonardo da Vinci (losing one's self in the contemplation of a wad of spittle and an old wall until the eye organizes it into a second world; a world that can be revealed equally directly through the medium of painting . . .)."*

I saw Dali often again after that first meeting. I liked the incredible humor which always provided the dominant note to his ideas, his complexes, his untrammeled imagination; and I admired the discipline of his eternally active brain—a ceaselessly turning outboard motor, as Picasso described it. And occasionally I also liked his painting . . . His megalomania was provided with a splendid springboard in *Minotaure,* which opened its pages freely to him. The articles he contributed—under titles that were intentionally startling, and written with a pseudoscientific precision—in which Dali gave free rein to all of his fancies and obsessions, were frequently lit with dazzling flashes of insight. The reader may have been aware that he had crossed the frontiers of an empire of madness, but it was nonetheless impossible for him to escape completely from a taut, persuasive, and almost always convincing dialectic. This was notably true in the case of "Millet's Angelus," which appeared in *Minotaure,* and formed the introduction to a long essay titled *The Tragic Myth of Millet's Angelus.* Who would have thought that this innocuous period picture—a pious depiction of a peasant couple, with heads bowed, absorbed in the evening prayer, and as widely reproduced as pictures and statues of the Virgin of Lourdes—was in reality the depiction of perversion itself, the consummate example, the

* It is only necessary, in fact, to substitute in Dali's definition the term "creative artist" for "paranoia" and it becomes valid for all the great creators of forms, and even for all of the great styles, beginning with the primitive man who discovered the form of a bison in the uneven surfaces of the wall of a cave.

"monument" to sexual inhibition? "How," Dali wrote, "could the sublime symbolic hypocrisy of this darling of the masses, the *Angelus,* have been separated from so flagrant an example of subconscious 'erotic fury'?" He told me that he had been set on the path of this discovery by reading Freud's revelation and interpretation of the vulture that appeared to Leonardo in a dream and was used by the artist as an invisible part of the composition of *The Virgin and St. Anne,* in the Louvre. According to Dali, it should be obvious to anyone that this pitchfork thrust into the ground beside the man and this barrow laden with open potato sacks behind the woman symbolized the masculine and feminine sexes. And he attributed the phenomenal popularity of the painting to its latent eroticism.

Dali was so obsessed with the subject that, for many years, he introduced the *Angelus* into his own paintings, and made a collection of every object he could find that bore a reproduction of this "twilight sham." It was as a result of this that, one day in his apartment, I photographed a coffee service in which every cup, every saucer, was imprinted with Millet's "scandalous" picture. And the simple fact is that no one who had read Dali's interpretation could any longer regard this prayerful couple as innocently as he had before. His perverse dialectic had found its mark. Suddenly, many of Millet's other paintings—*The Gleaners, The Hay Binders, The Sower,* etc.—became suspect, charged with disguised, subconscious erotic impulses. William Tell was another of Dali's disconcerting obsessions, and the familiar legend has taken on another meaning since he unveiled its "tragic myth." Dali saw in it the act of paternal vengeance, the symbol of his own quarrels with his father, which had resulted in a complete break between them. In the story of William Tell, he unmasked the monstrous legend of incestuous mutilation of a son by his father.

Another of Dali's discoveries was Art Nouveau, in which he discerned a "psychopathological" quality that stimulated his frenzy to the point of paroxysm. It was through him that I first heard about the work of Gaudí, the architect of La Sagrada Familia, the unfinished expiatory church in Barcelona. Dali's admiration for the Catalan creator of Art Nouveau was limitless. As a child he had often been taken for walks in Barcelona's Güell Park—which was also Gaudí's work—and he confided in me how strongly he had been impressed by it, saying that the enchantment of this *demented* architecture had marked him for the rest of his life.*

Dali was persuaded that the landscape of the Costa Brava, and especially that of Cape Creus—that "geological delirium" —which he himself had always before his eyes at Cadaqués, had also inspired Gaudí. In the curving forms of Gaudí's stones and the convoluted rhythms of his wrought iron, he found an echo of the convulsive lines of the beaches, the corroded grottoes, the jagged rocks, and even the furious pounding of the waves. His houses, "created for madmen, for erotomaniacs," had the look of having been molded in spun sugar for some display piece, and Dali likened them to the "exhibitionist and ornamental" cakes and tarts of a pastry shop. All of the 1900 style of art, at the opposite pole from the utilitarian and rational architecture Dali detested, now seemed to him to represent the ultimate form of an *antiplastic* art—"the expression of the darkest, most inadmissible desires." In an essay he wrote for *Minotaure* called "The Terrifying and Comestible Beauty of Art Nouveau," one of his best texts, Dali identified himself to such an extent with Art Nouveau that in "psychoanalyzing" it he was in reality performing an act of self-revelation.

I shared the task of illustrating this text with Man Ray. He photographed the architecture of Gaudí in Barcelona, while I did that of Parisian Art Nouveau. I began with the 1900 busts and vases Dali had bought in the flea market; florid shapes that were half woman, half water lily, the body emerging from extravagant flower forms, the hair becoming lost in aquatic growths. "Sculptures of everything that is extrasculptural," Dali wrote, "water, smoke, the iridescences of pretuberculosis bacilli and nocturnal pollutions, the woman-flower-flesh-peyote-jewel-cloud-flame-butterfly-mirror." He thought that the faces of these "hysterical" sculptures were actually those of the madwomen Charcot had treated through hypnotism at the Salpêtrière at about the same time, in an experiment that was a forerunner of Freud's

* Gaudí's influence on Miró was also considerable. But in his case, he was primarily impressed by the important role Gaudí accorded to *color* in his architecture; by the multicolored mosaics and gleaming ceramics. Walking in the Güell Park with me, and pointing out the curving benches, incrusted with broken bits of glazed earthenware, arranged so that they sometimes resembled pre-Miró Mirós, the artist said, "All my art comes from there . . ."[11] As for Picasso, he always said that Gaudí had had no influence on him. Certain elements of his architecture, however—primarily the chimneys—seem almost a prelude to cubism.

more famous discoveries. After this, I photographed some 1900 houses, with their distorted façades and "columns of feverish flesh"; and also the wealth of ornamentation on the entrances to the Métro,[12] which so fascinated Dali.*

I collaborated with Dali again on *Phénomène de l'extase* and *Les Sculptures Involontaires:* old bus and Métro tickets, instinctively rolled and twisted; bits of soap and absorbent cotton, "sculptured" involuntarily . . . I also photographed some automatons for the text of *Au Paradis des Fantômes,* by Benjamin Péret, perhaps the purest, the most intransigent of the surrealist poets. I liked his eternally curious mind and his fertile imagination, constantly dreaming up new amusements and surprises. One day he took me with him to the Concours Lépine, a veritable jungle of chimerical inventions, of childish, fantastic dreams, some of which seemed really demented. We walked around the stands of the "inventors"—among whom Marcel Duchamp had once figured, with his turning graphic disks, cutting spiral forms in space—and among the inevitable automatic cradle rockers, the gadgets for threading needles, the creams to do away with corns on the feet, the stitch counters for women who knit, we unearthed a dozen or so absolutely insane objects, whose involuntary humor and utter uselessness made them worthy of a place among the most frenzied of surrealist creations.

Among others, we saw an "insectodrome" for "obstacle races for cockroaches or other insects," with parallel tracks, an electric signal marking the arrival of the winner, and individual prods to stimulate the competitors; a "street-cleaning cane" for a dog, hollow on the interior, and provided with a little revolving shovel which gathered up what the dog had deposited on the sidewalk and pulled it into the interior of the cane—the dog carried the cane himself, fastened to his body by a system of elastics between the tail and the ears; a gramophone set into a model of the Opera, with the record turning on the stage and presumably giving the illusion of being present at an actual performance; a portrait of President Lebrun executed entirely in five- and ten-franc postage stamps, a hen that laid cigarettes, etc., etc . . .

* "One day, in the heart of Paris, I discovered the 1900 entrances to the Métro, which, unfortunately, were already being demolished, to be replaced with horrible anonymous constructions. The photographer Brassaï made a series of photos of the decorative elements on these entrances, and no one could believe his eyes—Art Nouveau seemed so completely surrealist." (*The Secret Life of Salvador Dali*)

This series of photographs appeared in another review, with a text by Benjamin Péret. I also photographed for *Minotaure* the sculptures of Alberto Giacometti, in his studio on the rue Hippolyte-Maindron, which even at that time resembled a plaster grotto invaded by stalagmites. Giacometti had joined the surrealist group two years before. Among other objects of "symbolic functioning" which purported to be the depiction of dreams, of subconscious emotions and repressed desires were *Le Palais* and *L'Heure des Traces,* which was also known as *La Boule Suspendue.*

I also illustrated several articles of André Breton's which were published in *Minotaure.* Among the most important of these—"*Le Message Automatique,*" with drawings done by various mediums, "*La Beauté Sera Convulsive,*" "*Château Etoilé,*" etc.—was "*La Nuit de Tournesol.*" One of his poems of 1923, very obscure and almost forgotten, had taken on an entirely new meaning and importance in Breton's eyes on the day he recognized in it a thinly veiled description of one of the major amorous adventures of his life, which was to take place twenty-one years later. He discovered with emotion that the object of his love had been unconsciously described in the poem—and also a nighttime walk with her to the vegetable and fruit markets—sometimes even down to the smallest details. The woman with the long "ash-blond hair" did a dance number in a music hall in which she represented a water nymph, and the lovers' nocturnal promenade led them to the water nymphs of Jean Goujon's Fountain of the Innocents in Les Halles, just as the poem had indicated. The text of the "*Tournesol*" article—the title was inspired by the Tour Saint-Jacques, rising from the city like a sun—takes each premonitory verse of the poem, one by one, and confronts its hidden content with the actual events which, according to Breton, were its belated fulfilment. According to the central theme of the "communicating vessels"—a theme which is very close to Goethe's "elective affinities"—our subconscious governs not only our dreams, but also our real life, occasionally anticipating the events which occur to us, our chance encounters, changing the accidents of our lives into "objective accidents." "Auto-analysis," Breton thought, "can sometimes exhaust the content of real events, to the point of making them depend entirely on an anterior activity which was in no way controlled by the mind."

To illustrate "*La Nuit de Tournesol,*" Breton had asked me for a photograph of Les Halles at night, another of the flower market, and a third of the Tour Saint-Jacques. The text appeared in *Minotaure*—and later in *L'Amour Fou*—with these illustrations. Contrary to what the author of *Nadja* thought at the time, however, these photographs had not been made specially for him. I had had them for some time—even one of the Tour Saint-Jacques as he had described it, "beneath its ghostly veil of scaffolding."*

* My other contributions to *Minotaure:* sculptures of Aristide Maillol, Henri Laurens, Despiau, and Lipchitz; a series on Ambroise Vollard; "*Nocturnes de Paris,*" which appeared with Young's "*Les Nuits*"; studies of the nude, accompanied by a text of Maurice Raynal. It was in Numbers 3 and 4 of *Minotaure* that I published my first article on graffiti. Its title, "From the Walls of Caves to the Walls of Factories," was suggested to me by Paul Éluard.

## 1939

All during the month of August, war seemed imminent. No one any longer believed that the catastrophe could be averted. Everyone expected the worst . . . And on November 15 of that year, the largest retrospective exhibition of Picasso's work—a sort of apotheosis, really—was to open at the Museum of Modern Art in New York, under the title: "Forty Years of His Art." Picasso wanted to spend the summer in Antibes. But he had scarcely arrived there, in July, when he learned of Ambroise Vollard's accidental death. It was a great blow to him. Although the celebrated art dealer no longer bought his canvases and drawings, he still published many de luxe editions with illustrations by Picasso. Vollard had come to see him several times in June, to discuss their new projects . . . Picasso was particularly interested in the idea of collecting all of his own writings into a single volume, to be illustrated with the prints he had done in color. And Vollard had accepted the idea enthusiastically. His death put an end to their collaboration. Picasso came back to Paris, but returned to Antibes immediately after Vollard's funeral and set to work again.

He had been impressed and fascinated by the sight of men spear-fishing at night by the light of torches, reflected brilliantly in the dark waters of the sea beyond the ramparts of the town, and was working on his large canvas, *Pêche de Nuit à Antibes,* when the French government issued its order for general mobilization. The imminence of war and his anxiety about the fate of his works decided him to return at once to Paris—a Paris that was almost unrecognizable, caught in the midst of a stampede, already deserted by three quarters of its population.

I met him then at Saint-Germain-des-Prés. He was a worried man, seeming helpless, not knowing what to do . . . He ordered dozens of crates and began packing up his pictures and thousands of books and other objects from the rue La Boétie and his new studio on the rue des Grands-Augustins. But his works were too scattered: there were still some at Boisgeloup, and at Le Tremblay, in the studio Vollard had rented to him in 1936, when Picasso had abandoned the little château to Olga, after their separation. There were too many things to be saved, to be put somewhere in a safe place. Discouraged by the exhausting, thankless task—which gave every promise of being as complicated as the dismantling of the Louvre—he abruptly gave up working at it. Although he is normally very much concerned about the fate of his work, he sometimes pretends a total indifference regarding it. "After all," he said one day, "the only thing that's important is the legend created by the picture, and not whether it continues to exist itself." And this is doubtless what he was thinking when he left Paris for Royan, without concerning himself further about the cases and paintings left behind, at the mercy of the bombings everyone expected. He arrived in Royan on the second of September. On the third, war was declared and Europe plunged into her ordeal. Germany, with the help of the Soviet Union, was already crushing Poland.

It was at this moment that *Life* magazine sent me an urgent request for a series of photographs of Picasso, to be published in conjunction with the opening of his exhibition, two months later in New York. But how was I to take them? How could I even arrange to see him for the necessary length of time? I learned from friends that he had come back to Paris on the seventh of September, but just for one day. As a foreigner, he had had to obtain a government authorization to remain in Royan. Fortunately for me, however, he was not able to obtain enough canvas for his work in the shops of Royan, so he decided to return to Paris a second time. He arrived on the twelfth of September, and stayed for two weeks.

I went to see him one morning, at the rue des Grands-Augustins. He was in excellent humor. It was true that Paris had already assumed her mournful wartime look, shrouded in black every night,[13] all of her lights extinguished, all of her windows sealed, her great avenues lit only by the ghostly blue bulbs of the street lamps. But the turn of events of the "phony war" had somewhat reassured people. The danger of bombing seemed remote, for the time being at least. The daily aspect of the city was becoming more normal. The cafés, the movie theaters, and many shops which had closed their doors in the first upheaval—even the Café de Flore was among them—were beginning to reopen. Profiting from his enforced return to the capital, Picasso was again attempting to collect his paintings and drawings, so that they could be safely stored away, and the most beautiful pieces from his collection were already in the safe-deposit vaults of a bank, sharing the protection offered to bars of gold. He was very busy with all of this, but he agreed to give me an entire day for my photographs.

I wanted to photograph him in the new studio, although he was not yet living there, and in the cafés of Saint-Germain-des-Prés, which he had acquired the habit of visiting regularly in the five years since his separation from his wife. The middle-class life of the rue La Boétie, with its constant gatherings of the same people and its air of worldly success, had flattered his vanity and distracted and amused him for a time, but in the long run it had become simply a burden. Those who thought that he had put his youth behind once and for all, forgotten the laughter and the farces of the early years, voluntarily abandoned his liberty and his pleasure in being with his friends, and allowed himself to be duped by the pursuit of "status," found that they were mistaken. *La vie de bohème* regained the upper hand . . . Bruised and battered in the conjugal wars, disgusted even with painting, living alone in his two apartments, he had sent out a call for help to the great friend of his childhood, Jaime Sabartés, who at that time had been living abroad for many years, first in Montevideo and later in the United States. Picasso asked him to return to Europe and come and live with him. It was a cry of real distress; he was going through the gravest crisis of his life. And Sabartés came, installed himself in his friend's apartment on the rue La Boétie, and began the task of filing his papers and books, deciphering his poems, and carefully typing them. From that point on, they were almost always seen together, like the traveler and his shadow; the man with the most brilliant eyes in Paris accompanied by the most myopic man in Paris—at the

Brasserie Lipp, at the Deux-Magots, and at the Café de Flore, the three centers of attraction at Saint-Germain-des-Prés, which was even then beginning to take the place of Montparnasse.

For Sabartés, passing long hours in crowded, smoke-filled, poorly ventilated rooms was constant torture. And they rarely left before midnight. But was there anything he would not have done to please his friend? They would come to the crossroads of Saint-Germain-des-Prés, sometimes in a taxi, and sometimes on foot, usually accompanied by Elft, the dog who shared this "time of the cafés." After a brief, but well-publicized appearance at Lipp or the Deux-Magots, they would arrived at the Café de Flore and sit down at a table with Christian and Yvonne Zervos, Nush and Paul Éluard, the Braques, or other friends. The ceremonial was always the same: the waiters, Jean and Pascal, would run to help Picasso off with his eternal trench coat (he still has it, as a matter of fact); Monsieur Boubal, the Auvergnat proprietor of the Flore, would greet him and light his ever-present Gauloise; Picasso would nod and speak to the blond and smiling Madame Boubal, perched in the glass frame of her cashier's booth, and order a half bottle of Evian, which he never drank. Sabartés might discuss the events of the day with Spanish friends, but he never ceased watching Picasso like a mother-hen; Elft would wander around among the tables, begging for lumps of sugar from the other clients, and his master would reprove them if they gave in, fearing that sweets were bad for the dog's eyes.

It was not at the Flore, however, but at the Deux-Magots, that he made the acquaintance of Dora Maar, one day in the autumn of 1935, at almost exactly the same time Marie-Thérèse Walter gave birth to his daughter, Maya. On an earlier occasion, when she was sitting at a nearby table, he had been struck by the grave, tense countenance of this girl with the pale eyes and the look that was so fixed and attentive it was sometimes disquieting. She had been a member of surrealist circles since 1934. When Picasso saw her again in the same café, this time in the company of Paul Éluard, the poet introduced them. Dora Maar had now entered into his life . . .

At that time I had known Dora myself for five or six years. She was making a start, as was I, in photography. Neither of us as yet possessed a laboratory, and for some time we developed our prints in the same darkroom in Montparnasse, loaned to us by an American who was a mutual friend. Dora's father was an architect of Croat or Yugoslav origin, and her mother a Frenchwoman from Touraine. She had lived for a long time in Argentina with her parents, and spoke fluent Spanish. On several occasions we had exhibited our work together. But now her closeness to Picasso made my presence a rather delicate problem. Dora was in a better position than anyone else to photograph both Picasso and his work. And, at the beginning of their life together, she kept a jealous watch over this role, which she considered a prerogative, and which she assumed with assiduity and talent. It was she who photographed his sculptured pebbles and certain of his statues, and helped him with his photographic experiments in the darkroom. The series she made of the different phases of the evolution of *Guernica* will undoubtedly remain as an invaluable record of Picasso's creative processes. Dora was inclined to sudden outbursts of temper and anger, and in order not to provoke this I was extremely careful not to trespass on what was now her domain. Our relationship remained friendly but distant for quite a long time—approximately the duration of the Spanish Civil War. But curiously enough, as Dora began to lose interest in photography and devote herself entirely to painting—she had done some painting even before becoming a photographer—her attitude also changed. With the disappearance of professional jealousy, there was no longer any obstacle to our friendship.

And so, on that day in September 1939—it was the eighteenth or the nineteenth, I think—I began the series of photographs for *Life*. We went first to Lipp, where Picasso often ate. Sabartés was with him. The clientele of this old brasserie was noticeably different from that of the Deux-Magots, and even more so from that which frequented the Café de Flore: here there were deputies, senators, cabinet ministers, prominent lawyers, members of the Academy and the Institute, stars of the theater, well-known authors, and artists who had "arrived." The average age of the clients was also appreciably greater than that of the habitués of the Flore, which was the stronghold of the young poets and artists, of revolutionary, "avant-garde" actors and film-makers, but also of young men and girls, most of them in search of a role or a career, or just love and adventure. "The spirit of the Flore" would be as hard to analyze as perfume, but it did have several dominant strains: Jacques Prévert and his "band"; Jean-Paul Sartre and Simone de Beauvoir, still far from the existentialist movement, but already using the marble tops of the tables to cover sheet after sheet of paper with their writings; Picasso and his circle of friends . . . As for myself, having paid my tribute to the life of Parisian cafés during the years in Montparnasse, I was not a real habitué of the Flore, but I had many friends and acquaintances there.

I took some photos of Picasso having lunch at Lipp, seated on the banquette—in front of the wall of ceramic tiles done by Léon-Paul Fargue's father—and chatting with Matisse's son, Pierre.[14] Marcelin Cazes, the proprietor, watched me at work; a trifle worried, I think, that I might disturb the lunchtime repose of his other clients. Then, as was the custom, Picasso crossed the Boulevard Saint-Germain, flanked by Sabartés, to have his coffee at the Flore, where he happened to have several appointments that afternoon.[15] He signed some autographs, dedicated a group of his prints to a South American woman writer, and at about three o'clock we left and went to the rue des Grands-Augustins.

This street, in one of the oldest corners of Paris, still bears the name of a convent that was razed in 1791. Before that time, the convent lands extended as far as the rue de Nevers, the rue Guénégaud, and the rue Christine, where Gertrude Stein and Alice B. Toklas lived. The little private *hôtel* occupied by the restaurant Lapérouse, at the corner of the rue and the Quai des Grands-Augustins, dates from the fifteenth century. I was already acquainted with the aristocratic seventeenth-century building at Number 7, and with the two upper floors which had become Picasso's studio. In earlier years Jean-Louis Barrault had used them as a rehearsal hall for forthcoming plays, and I had sometimes been present at these meetings in the "Barrault attic." It was the actor, in fact, who had told Picasso that this singular locale was available, and he had promptly fallen in love with it. On a considerably larger scale, it reminded him of the Bateau-Lavoir, for which he has retained a secret nostalgia throughout his later life. The interior of the rooms could have given him the impression of being on a ship, complete with its gangways, its vast storerooms and its hold. But there was still another attraction to this house: Balzac had used it as the locale for his *Chef-d'Oeuvre Inconnu*. It was in this building—which was the Hôtel de Savoie-Carignan before the Revolution—that he located the meeting of the artist Frenhofer with François Porbus and Nicholas Poussin; and it was here that his hero, led by his thirst for the absolute to move further and further away from the representation of nature, created and destroyed his masterpiece, and died. The description Balzac gives of the house, and of its dark, steep staircase, is still extremely striking in its resemblance. Moved and stimulated by the thought of taking the place of Frenhofer's illustrious shade, Picasso rented the studio. That was in 1937. And in the same spot where the "unknown masterpiece" was created, he painted his well-known masterpiece, *Guernica.*

In the place the celebrated canvas had occupied two years before, there now stood another panel, almost equally large: the *Femmes à Leur Toilette.* The work in tapestries done by Marie Cuttoli had interested Picasso greatly, and several of his canvases had been reproduced in Aubusson with extraordinary fidelity. He had now decided that he wanted to create a cartoon designed expressly for a tapestry, and had had the idea of resorting to the procedure of a collage. After collecting an enormous quantity of printed and flowered papers, he had formed the garments of the women directly from these—but not only their garments; their hands, their faces, and all of the different elements of the picture. I made a portrait of him, standing in front of this unfinished work. The creases and folds of his raincoat seem to be a part of the "collage" itself, and an arm which is actually on the canvas seems to belong to his own body.[17] *

I also took several photos of him in the opening of the window, with the landscape of rooftops he would later paint as a background; and some others seated beside the enormous, pot-bellied stove he had bought from a collector.[18] Then he showed me his recent paintings. Done in very strong relief, the majority of them represented every possible variation and deformation of the features of Dora Maar: a nose in profile, with flaring nostrils, linked to a full-face nose; an eye in profile turned toward an eye which stares fixedly out at the viewer. Only the slender hands, with their pointed fingers, and the ruby varnish of the nails, had occasionally been treated with a little more indulgence.

Picasso then led me through a wing of this vast establishment to a little room which served as his "printing shop." There was an old hand press in here; enormous, and a thing of great beauty.

* This project for a tapestry was never carried out. When I asked Marie Cuttoli the reasons for this recently (1963), she told me that Picasso had insisted that the cartoon should not be taken out of his studio, and that all the work of transcription must be done there. But, for technical reasons, this was not possible.

The ink left on the handles by the thousands of hands that had manipulated them at one time or another had accumulated over the years and was now hard as stone, forming huge black embossments.

PICASSO: It's beautiful, isn't it? Almost a museum piece . . . It used to belong to Louis Fort, the printer who pulled all of my plates after Eugène Delatre died. I loved this press, so I bought it. But I had to leave it at Boisgeloup for a long time. Now that I have the room for it, I had it brought here. Lacourière installed the rest of the equipment for me. I have everything I need to work —a full set of acids and even a case of resin for aquatints.*

Several days later, I received a telephone call—someone calling for Picasso: "He would like to see you again, before going back to Royan. He wants to come to you. Can he come right away? Could you see him at home in half an hour?"

My apartment was turned completely upside down. I was in the midst of "getting things in order," and there were piles of books, files, and sheaves of photos scattered everywhere. Picasso came directly there—81, rue du Faubourg Saint-Jacques—from the Café de Flore, so he arrived before I had a chance to do anything about it. The Hispano-Suiza was waiting for him in the street. I showed him the series of pictures I had taken at Lipp, in the Flore, and in his studio. He was delighted with the portrait that showed him beside the extraordinary stove, and which was later published in *Life*. He wanted to see more photographs; that was why he had come. I began bringing them out to show to him, and he asked for more and still more, seeming avid to know them all. I came at last to the series I had done of the Paris underworld in 1932–33: pimps and their girls, petty gangsters, perverts, filthy dens of night spots and their entertainers, rooms for opium smokers, bordellos . . .

PICASSO: When you see what you express through photography, you realize all the things that can no longer be the objective of painting. Why should the artist persist in treating subjects that can be established so clearly with the lens of a camera? It would be absurd, wouldn't it? Photography has arrived at a point where it is capable of liberating painting from all literature, from the

* In spite of all this equipment, Picasso never worked there on this press. Because of the cold, he preferred going to Lacourière's, in Montmartre, where the studio was always well heated.

anecdote, and even from the subject. In any case, a certain aspect of the subject now belongs in the domain of photography. So shouldn't painters profit from their newly acquired liberty, and make use of it to do other things?

I went over to a cupboard, and brought out several old portfolios, containing the drawings I had done in Berlin in 1921. Picasso was surprised. He did not know I had ever done any drawing. He looked at them attentively, seemed astonished, and said to me: "You're a born draftsman . . . why don't you go on with it? You own a gold mine, and you're exploiting a salt mine."

A lively discussion ensued. I tried to explain to him why I had decided in favor of photography. He interrupted me often, and I listened to his objections and his reproaches. And later, at every one of our meetings, the first question he put to me was always: "And the drawing? Have you gone back to your drawing?"

Since it was wartime, I had to obtain the military censor's seal before I could send my photographs to the United States. I was completely dumbfounded to learn that one of them had been denied release. Had it become betrayal of a State secret, a breach of military security, to show Picasso's hand holding a paintbrush?[19] I racked my brain for the reasons, but in vain. Then I began to study the "palette" which also figured in this photograph. Picasso, who has rarely held a palette in his hand, has always managed one way or another, by setting it on a chair, a table, or even on the floor. But most of the time he doesn't even use one. At the rue des Grands-Augustins, he mixed his colors on a folding table covered with a thick layer of newspaper. As soon as this paper became saturated with colors, linseed oil, and turpentine, he simply picked it up and threw it away. When I examined this photo closely, I discovered that the page of newspaper—an issue of *Paris-Soir*—stained with his colors, contained one article on the Pope and another on a cardinal. Of the captions and text, half-covered with paint, you could still read:

THE POPE IS RENEW . . . HIS EFFORTS
IN FAVOR OF . . .

*He has addressed a note to France, England, Italy, Germany, and Poland. The Vatican considers that an alliance between Paris, London, and Moscow would open the doors to bolshevik penetration of Europe. (See late bulletin.)*

Of the second article, you could still read this:

CARDINAL VILL . . . PRESIDES OVER
JOAN OF ARC SERVICES AT DOMREMY

*The church of . . . is now a basilica. The saint from Lorraine receives the homage of both the Supreme Pontiff and . . .*

What was there in this that could have upset the censors? Did they imagine a deliberately sacrilegious act in Picasso's hand smearing paint over Joan of Arc, Cardinal Vill . . . , and the Supreme Pontiff? Did they want to avoid a diplomatic incident with the Vatican? Did they scent some kind of joke, which, in view of the situation, they could not permit? Whatever their reasons, my photograph was denied a permit to cross the Atlantic, and confiscated.

The phony war became that war which was not phony at all, and the Paris we loved became a Paris of green uniforms and swastikas floating above the public buildings and the great hotels, headquarters for the Kommandantur and the Gestapo; a Paris without taxis, without cigarettes, without sugar, without chocolate; a Paris of rhubarb and turnips and saccharine; a Paris of queues and ration tickets, of curfew and jammed radios, of propaganda newspapers and films; a Paris of German patrols, of yellow stars, of alerts and searchs, of arrests and bulletins of executions.

At the beginning of the war, Picasso had managed to get some work done in the villa he had rented at Royan, *Les Volières*. He remained there for almost a year, making three further trips to Paris, in search of paints, brushes, canvas, and reams of paper. In the summer of 1940 he watched the German troops enter Royan, and on the twenty-fifth of August he returned to the capital to stay. In occupied Paris, life was difficult, even for Pablo Picasso. No gasoline for his car, no coal to heat his studio. Like everyone else he was forced to adjust himself to the grim existence of wartime: standing on lines for everything, taking the Métro or the infrequent, crowded buses, to go from the rue La Boétie to the rue des Grands-Augustins. It often happened that he made the trip both ways on foot. He could be found almost every night at the Café de Flore, that friendly and well-heated refuge where he felt completely at home; better than he would have been at home.

In 1942, weary of this daily shuttling back and forth between the right bank and the left, his dwelling and his studio, he decided to settle definitely in the rue des Grands-Augustins. He bought electric heaters, which were useless, because of the constant curtailments of the current, and installed gas heaters which were just as ineffective, and for the same reasons. But from this point on, he devoted himself entirely to his work and gradually deserted Saint-Germain-des-Prés. The "time of the cafés" had ended. It had lasted *eight years . . .*

I arrive at No. 7, rue des Grands-Augustins, happy at the thought that I will be seeing Picasso again in his new surroundings. There have been some changes since my last visit. Since the main entrance has been condemned for lack of repairs, you now climb up to the "attic" by a narrow spiral staircase, whose worn and rickety steps and general air of gloom remind you of climbing up inside the tower of Notre-Dame. You climb and climb, you pass the door to the "*Association des Huissiers de la Seine,*" the owners of the building; and at last you come to a gigantic ICI, drawn by Picasso on a scrap of cardboard to indicate the location of his doorbell.

Marcel, the chauffeur, opens the door for me. For many years now, he has been not only Picasso's man, his Jack of all trades, but also a person in whom he has complete confidence. He stretches the canvases, fits the frames, prepares the crates, packs, unpacks, does all of the shipping . . . After making my way through the green plants of the little entrance hall, I walk down the vestibule, where every nook and corner, every chair, the one long table, is covered with books, catalogues, letters, photos. With every new delivery of mail, the piles rise like stalagmites. In the opening of the door leading to the studio, the first picture you see is a Matisse—a large still life of oranges and bananas which dates from before the First World War. A little Douanier Rousseau is just next to it: *Allée du Parc Montsouris,* with its tall poplars and tiny personages clothed in black.

A multitude of statues now fills the enormous hold of the ship, some of them old acquaintances from Boisgeloup . . . But for an instant, my heart seems to stop—dazzlingly white in their shed up there, they have become darker here, somehow smaller . . . They had all been cast in bronze! I think of André Breton, who praised Picasso for "wasting" the perishable plaster! And by what kind of miracle has he managed to obtain so much metal at a time when the German occupant is tearing from its pedestal every bronze statue in Paris, France and Navarre, and despoiling the bistros of their handsome *zincs*, even when it isn't zinc, but copper?* Some of these original plasters had been cast in 1939, for his exposition in New York. But the others? I can see more than fifty new bronzes, of which at least twenty are very large. I have still not recovered from my surprise when Picasso arrives. Wearing a pair of shorts and a striped sailor's shirt—anyone would think he was a carnival wrestler, prepared to challenge the audience—he seizes me by the shoulders, embraces me, fixes me with that piercing eye.

PICASSO: Tell me the truth! We haven't seen each other in a long time . . . I've changed, haven't I? Look at this—look at my hair. When I come across an old snapshot of myself, I get frightened . . . Why don't you come to see me more often? It's not very nice of you . . . Of course not, you wouldn't disturb me . . . I don't go to the cafés anymore, so I like to see my friends right here, at home; I don't want to lose touch with them. I've arranged things—mornings for my friends, afternoon and night for work . . . I have some good lights now, and I often work at night . . . But I'll tell you why I wanted to see you now: a publisher has come to me with a project for an album of my sculptures. But he wanted to impose his own photographer on me. I wouldn't go along with it. I insisted that it had to be you, and I would be happy if you would do it. I like your photographs of my sculptures. The ones they took of my new things aren't very good at all. I'll show them to you . . . Where are those photos?

Sabartés looks for them, Marcel looks for them, Picasso looks for them . . . "But they were here, right on this pile, just yesterday. I saw them with my own eyes. And I left them there, on top, purposely . . ." Everyone rummages through the mountains of papers. Until at last they are found, submerged beneath the newest avalanche.

PICASSO: Look at them . . . My *Tête de Mort* looks like a walnut. We could do something better than that. What do you think?

We look at some of my old photographs of his sculptures.

* Contrary to what was generally thought, the majority of these uprooted statues were not transformed into cannon. They were destined for use in the colossal statues of Arno Breker, Hitler's protégé and official sculptor of the Third Reich.

6. PRECEDING PAGE In his rue La Boétie studio, 1932

*And everything is centered on the flashing intensity of that gaze, piercing you, subduing you, devouring you . . .*

7. Rue La Boétie studio, 1932

*. . . and the towers of empty cigarette boxes, which he piled one on top of another every day, never having the heart to throw them out . . .*

8. Rue La Boétie studio, 1932

*. . . stacks of paintings, mysterious bundles revealing glimpses of other canvases by the Douanier Rousseau, and a group of African statuettes.*

9. Rue La Boétie studio, 1932

*. . . paints and brushes scattered across the floor, the tubes squeezed and twisted, left there strangled, with the feverish imprint of Picasso's fingers on their contorted forms.*

10. Salvador Dali and Gala in his Paris studio, 1932

*...a tiny moustache; great, sparkling, hallucinatory eyes; the jet-black hair of a gypsy, gleaming with brilliantine.*

11. Joan Miró in Barcelona's Güell Park, 1955

*Walking in the Güell Park with me, and pointing out the curving benches, incrusted with broken bits of glazed earthenware . . . the artist said, "All my art comes from there . . ."*

12. The ornamentation on the entrance to the 1900 Paris Métro, which so fascinated Salvador Dali

13. Saint-Germain-des-Prés church and the café des Deux-Magots, 1939

*Paris had already assumed her mournful wartime look, shrouded in black every night…*

PICASSO: They really were more beautiful in plaster. At first, I wouldn't even hear of having them cast in bronze. But Sabartés just kept saying, "Plaster is perishable . . . You have to have something solid . . . Bronze is forever . . ." He's the one who persuaded me to have them done in metal. And at last, I gave in. What do you think of them?"

MYSELF: Some of them have lost in the change. Especially your monumental heads. Those great curved surfaces, white and stark —it's as if they had been eaten into by the reflections and irregularities of bronze. I can picture them in white marble, or rose. That would have betrayed them less, I think . . . But how did you manage to have all this done, in bronze?

PICASSO: That's a long story. Some devoted friends moved the plasters to the foundry—at night, and in hand carts. But they risked a good deal more, bringing them back here in bronze, right under the nose of the German patrols. The "merchandise" had to be very well camouflaged . . .

We make a tour of his new pieces of sculpture. I am astonished at the number of them . . .

PICASSO: Since Boisgeloup, I hadn't done much in the way of sculpture. Then, all of a sudden, it caught me again. I've done all of this in the last three years, during the occupation. Since I couldn't leave Paris, I made my bathroom into a sculpture studio—it's the only room in this barracks that can be heated. That's where I did most of these. There are a lot more—some little bronzes that I have in a glass case, and some others I couldn't manage to have cast, in a shop not far from here, in a courtyard right next to the Restaurant Catalan. These plasters are the most recent ones. This big old man—I did him in February.

And Picasso points out *L'Homme à l'Agneau*, dominating this people of statues from his over-six-foot height . . . naked, planted firmly on his long and skinny legs, a round, bald head—the peevish face resembles that of Ambroise Vollard—the giant clutches a lamb in the vise of his powerful arms. The left hand clutches the backbone of the weighty, struggling animal, the right hand has caught three of his hoofs, but the fourth has escaped . . . Modeled very freely from little balls of clay, like some of the great Etruscan terra cottas, *L'Homme à l'Agneau* seems to have been created almost spontaneously.

Beside him, on a revolving stand, a large head of a young girl with a closed, tense face, square jaws, a powerful profile, a mass of hair falling back and down the neck. Unquestionably a portrait of Dora Maar.* On another such stand, the tail of an all-white cat forms an exclamation point. There is another cat, in bronze, standing squarely on its four feet, with a swollen belly.

PICASSO: I don't like pet cats, purring on a couch in a living room, but I adore cats that have gone wild, with their hairs bristling at the ends. They chase birds, stand on ledges, run through the streets like demons. They turn and stare at you with those ferocious eyes, ready to leap at your face. And have you ever noticed that female cats—free cats—are always pregnant? Obviously they don't think of anything but making love . . .

I see the cocks of Boisgeloup again, and then there is an odd, splendid sort of woman.

PICASSO: What do you think of her? One day in the flea market I found a 1900 *haute couture* mannequin—a real figure from the nineties—a high bosom, beautifully rounded rump, wonderfully sculpted, but without arms or a head. So I gave her some arms and a head. The left arm came from Easter Island—it was a gift from Pierre Loeb—and I did the right arm and the head. All I had to do was add them on.

And here is a curious bovid head, with long horns . . .

PICASSO, *amused, observing my reaction:* Guess how I made that head of a bull. One day, in a rubbish heap, I found an old bicycle seat, lying beside a rusted handlebar . . . and my mind instantly linked them together. The idea for this *Tête de Taureau* came to me before I had even realized it. I just soldered them together. The thing that's marvelous about bronze is that it can give the most diverse objects such unity that sometimes it's difficult to identify the elements that make up the whole. But that's also a danger: if you no longer see anything but the head of a bull, and not the bicycle seat and handlebar that formed it, the sculpture would lose its interest.

A tubular statue, very long and thin, attracts my attention, because of its novelty. The body is a slender shaft—some kind of corrugated paper must have been used to impress its grooved

* This head, later cast in bronze, is now the monument to Guillaume Apollinaire in the square of the church of Saint-Germain-des-Prés.

pattern—the neck, a wooden roller emerging from a dessert mold, transformed into a little fluted ruff. As for the head, it is a square slab, doubtless the cover of a box. The left arm is crooked, holding a sort of vase; the right arm, lifted vertically, holds a ball in its hand. Picasso has named it *Femme à l'Orange.*

Sabartés calls Picasso. We'll continue with the review of the sculptures another day.

PICASSO: Would you like to photograph my statues? I would like very much to have you do it.

Since he asks me what I am doing at the moment, I explain my situation to him as briefly as possible. I have refused to ask for an authorization to photograph from the Germans—although they had urged me to put in an application—so I have no right to publish any of my photos. I am unemployed and doing other things.

PICASSO: We're in the same boat. I have no right to exhibit, or to publish anything. All of my books are forbidden. It's against the law even to reproduce my work. So—see if you can work out something with the publisher, and come whenever you want to.

## *Late September, 1943*

This morning I set to work on the first statue: the *Tête de Mort.* A fascinating work. More a monumental, petrified head with vacant orbits of eyes, a nose that has been eaten away, and lips erased by time,[20] than any grimacing, fleshless skeleton. It resembles a block of vagrant stone, pitted with cavities, eroded and polished by its journeyings from age to age. Is it the war that has brought forth this monolith in Picasso's work?* I turn and re-turn it, studying every angle; I take several photos of it. Picasso insists on helping me, watching me work. My "method" intrigues him. I rarely look into the frosted-glass viewer, I measure distances with a piece of string, and I sometimes use magnesium powder flashes for lighting. The explosion frightens and amuses Picasso. He nicknames me The Terrorist, and from this point on he always refers to me this way . . .

* The motive of the death's-head had its beginnings, I believe, in the skeleton of a sheep's head, done at Royan in 1939. It reappears with the skeleton of a bull's head in 1943, and continues with a series of still lifes with skulls in 1945 and 1946.

PICASSO: I don't understand . . . How do you know what the results will be? You have no way of judging the effect of your lighting.

MYSELF: I figure it out in my head . . . Why don't I use floodlights? Because multiple sources of light throw conflicting shadows. I like light from a single source, and I soften the shadows by using screens to reflect it.

PICASSO: But why it is that sculpture is so rarely photographed well?

MYSELF: There's always been a stupid tradition that says that a light-colored statue—marble, plaster, or something like that—should be photographed against a dark background, and a dark statue against a light ground . . . It kills them. They look as if they had been flattened out, and no longer have room to breathe. For a piece of sculpture to retain all of its original dimensions in a photo, the lighted parts of it should be lighter than the background, and the shaded parts darker. It's so simple . . .

PICASSO: It's the same thing for drawings: on a gray or beige ground, you use white for the light and black for the shadows. Is that what you mean?

MYSELF: It's the basic principle of classic drawing, ever since relief was first discovered and artists tried to achieve it. And even if this plasticity is no longer of any interest for painting, it's absolutely necessary for photography, when you want to achieve a maximum appearance of relief in a piece of sculpture . . .

## *Early October, 1943*

I bring the photos of the *Tête de Mort* to Picasso. Henri Michaux accompanies me. He has always wanted to meet Picasso, but left to his own devices he would never have done anything about it. I met him by chance the other day, in Montparnasse. We were both pleased at renewing a friendship that goes back twenty years, to 1924. Michaux, in fact, was one of the first people I met after my arrival in Paris. I had been without news of him since the 1940 exodus from Paris. But I had read André Gide's lecture, *Discovering Henri Michaux*, which Gide had published as a little brochure, in order "not to disappoint" the poet after the lecture itself was forbidden by the Vichy authorities. We had a drink together on the terrace of the Rotonde. Michaux told me about the time he had spent in the South, since the invasion, first at Montauban, then at Le Lavandou, in the Var. Now he is back in Paris, to stay. He questioned me, in turn, and I told him the various episodes of my journey across France, from Paris to the Pyrénées, with Jacques Prévert and some other friends; our stay in Cannes, and my "repatriation" to Paris in the autumn of 1940.

I introduce Michaux to Picasso, and show him the photographs of the unusual sculpture, the *Tête de Mort.* He likes them enormously, and I am confused by his compliments. Then he opens an enormous leather portfolio which had been lying on a folding table, and shows us his latest drawings and washes—birds, doves, and especially women. His line has never been so beautiful, sometimes fluid, sometimes insistent, always breathing sensuality. And what ardor, what fire! As if his pen had been dipped in some flaming lava, hurling out sparks, burning and devastating . . . In many of the wash drawings, the ground (even though it was thick and solid) is literally torn away, the ink biting into it so deeply that it has taken on the black color of coagulated blood . . .

And while Piscasso extracts from the portfolio, one by one, these sheets on which he has set down what are perhaps his most beautiful drawings—although everyone always says that for the most recent ones—I ask him how the ideas for his drawings take form; whether they are fortuitous, or premeditated.

PICASSO: I don't know. Ideas are just simple points of departure. It's rare for me to be able to pinpoint them, just as they came to my mind. As soon as I set to work, others seem to flow from the pen. To know what you want to draw, you have to begin drawing it. If it turns out to be a man, I draw a man—if it's a woman, I draw a woman. There's an old Spanish proverb: "If it has a beard, it's a man; if it doesn't have a beard, it's a woman." Or, in another version: "If it has a beard, it's Saint Joseph; if it doesn't have a beard, it's the Virgin Mary." Wonderful proverb, isn't it? When I have a blank sheet of paper in front of me, it runs through my head all the time. Despite any will I may have in the matter, what I express interests me more than my ideas . . .

I point out to Picasso that all of the men in this series are bearded, like Father Zeus.

PICASSO: Yes. They all have beards. And do you know why? Every time I draw a man, it's my father I'm thinking of, involuntarily. For me, a man is Don José, and will be all my life. He wore a beard, and every man I draw I see more or less with his features . . .

We discuss drawing for a time, and in particular the drawings of Matisse.

PICASSO: Matisse makes a drawing, then he makes a copy of it. He recopies it five times, ten times, always clarifying the line. He's convinced that the last, the most stripped down, is the best, the purest, the definitive one; and in fact, most of the time, it was the first. In drawing, nothing is better than the first attempt.

As he continued to take the washes from the portfolio, he comes across a diploma, done in handsome calligraphy.

PICASSO: It's my diploma as an academician! Yes, I'm now an academician. The Royal Swedish Academy elected me to membership. What do you think of that?

His delighted laughter still echoes in our ears when we leave. Michaux is experiencing the near-shock which the first impression of Picasso's overwhelming personality never fails to produce. But he remarks, with a touch of humor, "This man who complains so bitterly about so many people disturbing him at work would be very unhappy if no one disturbed him anymore. When he was showing us his drawings, he was in his element."

I say to Michaux: "If I had a choice among all the work he has done, I would take the drawings without hesitation. With that impassioned pen in his hand, his personality unfolds without the slightest constraint. It's there, I think, that his genius appears most clearly. His drawings are steeped in the same ink as his writing. In them, you can drink from the source itself."

Michaux shares my opinion. The spontaneity and brilliance of these drawings has moved him. "They smell of sulphur," he says.

He suggests that we go to lunch in a tearoom in the rue de Tournon, next to the Senate buildings, where he often has his meals. We cross the Boulevard Saint-Germain, which has become so provincial in appearance. Paris would seem almost a charming city, if the lists of hostages and executions that cover the walls did not constantly recall us to reality.

I tell Michaux that I can think of no one among the younger artists who could take the place of Picasso, Matisse, or Braque.

MICHAUX: Neither do I—I haven't seen a draftsman of the stature of Picasso, or a colorist like Matisse or Braque. But perhaps we no longer want the same thing, we're no longer aspiring to the same thing. Picasso is a genius, of course, but his "monsters" no longer disturb us. We're looking for other monsters, down different paths. The question of a "succession" may exist, but in another way.

I have to agree that Michaux is right. I expressed myself badly. I shouldn't have spoken of "taking the place of . . ." One is always wrong in attempting to prejudge the future, especially in matters of art. I should have said, "I don't see any young painters who might be the equivalent of what Picasso was at twenty."

The tearoom is very crowded. I suggest to Michaux that we go to my bistro in the Faubourg Saint-Jacques, just across from the Hôpital Cochin; a favorite meeting place for young doctors and artists, where I often encounter the sculptor Fenosa, and sometimes Germaine Montero, surrounded by a little band of Spanish republicans-in-exile, who listen to her, openmouthed, for hours on end . . .

As we walk up the Boulevard Saint-Michel and the Allée de l'Observatoire, Michaux confides to me that the plastic arts have interested him more and more, and now he is devoting himself almost exclusively to painting.

MICHAUX: I've had enough of poetry! It's the poor relation of the arts. Silent, and without echo. The verb is no more than an allusion, an innuendo. Artists who work with their hands are much happier. The object they create has a visible, palpable form; it is an echo . . . Something concrete, which answers you even after it is detached from you. The poem is mute; it sends back nothing . . .

MYSELF: If you adopt that attitude, you'll have to throw out music too. So long as it isn't being played, isn't it just a mass of notes? And you arrive at the paradox by which music becomes the art most wanting in echoes.

MICHAUX: And so it is, as long as it isn't played. Obviously, when a hundred instruments send back something you have imagined and created, that is a response. But will it be played? When and how? And that's precisely the question! Do you know that a young composer who writes a symphony today has just about one chance in ten of hearing his work once in his lifetime? Only the plastic arts have an immediate echo. It doesn't depend on a narrator or singer, or a printer, or musicians; it depends on nothing. What you create with your hands is fixed, has an existence of its own. That's why I'm painting now . . .

### *Tuesday, October 12, 1943*

Picasso, the publisher of the book, and I are going to go through all of the sculptures and select the statues to be included in the album. Among them is *L'Oiseau.* A child's scooter rusted and deformed, shorn of its wheels, suggested the idea of a bird to him one day, just as the saddle and handlebar of the bicycle had suggested a head of a bull. The little plank on which the feet are placed becomes the body of a wading bird; the steering shaft its long neck, and the fork which held the front wheel its head and beak. A triangular piece, intended for securing busts on their pedestal, serves for feet. Picasso has given him a red feather for a tail. We make notes on the majority of the sculptures without incident. But when we come to the scooter-bird, the publisher whispers in my ear:

"Don't bother to photograph it. It's more an object than a piece of sculpture."

Picasso, who hears everything, guesses everything, misses nothing, turns to him suddenly, points at *L'Oiseau,* and says sharply, "I insist absolutely that this *sculpture* must be in my album!"

When the publisher left the studio an hour later, Picasso was still seething with anger.

PICASSO: An *object!* So my bird is just an object! Who does that man think he is? To think he can teach me—me, Picasso—what is a sculpture and what isn't! He has a lot of cheek! I think I know more about it than he does. What is sculpture? What is painting? Everyone clings to old-fashioned ideas and outworn definitions, as if it were not precisely the role of the artist to provide new ones . . .

He would have gone on grumbling even longer, if Sabartés had not called him to the telephone. Baron Mollet comes in, more flighty than ever. With his denuded skull, his great, Punch-like nose, his unceasing flow of talk, he resembles the great clown Grock more than ever. The object of his visit? To propose to Picasso the purchase of an "extraordinary" cabinet, for "almost nothing." He has just unearthed it in a nearby antique shop.

BARON MOLLET: It really isn't expensive! It's a unique opportunity! Pablo, will you come to see it at three o'clock? It would be wonderful for you . . .

I have known him for a long time, and this isn't the first time I have seen him here. An old friend of Picasso's from the days in Montmartre, he often drops in totally unexpectedly. Known to, and knowing, everyone in Saint-Germain-des-Prés, he has been, in turn, the friend or *confidant* of Apollinaire, Max Jacob, Cendrars, Fargue, Cocteau, Modigliani, van Dongen. He calls them all by their first names: Pablo, Guillaume, Max, Blaise, Léon-Paul, Jean, Amadeo, Kaes . . . But this man, who invented and personified the idea of public relations at the beginning of the century, spreading the news from the Café Napolitain to the Closerie des Lilas, establishing liaison between Montmartre and the Boulevards, Montmartre and Montparnasse; this man who is always content, without work and without money, this great collector of minds, of talents, of intelligences, has also known how to make himself loved by the new generation of poets, painters, and writers—Raymond Queneau, Jacques Prévert . . .*

Curiously enough, Prévert arrives at this moment, a cigarette thrust between his lips. Picasso shows him the marvelous drawing and washes. We are looking at the series of doves, when a live dove appears on the landing of the staircase.

JACQUES PRÉVERT: And there he is—our mysterious personage. When you speak of the devil . . .[21]

Picasso invites us to come upstairs, because his little apartment and the studio where he does his painting are on the upper floor, and spreads out his most recent canvases. When he is called to the telephone, he leaves us alone. Prévert is fascinated by one painting: the big window of the studio, opened to the staggered roofs and chimneys of Paris. It is primarily the undulating line of the radiator sections, with its rounded handle and long pipe, that has preoccupied Picasso. He had painted it three months ago, on the third of July.

* In 1963 he published his memoirs, just as they came from his pen and his memory, and Raymond Queneau contributed a preface.

JACQUES PRÉVERT: Look at that! Any other painter would have omitted the radiator, thinking it was ugly, vulgar, "unesthetic." He would have stressed the "picturesque quality" of the old walls and roofs. But it's precisely that radiator that dominates this canvas. Picasso wants to tell the truth, before anything else. Look, he's even painted that old rag hanging on the wall.

I agree with him. I too prefer the canvases born of direct inspiration, from things he has seen in his own surroundings, like this *Mère et enfant* painted in May. I explained to Prévert that Picasso painted the child first, taking his first steps, having a hard time balancing his plump little body. "He would have fallen," Picasso had said to me, laughing, "because he doesn't know how to walk yet. So I added his mother to the canvas later, to hold him up." There is also a painting of a chubby little boy, seated on the ground beside a chair on which two doves have perched. The canvas is dated in the month of August of that year.*

We also admire a canvas of a dark brown sideboard in the Restaurant Catalan, with heavy, baroque moldings. Picasso had painted it twice in the month of May, against a yellow background.

MYSELF: There's absolutely nothing gratuitous in the picture. Everything in it was inspired by reality.

JACQUES PRÉVERT: Why, of course! Picasso—more than any artist who might be known as a painter of reality—reacts to the things around him. Everything he does is a response to something he has seen or felt, something that has surprised and moved him . . .

Picasso returns. Prévert picks up a little book lying on a chest, and begins to leaf through the pages.

PICASSO: That's my bedside book. It's incredibly funny! And as beautiful as Jarry! But you can't tell whether the humor is conscious, willful, or completely involuntary. It's about Marshal Pétain. But really, you get the impression that the author doesn't give a damn about the great man and has just disguised it as a tribute to him.

The cover of the book bears the title: *The Great Man Alone*. It was written by René Benjamin.

* This painting was premonitory: four years later, Françoise Gilot bore him a son, Claude.

PRÉVERT, *reading aloud:*

*The Marshal is calm and virile,*
*Opinion feminine and nervous.*
*The Marshal thinks.*
*Opinion feels.*
*The Marshal wants to create.*
*Opinion turns away and grumbles . . .*
*Some wretched people have been seen tearing down his portrait . . .*

PICASSO: It's the conversations you have to read. The one about the Marshal's luncheon with a priest on his right and a cabinet minister on his left, for instance. Read that . . .

And Prévert, in his quick, jerky style, reads aloud:

*"Monsieur le Maréchal," the priest said, "you haven't introduced me to Monsieur le Ministre. Excuse me, but I still don't know—what is he the minister of?"*

*"What do you think?" the Marshal asked slyly.*

*"Ah, that's a difficult question," the priest answered, blushing.*

*"Either that or it's a minister who doesn't make much of an impression," the Marshal said seriously.*

*"I didn't say that," the priest said quickly. "Good heavens, no."*

*"Well, then," the Marshal said sadly, "it's just that you're not a connoisseur of ministers."*

*"Monsieur le Maréchal," the priest said, obviously very upset, "you invited me to lunch last year with M. A. I knew who he was!"*

*"Who was it?" the Marshal asked thoughtfully.*

*"Why, one of your ministers!"*

*"Think of that," the Marshal said happily, "I had forgotten him."*

*The maître d'hôtel leaned over the Marshal's shoulder, holding out a bottle for his approval, and murmuring, "Clos du Maréchal."*

*"Taste that," the Chief of State said, "and don't worry about ministers anymore. They pass. Wine remains."*

PICASSO: It's amusing, isn't it? There's also a passage where the young Cabinet attachés are sitting around a table discussing what the Marshal should wear to visit the bombed cities. Where is that passage? Here it is:

*What should he wear? Everyone gives his opinion. Khaki? That color is as nondescript as its name. Better even in civilian clothes. In civilian clothes? Cries of protest. A Marshal in civilian clothes is no longer a Marshal! Suppose he wears his horizon blue uniform from the other war? Ah, bravo! Everyone is entranced with that picture.*

"That luncheon ends with a scene that is straight out of Jarry," Picasso says. "You've got to read that!"

And Prévert, who is completely at home with the priest, the cabinet minister, and the Marshal, begins to read this page which, as he recites it, seems almost like one of his own poems:

*The Marshal, who was eating an apple, began to laugh, and he choked; coughing, and trying desperately to catch his breath. Everyone at the table is anxious. But he still has the strength to say, "It's nothing."*

*Nonetheless, Dr. Ménétrel stands up.*

*Everyone turns and stares at him.*

*At last, the Marshal swallows some water.*

*His breath returns.*

*And his voice, too.*

*"It's your fault," he says to the priest, in an acid tone.*

*The priest practically jumps out of his chair.*

*"You didn't say grace."*

*"Good heavens," murmurs the priest.*

*"Well, do something about it—say it now!" the Marshal orders, and stands up.*

*Everyone else stands up.*

*The priest murmurs a few confused words of Latin and makes the sign of the cross . . .*

*The young attachés are dumbfounded.*

*They will never know what the Marshal will wear for his trip. Perhaps he will dress as a Chinese . . .*

PICASSO: I don't know how many times I've reread that. I know it by heart. And the dinner with Maurras, deaf as a pot and wearing a leopard skin—you can read it yourself; I'm not joking! —where there's a woman named Espérance, who's one of his admirers. It's really high comedy. And the audience for the six workmen! The Marshal making his speech on the "Charter of Labor"; the young men asking his permission to sing the Marseillaise for him; and Pétain answering them, "Only the fourth stanza!" And the Marshal's interview with the Minister of Health, after his return from an inspection of the bomb damage in Lorient. You have to read that. It's the best part!

And Prévert reads this passage aloud:

*"I've just come back from Lorient."*
*"What's left of it?" the Marshal asks heavily.*
*"Nothing," the minister answers, in the same tone.*
*"And what do the people say?"*
*"Nothing, Monsieur le Maréchal," the minister says.*
*Then he adds:*
*"They think . . . well, c'est la guerre."*
*The Marshal murmurs:*
*"That's good."*
*"In any case," the minister says, "I told them that you loved them."*
*"That's good too," the Marshal says, "provided they understand that it's true."*

I tell Picasso that I am still missing all of his statues of the blue period, particularly the little one of a kneeling woman combing her hair. "It seems to me that I saw it in your apartment on the rue La Boétie, in the first room, on the mantelpiece."

PICASSO: It's one of my very first, if not my first piece of sculpture. I did it at the same time as the little *Femme Assise*, in 1899, I think. One day I was desperately in need of money, and I sold almost all of my old sculptures to Vollard. He's the one, in fact, who had them cast in bronze. In addition to those two women, there was a head of an old man, a woman's head, and the Harlequin in a cap that I must have done seven or eight years later.

MYSELF: Couldn't I photograph them at Vollard's?

PICASSO: I would have liked to have all of them in this book. But, alas, Vollard's successor, Fabiani, doesn't want them reproduced. Did you know Vollard?

MYSELF: I visited his house on the rue Martignac several times. The first time was with Tériade and Maurice Raynal, in 1932. He was having the whole house repainted, and there was a big sign on the entrance, saying: *Beware of the painting!* I took a photo of it, as a matter of fact.

JACQUES PRÉVERT: *Beware of the painting!* What a marvelous sign for an art dealer!

MYSELF: Raynal wanted to ask Vollard for an article on Cézanne for *Minotaure.* He was skeptical about getting it, though, and we really expected a refusal. But Vollard was in a very good mood that day. He greeted us with something almost resembling warmth. I had difficulty recognizing the surly bear I had heard about in this amiable man . . . And, a rare favor—he opened up his famous "little room," where he hid the pictures he didn't want to show to anyone.

PICASSO: Vollard was very, very secretive. He knew how to surround his paintings with mystery, and thus raise their prices. In the rue Laffitte, he buried almost all of them behind a partition at the back of the shop, and refused to allow anyone to go through it.

MYSELF: It was odd to see this giant of a man bending over double, sometimes down on his hands and knees, bringing out unknown Cézannes, one by one, at least a dozen of them . . . And he gave me *carte blanche.* I could photograph anything in the house I wanted to, with the exception of the treasures in the little room. I even took some pictures in his office, where there were several Maillol and Renoir bronzes, lying around on the floor among empty frames and reams of paper and books. Your little kneeling woman was there, too . . . I had to promise Vollard to submit any photos I took in the house to him, for approval. He was delighted with them, and particularly liked the portrait I did of him, with his little black cap on his head. He used it for the cover of the American edition of one of his books, as a matter of fact. I didn't flatter him, though. The face is dark and hairy above his enormous body, and the eyelids are half-closed over those sly, peasant eyes.[22] I suppose he found that he was more jovial in my portrait than he normally was. He told me something that Matisse had often repeated to me: "I'm always taken for a sad, sullen man. The truth is that I'm very gay by nature, even if my exterior gives a different impression."

But this is what happened—the thing I really wanted to tell you. Suddenly, while he was looking at my photographs, he let out a shout. "Good God! Did you photograph that? But this is awful! I hope you haven't shown this photo to anyone else." I reassured him, and he said, "Destroy this negative the minute you get home; please, for my sake." He didn't give me any explanation. I think it was because of a Maillol nude that Vollard could reproduce in only a limited number of copies, according to their contract. But, in my photograph, you could see several of them . . .

PICASSO: When I was young, and needed money, he exploited me . . . One day he picked up thirty of my canvases and carried them away for two thousand francs. And later on, he paid me a thousand francs for some of my best drawings.

I go to lunch with Jacques Prévert at Les Vieilles, in a passage off the rue Dauphine. Their food is good, and their Beaujolais is excellent. Jacques, who adores cheeses, orders one of those creamy camemberts that melt in the mouth, as a first course. And we talk about Picasso . . .

MYSELF: At the time of the invasion, he could have left if he had wanted to; gone wherever he wanted to—Mexico, Brazil, the United States. There was no lack of money or of invitations. Even during the occupation, the American consul urged him several times to leave France. But he stayed. His presence here is a stimulant and a comfort; and not only for his friends, but even for people who don't know him at all.

JACQUES PRÉVERT: I agree with you completely. We have to be grateful to him. It was an act of courage. And this man is not a hero. He is afraid, just as everyone who has something to say or something to defend is afraid. It's easy to be a hero, when you're not risking your life. In his case, he could—and still can—lose everything. Who knows how this war will turn? Paris may be destroyed. Unpopular as he is with the Nazis, he could be interned, deported, held as a hostage. Even his work—"degenerate" art, "bolshevik" art—is condemned already, and can be burned in one of their fires. No one in the world, not even the Pope or the Holy Ghost, could prevent that auto-da-fé, if *they* ordered it. And the closer Hitler and his legions come to the end, the more reason there is to think that their fury will become murderous and destructive. Picasso can't guess how they may react, can he? But he has taken the risk. He came back to occupied Paris. He is here. Picasso is quite a man.

*Tuesday, October 19, 1943*

When I arrive at Picasso's this morning, all of the faces are taut and strained. Marcel, the chauffeur, is chewing his lips; the normally mischievous smile of Inés, the housekeeper, has disappeared; Sabartés is silent. They are all standing in the only heated room of the studio, gathered around the big, paper-strewn, provincial table, as if it were a bier. Picasso, who is usually so effusive, scarcely nods to me. His features are drawn, his brow furrowed, he studies the faces around him like a judge of the Inquisition. What can have happened?

PICASSO, *attempting to control his anger:* My little pocket flash-light has disappeared! I left it right here, on this chair . . . I am ab-so-lute-ly sure of it. And it isn't there now! And if it isn't there, it's because someone took it! I spent the entire night looking for it . . . I-will-not-tolerate things disappearing like that, in my house. I demand ab-so-lute-ly that it be found, at once!

No one says a word. No one dares. Only Sabartés, accustomed to his friend's fits of rage for many, many years, retains some sense of balance and philosophy. He leans toward me and whispers, quite casually, "He did it himself, unquestionably . . . He must have put it someplace, and then forgotten it. Now, he's accusing everyone else . . . That's him . . . I know him . . ."

Christian Zervos, the publisher of *Cahiers d'Art,* comes in. For some time he has been fascinated with Picasso's magnificent drawings, and wants to publish an album of them. Picasso opens the heavy, Cordovan leather portfolio, embossed with corners, studded with nails, like the portal of a cathedral, and brings out his drawings, one by one.

PICASSO: I was lucky—I managed to get my hands on a supply of splendid Japanese paper. It cost me the eyes of the head! But without it, I would never have done these drawings. The paper seduced me. It's so thick that, even when you scratch deep into it, you barely touch the inner layers . . .

And it was, really, the voluptuous quality of this paper that had conjured up in his mind these undulent, supple, passionate women . . . The seductive quality of basic matter has always played an important part in his work.

Having gone through all of the drawings with Zervos, Picasso said to him, "You want to publish these? It's a very good idea. But you would have to publish the entire series, without leaving any of them out. And I would think they should be reproduced just as they are, in the same size. Then they could make a wonderful album—don't you think so?"

Zervos wants to take the whole series of drawings with him. Picasso doesn't want to let it go just yet. He is always a little reluctant to part with his work. In any event, they count and recount the drawings. According to Zervos, there are a hundred and twenty; according to Picasso a hundred and twenty-one. His count is correct.

## *Wednesday, October 20, 1943*

The table, which yesterday was covered with dust, has been completely cleaned. Catalogues, folders, books, letters, have been carefully dusted and arranged in piles, according to their size. Picasso comes in, delighted at my expression of surprise.

PICASSO: I spent the whole night looking for my pocket flashlight, again. I can't stand having things stolen from me. So I went to work on this pile of books, too—the flashlight might have been somewhere in there. I cleaned it all up, straightened everything out . . .

MYSELF: And what about the flashlight?

PICASSO: I found it. It was upstairs, in my bathroom.

Picasso has an errand to do in the city, and goes out. Shortly afterward, a woman comes in, carrying a carefully wrapped package under her arm. She wants to see Picasso "in person." She has something to show him which she knows will interest him. She can wait, all morning if necessary.

When Picasso returns, two hours later, she unwraps the package and takes out a small painting.

"Monsieur Picasso," she says, "I wanted to show you this—one of your old paintings."

He always shows some emotion when he comes across one

of his works that has been lost to him for a long time, and he is clearly moved by the sight of this little canvas.

PICASSO: Yes, it's a Picasso, all right. An authentic one. I painted it at Hyères, during the summer of 1922.

THE VISITOR: Then could I ask you if you would sign it? Owning a real Picasso that isn't signed is terrible! People who see it in our home may think it's a forgery.

PICASSO: People are always asking me to sign my old paintings. It's ridiculous! I've always marked my pictures in one way or another. But there were periods when I put the signature on the back of the canvas. Everything I did of the cubist period, up to about 1914, has my name and the date on the back of the stretchers. I know there was a story that when Braque and I were at Céret we decided not to sign our pictures any longer. But that's nothing but a legend! We didn't want to sign them directly on the painting itself, because it spoiled the composition. And even later, I sometimes signed my canvases on the back, for that reason or another one. If you don't see my signature and the date, madame, it's because it's hidden by the frame.

THE VISITOR: But since the painting is yours, Monsieur Picasso, wouldn't you do me the kindness of signing it for me?

PICASSO: No, madame, absolutely not! If I signed it now, I would be committing a forgery myself. It would be my signature of 1943, applied to a canvas painted in 1922. No, I can't sign it, madame; I'm sorry.

The woman gives up, and rewraps her Picasso. After she has left, we continue discussing the matter of signatures. I ask if he deliberately chose to use his mother's name: Picasso.

PICASSO: My friends in Barcelona always called me by that name. It's more unique, more musical than Ruiz. That's probably why I adopted it. But do you know what attracted me to the name? I'm sure it was the double *s*, which is very rare in Spain . . . The name Picasso is of Italian origin, but you knew that. And your name, or the name you use, can be important. Can you imagine me being called Ruiz? Pablo Ruiz? Diego-José Ruiz? Or Juan-Nepomuceno Ruiz? I don't even remember how many Christian names I was given. Have you ever noticed that there's a double *s* in Matisse, in Poussin, in Rousseau?

Then Picasso asks me if the double *s* in my own pseudonym, Brassaï, had had anything to do with my choice of it.

"It's the name of the town I was born in in Transylvania," I told him, "but it may be that the sound of the double consonant had something to do with it too . . ."

Another visitor arrives: the poet Georges Hugnet. He has just discovered one of Picasso's old gouaches, and is thinking of buying it.

"It's one of your most beautiful gouaches: a holiday scene, with dancers in a village square. It was offered to me for a hundred and fifty thousand francs."

PICASSO: That's really not expensive! I remember it very well. I painted it at Juan-les-Pins. It was a feast day on the Îles de Lérins, at Sainte-Marguerite. There were some old men. They were dancing almost nude . . . That's it, isn't it? Yes, then go ahead and buy it. You'll be getting a bargain.

Georges Hugnet leaves us to go and buy the gouache. I show Picasso my twenty "arrondissements": a series of nudes I had done ten years before; nudes done entirely in curving lines and contours, in "roundings." Because there were twenty of them, I had nicknamed them my arrondissements, after the twenty districts of Paris. Picasso spreads them out on the floor . . .

MYSELF: The thing that has always fascinated me in the female body is the aspect of it that seems to be some sort of vase, or musical instrument, or fruit. In the art of the Cyclades Islands, this characteristic is very noticeable: woman was transposed into a kind of violin. And I was surprised when I first noticed how much the fruit of the coconut palm—the largest fruit there is—resembles the lower torso of a woman.

PICASSO: That enormous coconut you're talking about really is the strangest fruit I've ever seen. Have you ever noticed the one I have? Someone made me a present of it one day. I'll go get it for you . . .

In a few moments Picasso returns, carrying a huge coconut. Mine is in its natural state, with a rough and hairy outer covering. His has been polished, so that it resembles the surface of some exotic wood.

PICASSO: It was a good idea to do the female body in portions, this way. Details are always fascinating . . .

Then he studies some of the nudes in which the female form has been transformed into a landscape . . . One contour which outlines the body and, at the same time, sketches a relief of hills and valleys interests him greatly. The eye passes directly from the sinuous line of the feminine body to the curving line of the valleys. Picasso remarks that, in some of the photos, the presence of "goose-flesh" evokes the skin of an orange, the granulation of stone, or the network formed by waves when they are seen from a distance. One of the attractions of photography is the thought of mingling such similarities, such visual metaphors. We begin to talk about stones: sandstone, granite, marble . . .

PICASSO: It seems strange to me that we ever arrived at the idea of making statues from marble. I understand how you can see something in the root of a tree, a crevice in a wall, a corroded bit of stone, or a pebble . . . But marble? It stands there like a block, suggesting no form or image. It doesn't inspire. How could Michelangelo have seen his *David* in a block of marble? If it occurred to man to create his own images, it's because he discovered them all around him, almost formed, already within his grasp. He saw them in a bone, in the irregular surfaces of cavern walls, in a piece of wood . . . One form might suggest a woman, another a bison, and still another the head of a demon . . .

We were back in prehistoric times . . .

MYSELF: A few years ago, I went to the valley of Eyzies, in the Dordogne. I wanted to see the art of the caves in its own habitat. And one thing surprised me: each generation, knowing nothing whatever of the generations that had preceded it, nonetheless laid out the caves in the same manner—thousands of years apart. The "kitchen," for instance—it's always in the same relative location . . .

PICASSO: Nothing extraordinary about that! Man doesn't change. He keeps his same habits . . . All of those people selected the same corner for their kitchens instinctively. Don't men always choose the same sites to build a city? Beneath the cities, there are always other cities; other churches beneath the churches, other houses beneath the houses . . . Races, religions may change, but the marketplaces, the dwellings, the places of worship or pilgrimage remain the same. Venus is replaced by the Virgin Mary, but the same life goes on.

MYSELF: During the excavations in the lower levels of the valley at Eyzies, the archaeologists had the fine idea of preserving one section, four or five meters in depth, just as they found it, with layers that had been placed on top of each other over a period of thousands of years. It's like one of those pastries—a *mille-feuille* . . . The "tenants" left their cards on every layer: fragments of bone, teeth, tools made of flint. With a single glance you can survey I don't know how many thousands of years of history. It's very impressive . . .

PICASSO: And thanks to what? Thanks to dust! The earth doesn't have a cleaning woman to dust it off. So the dust that falls there every day stays there. Everything that has come down to us from the past—it's dust that saved it. Look; even here, on these piles of things, in just a few weeks there's a thick layer of it. In some of the rooms at the rue La Boétie—do you remember?—my things were already beginning to disappear, buried in dust . . . Do you want me to tell you something? If I've always forbidden anyone to clean my studios, or dust them, it wasn't just because I was afraid they would disturb my things—it was primarily because I always counted on the protection of the dust. It's my ally. I've always let it fall wherever it likes. It's like a protective layer. When there's no dust in this spot or that one, it's because someone has been meddling with my things. I can see right away that someone has been there. And it's because I live constantly with dust, in the midst of dust, that I usually wear gray suits—they're the only ones that don't show any trace of it.

MYSELF: It takes a thousand years of dust to make a layer one meter thick. The Roman Empire is buried two or three meters beneath the earth. In Rome, in Paris, in Arles, it is down in our cellars. And the prehistoric layers are even deeper. If we know anything at all about the first men, it's because of the "protection" of the dust—you're right about that.

PICASSO: In reality, we know very little. What is it that lasts, when it's buried in the earth? Stone, bronze, ivory, bone, sometimes pottery . . . Never the objects made of wood, nothing of the fabrics, the hides. And that completely falsifies our ideas about the first men. I don't think I am mistaken in believing that the most beautiful objects of the "stone age" were made of hide, of fabric, and especially of wood. The stone age should be called the age of wood. Among the Negro statues of Africa, how many are there in stone, in bone, or in ivory? Perhaps one in a thousand! And prehistoric man had no more ivory at his disposal than the Negro tribes . . . perhaps even less. He must have had thousands of wooden fetishes—all gone, disappeared . . .

MYSELF: Do you know what the earth preserves best, Picasso? Greco-Roman money . . . I followed the excavations at Saint-Remy, where they've been unearthing a Greek village. With every shovelful of earth, they dig up another coin.

PICASSO: It's crazy, the number of Roman coins they find! It makes you think all the Romans must have had holes in their pockets. They sowed coins everywhere they went—even in the fields. Perhaps they planned on raising money.

MYSELF: An excavation always gives me the impression of a mold that is being broken so the sculpture inside can be taken out. At Pompeii, it was Vesuvius that did the work of making the mold. Houses, men and women, animals—they were all caught instantaneously in that boiling matrix. There is nothing quite so startling as the sight of those contorted bodies, caught forever in the moment of death. I saw them, in the glass cases they've preserved them in at Pompeii and Naples.

PICASSO: Dali was obsessed with the idea of monstrous castings of that kind; of that instantaneous end of all life because of a cataclysm. He talked to me about a mold of the Place de l'Opéra, with the Opéra, the Café de la Paix, the chic prostitutes, the automobiles, the pedestrians, the cops, the news stands, the flower stalls, the street lights, the big clock still marking the time . . . Imagine that in plaster or bronze, life-size . . . What a nightmare! For myself, if I could do such a thing, I would rather do Saint-Germain-des-Prés, with the Café de Flore, the Brasserie Lipp, the Deux-Magots, Jean-Paul Sartre, the waiters Jean and Pascal, Monsieur Boubal, the cat, and the blond cashier . . . What a marvelous, monstrous casting that would make!

*Monday, October 25, 1943*

Picasso wants me to see the showcase, or, as Sabartés calls it, the "museum." It is a large, locked armoire of metal and glass, occupying a little room adjoining the studio. Picasso takes out his imposing collection of keys and opens it. Fifty or so of his bronze statuettes are heaped on its shelves, along with his carved woods, his engraved pebbles, and other objects that are either curious or rare. Among them, my eye is instantly caught and held by a conglomerate of drinking glasses, twisted, deformed, pleated, and folded around each other into a single mass. Could it be some kind of "experiment" of Picasso's? Seeing that this strange object has aroused my curiosity, he reaches into the case and takes it out for me, infinitely carefully . . .

PICASSO: I see . . . These glasses intrigue you. Magnificent, isn't it? Well, they are wine glasses! They come from Martinique. You are too young to remember the terrible cataclysm that destroyed the city of Saint Pierre: the eruption of Mount Pelée—in 1902, I think it was. In a single night, the volcano blotted it out completely. But even though it destroyed so many human lives, it also created something: strange objects like this one, found in the ruins . . . I was intrigued and dumbfounded by its beauty, just as you were . . . So it was given to me as a gift. All these glasses recast by the heat of the earth—it's as beautiful as any work of art, don't you think so?

I notice the *Verre d'Absinthe,* and remember how daring a work it was considered at the time. It was the first time that so simple an object had become a piece of sculpture! And it was also daring in the manner of its treatment: to create the illusion of transparence, Picasso had split the glass in two.

PICASSO: I modeled it in wax. There are six bronzes of it in existence . . . I colored each one of them differently.

There is also a cast of the Venus of Lespugne in the showcase—in fact, there are two specimens of it: one damaged, like the original itself, the other completed and restored. Picasso adores this first of all goddesses of fertility, the quintessence of feminine forms, whose flesh seems to swell and expand around a central core, as if aroused by the desire of man . . . And here is the white skeleton of a bat, attached to a black support in an attitude of crucifixion . . .

PICASSO: I love bats! Women are afraid of them. They think they're going to get caught in their hair, or something like that . . . But I think they may be the most beautiful of animals—there's a fineness about them that's extraordinary. Have you noticed their eyes; how brilliant they are, sparkling with intelligence—and their skin, soft and silky as velvet? And look at those tiny, delicate bones.

MYSELF: I was certain that you liked skeletons! I used to study them; I amused myself by taking them apart and putting them together again. If you really want to understand the genius of creation, there's no better way to do it than to rebuild a skeleton.

PICASSO: I have an absolute passion for bones. I have a lot of others at Boisgeloup: skeletons of birds, heads of dogs and sheep . . . I even have a skull of a rhinoceros. Did you see them, out in the barn? Have you ever noticed that bones are always modeled, not just chipped out? One always has the impression that they have just been taken from a mold, after having been modeled originally in clay. No matter what kind of bone you look at, you will always discover the trace of fingers . . . sometimes enormous fingers, sometimes Lilliputian ones, like the ones that must have modeled the fragile little bones of this bat. On any piece of bone at all, I always find the fingerprints of the god who amused himself with shaping it. And have you noticed how the convex and concave forms of bones fit into each other—how artfully the vertebrae are "adjusted" to each other?

MYSELF: It was a great discovery, the vertebrae. The world of higher animals is entirely based on this master plan—or "invention," if you want to call it that. The thing I never cease to marvel at is the art with which nature has always found a means of creating an entire form, starting from this single "plan" and then deforming or transforming the vertebrae according to its needs. The entire skull is made up of vertebrae, fitted together like pieces of a construction toy, but they are such highly transfigured vertebrae that it took the eye of a poet to recognize and identify them.

PICASSO: What poet was that?

MYSELF: Goethe. He was the first person to discover and describe the cranial vertebrae. And it was the skull of a sheep he had picked up in a cemetery that set him on the path.

This subject fascinates Picasso. So I sketch out a diagram of a vertebrate: a long shaft with two hollow cylinders; one for the spinal marrow and the brain, the other for all the organs

14. At Brasserie Lipp, September 1939

*—in front of the wall of ceramic tiles by Léon-Paul Fargue's father—and chatting with Matisse's son, Pierre.*

15. At Café de Flore, September 1939

*Then, as was the custom, Picasso crossed the Boulevard Saint-Germain, flanked by Sabartés, to have his coffee at the Flore, where he happened to have several appointments that afternoon.*

16. With one of his bronzes in his rue des Grands-Augustins studio, September 1939

17. With *Femmes à Leur Toilette*, the design for a tapestry, September 1939

*The creases and folds of his raincoat seem to be part of the "collage" itself, and an arm which is actually on the canvas seems to belong to his own body.*

18. OPPOSITE PAGE In his rue des Grands-Augustins studio, September 1939

*. . . seated beside the enormous, pot-bellied stove he had bought from a collector.*

LE MOSAN

19. Photograph denied release by the military censors, September 1939

*Had it become betrayal of a State secret, a breach of military security, to show Picasso's hand holding a paintbrush?*

20. Picasso's *Tête de Mort*, bronze

*. . . a monumental, petrified head with vacant orbits of eyes, a nose that has been eaten away, and lips erased by time . . .*

21. Picasso's rue des Grands-Augustins studio, October 1943

*We are looking at a series of doves, when a live dove appears on the landing of the staircase.*
JACQUES PRÉVERT: *When you speak of the devil . . .*

22. Ambroise Vollard, 1933

*The face is dark and hairy above his enormous body, and the eyelids are half-closed over those sly, peasant eyes.*

to be protected . . . Three pairs of members are joined to this shaft, to enable it to move . . .

PICASSO: I understand the arms and the legs, but where do you get the third member?

MYSELF: It's the mandible, the lower jawbone. Like the other members, it isn't part of the shaft, it's plated onto it. It articulates on its joints exactly like the arms and the legs—but arms and legs that are welded together and have no power of movement at their ends, arms with no joints in the hands. In fact, the lower jawbone of birds does bend around a sort of "elbow," and in the case of serpents, whose jawbone also bends, there's another peculiarity: the two ends are not welded together at all, but simply linked by a very elastic tissue. That explains how serpents can swallow whole animals, much larger than themselves.

We go on discussing the matter of bones and skeletons for some time. The unchanging number of the seven cervical vertebrae astonishes Picasso.

MYSELF: It's almost as though nature had deliberately tied her own hands, forcing herself to get along with seven vertebrae and not one more . . . as if invention were tributary to obstacles. To make the neck of a giraffe, she had to lengthen the vertebrae enormously—with the result that the neck is stiff and inflexible—and at the other end of the scale, for the dolphin, which has practically no neck at all, she had to reduce them to slender, scarcely visible blades . . . Using just five fingers, she may make the hand of a man, the hoof of a horse, the paw of a dog, or those long, umbrella-like spokes that form the armature for the wings of your bat . . . People often reproach you, Picasso, for the liberties you take, for your deformation of forms, but if they took the pains to study what nature dares to do with one single, identical *motif!* If they really want to understand your work they should go to the Museum of Natural History and not to the art museums . . .

After this, I am left alone with the six little bronzes Picasso has taken from the "museum" for me to photograph. In this cluttered studio, I cannot find a single bare wall which will serve as a background, so I decide to pin up a square of pasteboard. And I need some thumbtacks. I ask Marcel for them. But, in this vast melting pot of art, where canvases come and go by the dozen, brushes and tubes of paint by the hundreds and thousands, there is not a single available thumbtack . . . Finally, after considerable difficulty, Marcel locates a few and digs them out for me with his battered penknife . . . When Picasso rejoins me a little later, his eyes fall immediately on these six miserable thumbtacks.

PICASSO: But those are *my* thumbtacks.

MYSELF: Yes, they are *your* thumbtacks.

PICASSO: Well then, I'll take them.

MYSELF: No, leave them alone! I need them for the background.

PICASSO: All right, keep them. I'll leave them with you. But don't forget to give them back. They are *my* thumbtacks . . .

## *Thursday, November 11, 1943*

Met Henri Michaux in Montparnasse yesterday. Even though he was in a hurry, he stayed with me for a while and we walked down the Boulevard Raspail together.

HENRI MICHAUX: I understand Picasso was impressed with your photograph of the *Tête de Mort*. It gives a new dimension to his sculpture. Your vision has reflected back on the object itself. It's impossible to look at it with the same eye any longer . . .

We part company in front of Rodin's statue of Balzac, having agreed to meet the next morning at ten o'clock at the Café Danton.

Michaux is there, waiting for me inside the café. We drink a dreadful cup of "coffee"—sweetened barley water. The last time, he had not been able to see Picasso's sculptures. But this morning I don't feel well enough. I have no desire to go to Picasso's. How can I tell him that? He will be disappointed. And then I learn that he has slept very badly and he too is apprehensive about the visit we had planned . . . "Could we put it off until tomorrow?" He had wanted to suggest it to me, and hadn't dared. Now both of us are relieved. And in any case, we would not have been able to see Picasso this morning. I had forgotten that it was a Thursday, and on Thursday Picasso is never at home. Intrigued by this, Michaux asks me the reason.

MYSELF: Thursday is a day he has set apart completely. No appointments, no visits from friends. If anyone happens to suggest that day to him for something, he answers: "Impossible, that's a Thursday." It must have something to do with a child . . . There's no school on Thursdays. Picasso had a daughter, Maria or Maya, by Marie-Thérèse Walter. She must be ten or eleven now. I imagine he spends Thursdays with the child and Marie-Thérèse . . .

We drink a second cup of the barley water and saccharine. Michaux is gloomy. He seems to be worried about something. I try to cheer him up by telling him little anecdotes and stories . . . It is eleven o'clock.

HENRI MICHAUX: For several days now, I haven't been myself at all. And I lose everything. First, my address book, then my travel card. It's become a regular thing. I lost my fountain pen, and yesterday it was my ration card. When I start to lose things, I get frightened. It's always the beginning of a black period.

MYSELF: You're too absorbed in your own work, too absent-minded.

HENRI MICHAUX: Yes, alas! And objects take advantage of it. They have only one idea: to get away from me, as quickly as possible . . .

After we have made an appointment for the next day, same place, same time, Michaux leaves me. Through the windows of the glassed-in terrace, I can see his slender silhouette as he walks away and then vanishes into the Boulevard Saint-Germain. He has scarcely left when I notice a pale blue scarf beside me. It's his, no doubt of that. Hiding slyly against the back of the banquette, it had seized the opportunity to get away from him.

### *Friday, November 12, 1943*

Henri Michaux is waiting for me at the café, with his wife, Marie-Louise. On the rue des Grands-Augustins, we pass in front of the Catalan, Picasso's preferred restaurant. It is closed. The other day, there was an unexpected visit from the rationing inspectors. Picasso and several other regular customers were caught *in flagrante delicto:* they were eating *Chateaubriands* on one of the three meatless days of the week. The restaurant was closed for a month, and even Picasso had to pay a fine.

HENRI MICHAUX: He'll die of hunger . . . Wasn't it here that Léon-Paul Fargue had his attack?

MYSELF: Yes, in April I think it was. He was having lunch with Picasso. He let something fall, and bent over to pick it up, but his arm wouldn't move. He was terrified.

HENRI MICHAUX: We would have been too, in his place.

MYSELF: When Picasso saw him, still stooping over like that, he got worried, and said, "What's the matter?" It wasn't until then that he noticed that the expression on Fargue's face had changed. It was all distorted. Picasso's sense of humor never leaves him entirely, and he said, "What's happening? Your face is all out of line!" They called an ambulance, and Picasso telephoned Fargue's wife, Chériane. She had to take the Métro to get here, and she kept telling herself: "If I see Picasso in front of the Catalan, it means that Fargue is dead." And Picasso was waiting for her in front of the door. But Fargue wasn't dead. He was lying there, almost unconscious—he had had a stroke. The ambulance came and took him away at last. For two days he was between life and death, and then he began to come back. I've been told he is doing better now.

HENRI MICHAUX: Better? That's just a manner of speaking. He's half paralyzed, can't move one of his arms or open one of his eyelids. His morale is very low. He's frightened. He lives in terror of a second attack. And since I'm always frightened myself, and worry constantly about what could happen to me, I was alarmed at seeing him in this condition. I really didn't know what to say to him. It ended with him trying to reassure *me*. It was very, very painful.

Picasso is not at home. But I show my friends around the studio. Michaux is particularly taken with one little statue: a peasant, mowing, a great straw hat on his head, round and luminous as the sun of the Midi. Even though the hat is nothing but an impression in clay of a little dented pastry mold, it somehow evokes Van Gogh, Provence, the sky of the Midi . . .[23]

HENRI MICHAUX: When you see something so beautiful, it makes you happy for the entire day . . .

After Henri and Marie-Louise leave, I begin to photograph some of the sculptures. At about eleven o'clock, a young man arrives, carrying a painting under his arm. When he unwraps it, I see a landscape of Provence, with a bare wall, a millstone, and some trees in the background. "I've just arrived from Aix-en-Provence," the young man tells me. "I wanted to show this canvas to Monsieur Picasso. It's a Cézanne. I think it might interest him. I don't want to sell it, just to hear what he thinks . . ."

Sabartés and Zervos come in at that moment, and we study the canvas together. A Cézanne? Hum . . . We are skeptical. Picasso suddenly appears. The news of an unknown Cézanne has drawn him out of his hiding place . . . He studies the canvas attentively. "It's a painting that has some qualities, but it is not a Cézanne." The young man insists: "It was found in his studio. My family has always considered it authentic. It's dated from the same period as *The Card Players*."

PICASSO, *irritably:* You can have a thousand reasons for thinking you are right, and cite me a thousand proofs. This picture was never painted by Cézanne! I know what I'm saying. The signature is obviously false. But that doesn't mean anything. Haven't I seen my own paintings come back to me with a forged signature? No false signature could prevent me from recognizing a real Cézanne! But that's not the case here. He had no gift, no skill at all for imitation. Every time he tried to copy other artists, it was a Cézanne he painted. You can wrap up your "family Cézanne" . . .

Even after the young man has left, Picasso is still grumbling: "As if I didn't know Cézanne! He was my one and only master! Don't you think I looked at his pictures? I spent years studying them . . . Cézanne! It was the same with all of us—he was like our father. It was he who protected us . . ."

### *Monday, November 15, 1943*

With a few friends standing around, Picasso is looking at some reproductions of his paintings. He is highly dissatisfied with them.

PICASSO: You got here just in time. We've been talking about photography. Tell me something—what causes all these little holes, those little areas of light or dark, in places that have the same color value in the canvas?

I explain that it may be caused by an inequality in the lighting, by a badly stretched canvas, by reflections from the paint, or by spots where the paint has dried in to the point where it has lost its luster. "When we look at a painting, we move around so that we can avoid these 'holes,' but the lens must remain in one fixed spot, and can't always do it . . ."

Young Étienne Didier and his mother come in just then. Étienne's cherubic face, his air of stubbornness, his constantly searching eyes make him resemble Picasso as a child. I had asked them to come, so that he might show his paintings to Picasso himself. Étienne has been drawing since earliest childhood, with a passion I have never seen in another child. He draws as if he were obsessed, getting his inspiration from everything he reads—Jules Verne, Fenimore Cooper—from adventure films like Zorro and Tarzan, and from films about war and flying. The Indians attack the fort, the Maharaja and his court go tiger hunting, the pirates plunder the ship, the stage coach is attacked in the mountain passes . . . Or it might be a tournament, the brutal impact of arms and armor. Arrows fly, sabers lunge, lances and picks pierce the chests of fallen men. Everywhere, there are heads cut off, houses in flames, dying horses. The constant violence reminds the viewer of Uccello, and he is, in fact, the master Étienne admires most.

Picasso finds an empty frame, places it on an easel, and slips the pictures into it, one by one. He studies them close-up and then from a distance, occasionally putting on his glasses to observe some detail better. He looks at them as though he had never before seen a drawing. His eyes never leave them. He is totally absorbed by what he is looking at, and indifferent to everything else around him. The entire force of his attention is concentrated here. The greediness of his curiosity and his power of concentration are perhaps the key to his genius . . .*

* One day he said to Sabartés: "People don't pay enough attention. If Cézanne is Cézanne, it's for that reason: when he is in front of a tree, he looks attentively at what is before his eyes; he stares at it, fixedly, like a hunter sighting on an animal he wants to bring down. Very often, a painting is no more than that . . . You have to give it all of your attention . . ." (Jaime Sabartés: *Iconographie*)

One of Étienne's gouaches represents a terrible battle of knights on horseback. But above the battlefield, wreathed in clouds tinged with gold and silver, floats the spirit of an ancestor: he is encouraging the fighters of his own clan. The thing that intrigues Picasso is the presence of a white dove carrying a message in its beak. He turns to Étienne, and asks, "What does the dove represent?" But the only answer he receives is a slight lifting of the shoulders, a gesture Picasso himself uses when someone asks him that kind of question. And whenever he questions the boy about other images or details, there is the same imperturbable reply: "I don't know . . ." "That's the way it is . . ." "It just came to me that way . . ."

PICASSO: It's prodigious! What abundance, what profusion! And what a gift as a painter! Look at that white horse! See how he has used the white of the paper! He hasn't used any color at all for the horse, but the horse is whiter than the paper!

For an hour, he goes on looking at these drawings and gouaches, marveling at them. Then he disappears, and returns a minute later with a kaleidoscope, which he offers to Étienne. In this enormous bark, crowded with thousands of objects of every kind, he has known immediately where to find the gift he was searching for.

PICASSO: So—come back in fifty years! I would like to know what will come of all this in fifty years. And in any case, be sure you take good care of these drawings . . .

I went to lunch at the home of Étienne's parents, on the rue Servandoni. And with a distinguished guest: the painter Charles Camoin. I am delighted to meet this man (although considerably more jovial, he resembles his friend Matisse) who is one of the rare people still living who was a close friend of Cézanne's. I would love to hear him talk about the hermit of Aix-en-Provence, and in an effort to bring up the subject I tell him about the young man who had come to see Picasso with his family's "Cézanne."

MYSELF: It's a rather curious story. If anyone had wanted to fabricate a fake Cézanne, he wouldn't have put his signature on a canvas that was so obviously not his work. He would have done a better job of imitation. Do you think that this picture, which was supposedly found in his studio, might have been painted by some young artist who was a friend of his, like yourself, and did the picture while he was with him?

CAMOIN: I doubt it. Cézanne didn't like people around him when he was working, and never permitted anyone to accompany him to the site of his "theme." Only Renoir and Émile Bernard were ever granted that privilege. And in Émile Bernard's case, as a matter of fact, it always ended in some sort of drama. The theme was something sacred and secret to him. He once offered to let me accompany him, but he did it by letter, and at a time when I was no longer anywhere near him—and probably for that reason.

MYSELF: But how did you discover Cézanne. Did you already know his paintings?

CAMOIN: Did I know them! I was a pupil in Gustave Moreau's class at the École des Beaux-Arts, and I can tell you that we were a good deal more acute than the pupils of that school generally are. Well, to get to the Quai Voltaire every morning, I had to walk down the rue Laffitte, where Vollard had his shop. Among the other paintings in the window, there were always a few Cézannes exposed to the laughter of the public. Every day I used to linger in front of that gallery, studying the pictures close-up and then crossing the street to look at them from a distance, and always finding it difficult to tear myself away from the pleasure they gave me. I was twenty-one years old.

MYSELF: And how did you happen to go to Aix-en-Provence?

CAMOIN: Chance willed that the city where I was assigned to do my three-year military service was Aix-en-Provence. I arrived there in the evening, filled with a truly violent emotion. At last I was in the city of Cézanne! "I must see this man immediately," I told myself. Naïve as I was, I thought he would be very well known and that anyone in Aix could show me the way to his house. Well—I questioned at least a dozen passers-by, and not one of them knew him. Guess where I was finally given his address. By a priest at the church!

I went directly there. Bad luck: the master was not at home. But I was asked to wait; he would surely be back soon. I sat down and waited for five minutes. They seemed interminable. Suddenly, when I thought of bothering him this way with an unexpected visit, and compromising whatever chance I had of gaining his friendship, I was so terrified that I leaped up and ran out of the house.

I had scarcely left when I began regretting my hasty action

and reproaching myself for my cowardice. I acted like a crazy man. I walked and walked, unable to make up my mind whether to go away or to go back to that modest little house which had such enormous prestige for me, simply because Cézanne was there. I had been on this merry-go-round for hours when suddenly I was seized with an overwhelming desire to go back. It was stronger than I was. My heart was pounding against my ribs, but I knocked at the door. It was the artist himself who poked his head out of a window, furious at being disturbed like this at night, and yet very intrigued at the sight of this impertinent soldier. It was eleven o'clock at night and he had been sleeping. Cursing and grumbling, he came down and opened the door for me, holding up a kerosene lamp to see my face. It was by that light that our eyes met for the first time. I stammered out a few words, and he asked me to come in. I went in, I followed him. He was wearing a nightcap, and his nightshirt hung down around the pants he had put on. He had scarcely set the lamp down on a table when he cried, "Look how marvelous that is! The yellow of the glass on the lamp, against that blue background! That should be painted! But what can you do—artificial light betrays the value of the colors completely. And I never paint at night anymore; I've even had to give up looking at pictures . . ."

I was still stammering with nervousness, but I tried to tell him of my enthusiasm for his work. He was very kind, and asked me to come back and see him again, even inviting me to lunch the next day. You can imagine my delight, my emotion . . . I was so encouraged by his welcome that I took a few of my little canvases with me. Cézanne looked at them attentively, and then, quite suddenly, he exclaimed, "But you are very good, young man! You are the one who is going to defend me in Paris . . ."

MYSELF: Haven't you ever thought of gathering together the things Cézanne said and wrote to you, Monsieur Camoin—as Émile Bernard did? He didn't really understand Cézanne at all, but his record of their conversations is of great value.

CAMOIN: No, alas, I never have. And I regret it enormously. But my memory is good, and a great many of his ideas and remarks are still clear in my mind. One in particular, because it was an enigma to me: "It's a man like you that I need." That's what he said to me during one of my regular Sunday visits. And later on, he often repeated it. What did he mean by it? I've racked my brain, but I have never known. I think now that, living in solitude as he did, and mistrustful of people, because most of them ridiculed both him and his work, he felt a need to unburden himself with someone he felt would understand him. But the surprising thing is that this remark, which he made in the course of a private conversation between ourselves, is mentioned in the book about him by Joachim Gasquet, the poet from Arles—a book that has a lot of things in it, by the way, but too romanticized and too rhetorical for my taste. It was undoubtedly Cézanne who repeated it to him, so he must have considered it of some importance . . .

MYSELF: But you exchanged a long correspondence with Cézanne after you left Aix . . .

CAMOIN: Unfortunately I have nothing very much of it left! Some time ago I was foolish enough to lend Guillaume Apollinaire a whole series of letters. I never saw them again. They are completely lost. Apollinaire never published them, although that was his intention. Among them was a copy of the very first letter I wrote to Cézanne after my departure for Avignon. I don't remember it very well any longer, but I am certain I expressed my gratitude to him. In any case, I ended it by telling him that there was a stanza lacking in Baudelaire's *Phares*. I loved that poem so much that I could think of no better way of speaking in praise of Cézanne than to associate my enthusiasm for the master of Aix with the masterpiece of Baudelaire. And I haven't changed my mind. I still feel that no one has ever written anything about painting quite so beautiful.

And, between the cheese and the fruit, Charles Camoin recites bits and pieces of the poem to us:

*Rubens, river of forgetfulness, garden of ease,*
*Pillow of cool flesh where no one loves,*
*But life abounds, flowing without cease,*
*Like the air in the sky and the sea in the sea . . .*

*Leonardo, profound and melancholy mirror . . .*

*Watteau, this carnival where hosts of shining hearts*
*Wander like butterflies in flame-like forms . . .*

*Delacroix, lake of blood haunted by angels of evil,*
*Shadowed by a wood of pines, eternally green . . .*

and then this final stanza:

> *This, O Lord, is the highest proof*
> *We can offer of our worth,*
> *This ardent cry that rolls from age to age,*
> *And dies only at the brink of your eternity . . .*

CAMOIN: It seems that Cézanne was moved and flattered by my letter. He was perfectly conscious of his own worth, so he doubtless judged the eulogy neither misplaced nor unmerited. It must have been as if he had perceived an echo of his inner conviction that he was the great painter of his time. He answered the letter immediately.

MYSELF: You told me a little while ago that you got Cézanne's address from a priest in the church at Aix. Was he really a religious man?

CAMOIN: Religion was a very personal thing with him. It's true that he went to mass regularly on Sundays, but he did it from atavism and as a matter of duty. "It's my form of hygiene," he used to say to me, with a sly little smile. But he had no use for the clergy. He called the village priests— Never mind, I won't repeat it here.

## *Wednesday, November 17, 1943*

Rare occurrence, there are no visitors today. I am busy rephotographing some of the sculptures.

PICASSO, *surprised:* What, are you doing them again?

MYSELF: Yes, the light is much better than it was the other day.

PICASSO: You are just like me. I'm always saying to myself: "That's not right yet. You can do better." It's rare when I can prevent myself from taking a thing up again . . . *x* number of times, the same thing. Sometimes, it becomes an absolute obsession. But for that matter, why would anyone work, if not for that? To express the same thing, but express it better. It's always necessary to seek for perfection. Obviously, for us, this word no longer has the same meaning. To me, it means: from one canvas to the next, always go further, further . . .

The other day, in the presence of Étienne and his mother, it was not possible for me to talk about the boy's drawings with

Picasso. This morning I brought with me a little gouache of *The Three Musketeers,* which he had done when he was seven. Étienne had thought it a failure and torn it up and thrown it in the wastebasket, but I had recovered it and pasted it together.

PICASSO: It's a little gem . . . The boy you brought here is prodigious. At that age, I've rarely seen such violence, such assurance, such a gift for painting. I was really struck by it. You can see to what extent he is pursued, obsessed, by images. But no matter how astonishing his drawing may be, this gift does not belong to him. Contrary to what sometimes happens in music, miracle children do not exist in painting. What might be taken for a precocious genius is *the genius of childhood.* When the child grows up, it disappears without a trace. It may happen that this boy will become a real painter some day, or even a great painter. But then he will have to begin everything again, from zero. As for me, I didn't have this genius. My first drawings could never be exhibited in an exposition of children's drawings. The awkwardness and naïveté of childhood were almost absent from them. I outgrew the period of that marvelous vision very rapidly. At that boy's age I was making drawings that were completely academic. Their precision, their exactitude, frightens me. My father was a professor of drawing, and it was probably he who pushed me prematurely in that direction . . .

*Thursday, November 18, 1943*

Since I worked very late last night, I do not arrive at Picasso's until about noon. As a rule, this is of no importance. He never leaves the studio before one o'clock. But when he is not there—today is Thursday—Sabartés shuts up shop at the stroke of noon. When I arrive, he is already coming down the stairs, accompanied by Marcel and a man I do not know. Who is he? I have already seen him several times at Picasso's. Sedately dressed in a blue suit, with the rosette of the Legion of Honor in his lapel, he sometimes sits for hours in the vestibule, simply waiting . . . Sabartés and Marcel leave us, and I walk toward the Métro with the unknown man. He tells me: "Picasso's paintings and drawings fascinate me; I love them. But I am much less receptive to his sculpture. What do you think of it?" I tell him that, in my opinion, Picasso's sculptural work is, in a sense, the foundation of his painting, and often is the place where his ideas are born and take shape. As for his plastic innovations, they will undoubtedly have an influence on the future evolution of sculpture . . .

Just as we are about to descend into the Métro, the man in the blue suit confides to me that he is a manufacturer of colors. "I furnish all of their colors to Braque, to Matisse, and many other painters. And to Picasso. I've been doing it for twenty years . . . I love painting, and I'm building up a collection of my own. Right now, I've decided on a still life of Picasso's . . . I'm in love with it. I've had my eye on it for a long time."

Then the man in the blue suit reaches into his pocket and takes out a large sheet of paper, which he carefully unfolds and hands to me. It is covered with Picasso's handwriting—less spasmodic, more studied than usual. At first sight, it resembles a poem. Twenty or so verses are assembled in a column, surrounded by broad white margins. Each verse is prolonged with a dash, occasionally a very long one. But it is not a poem: it is Picasso's most recent order for colors:

*White, permanent*———————————
*argent*———————————
*Blue, cerulean*———————————
*cobalt*———————————
*Prussian*———————————
*Yellow, cadmium lemon (clear)*———————————
*strontium*———————————
*Lake, madder*———————————
*blue and brown*———————————
*blue violet*———————————
*Black, ivory*———————————
*Ochre, yellow and red*———————————
*Ultramarine, clear and deep*———————————
*Umber, natural and burnt*———————————
*Red, Persian*———————————
*Green, cadmium, clear and deep*———————————
*Sienna, natural and burnt*———————————
*Green, emerald*———————————
*Japan, clear and deep*———————————
*Veronese*———————————
*Violet, cobalt, clear and deep*———————————

It made one think of Rimbaud's *Les Voyelles.* For once, all the anonymous heroes of Picasso's palette trooped forth from the shadows, with Permanent White at their head. Each had distinguished himself in some great battle—the blue period, the rose period, cubism, *Guernica* . . . Each could say: "I too, I was there . . ." And Picasso, reviewing his old comrades-in-arms, gives to each of them a sweep of his pen, a long dash that seems a fraternal salute: "Welcome Persian red! Welcome emerald green! Cerulean blue, ivory black, cobalt violet, clear and deep, welcome! Welcome!"

### *Wednesday, November 24, 1943*

I am awakened by the ringing of the telephone. The sepulchral voice of Henri Michaux. He asks if I can have dinner at his home tonight. Glad to have been aroused from sleep, I go to Picasso's. Baron Mollet and several others, including the manufacturer of colors, are already there.

PICASSO: Well, Brassaï, did you sleep well? We're going out in a little while, you know. It's too late to work . . .

MYSELF: I didn't intend to. I just wanted to pick up my cameras to—

PICASSO:—to take photographs somewhere else. You're being unfaithful to me.

MYSELF: I'll come back on Friday.

PICASSO: What, you're not working tomorrow either?

SABARTÉS: I know why. Tomorrow is Saint Catherine's day. He undoubtedly has some girl he plans to rescue from being an old maid.

MYSELF: It really doesn't matter—the editor has no paper to publish the book. Why should I rush?

PICASSO: Now don't get upset. We have all the time in the world. No one is rushing you.

MYSELF: The only thing I'm worried about is the cold in your studio.

PICASSO: Today it isn't very cold, and you're not working. But the day you make up your mind to get back to it, it will obviously be freezing.

Picasso glances at the time. He has just taken his watch from that useless pocket where men generally exhibit an equally useless handkerchief. He has always carried it that way, attached by a little chain to the buttonhole in the lapel of his jacket. Aside from a few old pensioners who play cards in the Jardin des Plantes every day, no one else still carries a watch that way. But he clings to his rooted habits, however obsolete they may be. Nothing in the world could persuade him to put a watch around his wrist like everyone else.

BARON MOLLET: Pablo, why don't you carry your watch in your vest pocket?

PICASSO: Because . . . Must I really tell you? All of my pockets have holes in them.

One after another, he turns out the pockets of his jacket, his vest, his trousers. Every one of them is ripped, torn, falling into shreds.

PICASSO: You see? I have no more pockets, and I have nothing in the pockets.

*Nothing in the sleeves*
*Nothing in the pockets . . .*

as Cocteau had sung in his *Ode to Picasso,* two years after their first meeting. A form of homage from the sorcerer to the magician . . . But if the pockets are empty now, it is because they have always been too full, stuffed with keys, knives, boxes of matches, cigarettes, lighters, string, bits of pasteboard and, if the place and occasion warranted, a pebble, a shell, a fragment of wood or cork, a root, a piece of glass worn and polished by the sea; things which are both common and rare, banal and marvelous, to the man who already sees in them the latent image of a dove, a bull, an owl, the head of a ram . . .

PICASSO: The only way I can be sure of not losing my watch is to attach it to the buttonhole. And when my pockets are the way they are now, I attach everything else to my belt.

He opens his jacket and his vest. Solidly attached to his belt by another little chain, there is an enormous bunch of keys, knives, scissors, all the paraphernalia of a cat burglar. Does he still have the secret pocket on the inside of his vest, where he used to bury the purse that contained his entire fortune, and seal it up with big safety pins? And isn't it astonishing that this man who cannot live without a feminine presence cannot find two feminine hands devoted enough to sew up his pockets?

MYSELF: I know what it means to have trouble with holes in your pockets. When I was out shopping one day, I put two eggs in one of my trouser pockets. I was living on the rue Servandoni then, and that particular day there was a big wedding at Saint-Sulpice. I was standing around with the rest of the idlers, watching for the bride to come out, when suddenly I felt something clammy sliding down my thigh. It was frightful . . . And the time it takes before all that yolk and all that white rolls out at your feet!

PICASSO: You should tell that story to Dali. He has held the monopoly on eggs ever since Christopher Columbus gave it up. Omelettes, fried eggs, scrambled eggs, hard-boiled eggs, soft-boiled eggs—Dali has used them for everything.

MYSELF: At the opening of one of his expositions in New York, the director of the gallery held out his hand to him, and Dali was holding an egg in his. The collision was inevitable—it must have been a horrible handshake.

PICASSO: People in the United States seem to love that kind of joke. And since Dali revels in them, he has found his promised land. Someone told me that the host at a very elegant reception had garlic rubbed over every doorknob in his apartment. It wasn't long before all the gilded and perfumed ladies began to smell garlic everywhere. When they discovered that the source of the odor was their own hands you can imagine what happened . . .

We begin gathering up our things to leave.

BARON MOLLET: Pablo, what a splendid overcoat! It's lined with lambskin . . .

PICASSO: I bought it a few days ago at the flea market. And guess how much I paid for it. Three hundred francs!

*Monday, November 29, 1943*

Last night I dined with Henri and Marie-Louise Michaux. We discussed the topic of the day: *Le Soulier de Satin.* After all sorts of difficulties, and months of discussion with the poet—to cut or not to cut this enormous work; to do it in a single evening, or in two—the Comédie Française at last put it on, on Friday. Staging this unique play of Claudel's—which is difficult enough to read—in the midst of the occupation; what a gamble. But Jean-Louis Barrault has succeeded in making a success of it, although less as a result of the staging than because of the warm and passionate voice of Marie Bell.

HENRY MICHAUX: *Le Soulier de Satin* is a very beautiful thing. I don't like the theater though, in any way; I might even say that I detest it. I rarely go. And when I am forced to go to a performance, out of simple courtesy, it puts me in a bad humor and I get away as soon as I can. The theater confronts me —both in the building itself, and on the stage—with a mass of people I spend my life avoiding. It's the perfect place for women who want to be seen in the right places . . . I didn't want to say no to Marie-Louise, but the evening was much too long and very tiring. But Claudel is a great poet. I have less sympathy for the man; he's too concerned with his fortune . . .

MYSELF: Do you know him?

HENRI MICHAUX: Scarcely. I was introduced to him at a reading at Adrienne Monnier's, and we exchanged a few words. He is a personality and he has courage. Doesn't it require courage to say what one thinks at present? People reproach him—and rightly so —for having written an ode to the Marshal. But didn't he also address a letter to the Rabbi of Paris, defending the Jews? Who else dared to do it? No one, that I know of . . .

Today, such a mob of people descended on Picasso that he took refuge in the studio, where I was photographing the last of the large sculptures.

PICASSO: I don't want to be rude to people, but I also don't like being forced to give up all my time to visitors. Why can't they leave me in peace? That's all I ask.

SABARTÉS: They are out there, solemn and sad as if this were a funeral. They are waiting for you. They have been waiting for you for an hour and a half. We have to do something.

PICASSO: But why did you let them in? Why didn't you tell them I wasn't here? They could have written to me, or left a message for me. But no, they're all the same, they all want to see me "in person" . . .

The conference goes on for several minutes. Picasso is still looking for some way out: "Tell them this . . . tell them that . . ."

SABARTÉS, *imperturbable, unshakable, inflexible:* It's too late now. We can't throw these people out now. We have made them wait too long. And they know that you are here . . .

Then, like a director struggling with a recalcitrant actor who is too frightened to go on stage and face the public, he pushes Picasso toward the door. Resigning himself to his fate, he asks only for a moment's grace, just long enough to run a comb through his hair and draw in a deep, deep breath. "All right, I'm going," he says, and disappears into the vestibule.

At about one o'clock, the house finally empties out. We are left alone. Kazbek, that strange, always silent and apparently sad dog, stretches his cadaverous frame and poses his delicate, interminable paws in front of him in an attitude resembling sculpture.

PICASSO: Have you noticed that he can assume poses that are so extraordinary they make you think of anything in the world except a dog? Look at him from over here. Doesn't he look more like a giant ray than a dog? Dora thinks he resembles an enormous shrimp. Man Ray took some photos of him. Maybe you will too, some day.

MYSELF: Have you ever seen Suzy Solidor's Afghan hound? Someone thought the dog looked like her, so he gave it to her . . . But he's not at all like Kazbek; he has very long hair . . .

PICASSO: That's a mountain breed, and mine comes from the plains, even though his name is the name of a mountain . . . He's absolutely naked . . . Only his ears have hairs.

MYSELF: They're very rare in France.

PICASSO: So rare that when I take him out for a walk, everyone looks at me and then asks about the dog. One day, in Royan, at the beginning of the occupation, a German officer stopped me in the street. I couldn't imagine what he wanted, but it developed that he just wanted to ask about Kazbek. I started to breathe again. Marcel takes him out most of the time, and he complains that people besiege him with questions. So I told him: "Once and for all, Marcel, when people ask you about the race of my dog, tell them that he's a *Charentais dachshund.* That will give them such a shock they won't bother you anymore . . ."

## *Tuesday, November 30, 1943*

Picasso is busy writing a dedication on a drawing he is giving to an old friend, the painter Ortiz de Zarate . . . A Renoir drawing has suddenly appeared on the easel in the vestibule. It has been offered to him for a million and a half francs. He hasn't yet decided whether he should buy it or not. The main topic of conversation is the Henri Matisse exposition at the Salon d'Automne. Someone in the group of those present says that the still life with oranges, which belongs to Picasso, is the most beautiful of all the canvases in the exposition. Picasso himself is not willing to admit this. He has scarcely left the group when someone else, whose name I don't know, remarks: "Picasso undoubtedly has his reasons for not deprecating the other Matisses . . . Several of them belong to him too . . ."

Today I set to work on a major task: *L'Homme à l'Agneau.* The fanatical eyes of this "good shepherd" are fixed unswervingly on me. He weighs a great deal. There is no question of moving him. I can do no more than turn him on his axis. And how am I to find a suitable backdrop? And how am I to light him? Standing in dead center of the room, he is completely in shadow.

Picasso comes into the studio, engaged in a lively conversation with a man of commanding appearance, elegantly dressed, and superbly bald. He introduces us. I catch only the first name, which Picasso never stops repeating, as a matter of fact: Boris, Boris . . . Boris is extremely attentive to the lighting I am trying to set up for *L'Homme à l'Agneau.* He smothers me with advice. "Do this . . ." "Don't do that . . ." "It would be better if you lit it like this . . ." His persistence annoys me. It also annoys Picasso, who intervenes: "You're wasting your time, Boris. Brassaï knows very well what he is doing. And your experience with footlights is of no use to him at all . . ."

I am left alone with the shepherd, who is giving me a good deal more trouble than the other statues. I take several photographs, full face, from a three-quarter angle, and in profile. Each time, when I must turn him around, I hold him carefully by the waist, because the ewe lamb he is carrying is very fragile, and leaps nervously in his arms . . . I have almost finished. But before I leave him, I want to turn him just one more time—perhaps I will glimpse an angle I have not seen before . . . I take him between my hands again and, very gently, begin the revolving motion. He has turned perhaps a quarter of the circle when I hear a dry, cracking sound, and one of the feet of the lamb falls and breaks into several pieces on the pedestal. The foot that was free of the shepherd's arms, thrust out adventurously . . .

For a long time now I have been expecting and fearing this accident. I knew that it must happen some day, fatally, inevitably. In three months that I have been lifting, turning, pushing and pulling at all of Picasso's sculptures, standing them on improvised, unstable pedestals—and most of the time carrying out these risky maneuvers with no help at all—it is a miracle that I had not yet broken any of them . . .

Once my first emotion has passed, I decide to tell Picasso what has happened. I know that he considers *L'Homme à l'Agneau* one of his most important works, and rightly so. What will his reaction be? He is certainly going to fly into one of those violent black rages which, personally, I have never had occasion to face. Perhaps it would be preferable to tell Sabartés first, and soften the blow? But I haven't seen him this morning. As I examine the debris of the foot, I realize that it was not very solidly attached to the body. The nail that was meant to hold it in place had cracked the plaster. The slightest shock would have caused it to fall. It was inevitable . . . And the Nemesis of sculpture whispers in my ear: "I tolerate nothing that ventures imprudently far from its base . . . I decapitate, amputate, mutilate . . . I wear away fingers, noses, ears, the legs of Hercules and the arms of Venus, anything that separates itself from the trunk . . . Huddled into itself, offering no projecting points to the weather or the winds, to vandals or photographers, resembling a crouching insect with all of its limbs in hiding, pretending to be dead—this is what I have decreed for sculpture . . ." I offer up the objection that this statue was meant to be cast in bronze, which allows for everything, tolerates everything . . .

I announce the news to Picasso. He doesn't shout, he doesn't explode. I see no flames in the nostrils of the minotaur. Could this be a bad sign? Haven't I been told that his cold furies, when he turns white with concentrated rage, are even more dangerous than those where everything happens immediately? He follows me, without having said a word. It is as a technician, an expert in his field, that he examines the wreckage. The pieces are fairly large, and none of them are missing. He has seen the nail, and the crack. "It isn't very serious," he says to me, calmly. "The socket was not deep enough. I'll redo it one of these days."

In the meantime, Sabartés has come back. Picasso tells him about the accident.

SABARTÉS: I know why you broke it. So that other photographers couldn't take a picture of it . . . And you are perfectly right! You should break every single one of Picasso's statues, as soon as you have photographed it. Do you realize how valuable the pictures would be?

An hour later, as I am leaving, Picasso says: "I wasn't angry, was I?"

## *Saturday, December 4, 1943*

Having finished with the large statues, I am ready to begin photographing the little bronzes and figurines in the "museum," but Picasso keeps the key to this himself. He will not entrust it to anyone, not even to Sabartés. From this point on, I can do nothing unless he opens the case for me. Yesterday, occupied with other things, he said, "I don't even have time to get out the sculptures for you. I'm sorry—but I will do it tomorrow, that's a promise . . . I just don't have a minute this morning . . ."

He did, however, find a minute to smile at me mischievously and say, "By the way, have you read the newspaper? There was a murder committed at the Hôtel de Nice last night. I'm very worried about it. Olga lives there, and so does Jacques Prévert. And it was a woman who was killed! I hope it wasn't Prévert who did it . . ."

Today, he has plenty of time, and is in a very good humor. I find him in the company of a weirdly dressed poet from Saint-Germain-des-Prés: bare feet in open sandals, a great leather sack slung across his back, and a cloak that is half-Nazarene and half-tramp. But he is young and handsome, and this clashes oddly with his attire.

Picasso opens the case and takes out a dozen or so of the little statues . . . I work alone in the studio all morning. As I am about to leave, I meet Sabartés. He is coming down from Picasso's apartment, carrying three little canvases in lovely tones of gray and rose.

SABARTÉS: They are part of my personal collection. This one is the latest protrait Picasso painted of me. What do you think of it? He did it at Royan, four years ago. I wanted to have it framed, but he insisted on taking care of that himself. And while he was about it he practically repainted the entire canvas.

I look at the painting he is holding out to me: Sabartés costumed as a Spanish grandee, with a fluted ruff like those worn by men of the sixteenth and seventeenth centuries around his neck, and a curious cap of black velvet, ornamented with a little blue plume. The portrait is a really astonishing likeness, although Picasso has completely rearranged the face, fixing the eye in the usual location of the ear and an ear at the base of the nose, and carrying audacity to the extent of depicting the familiar eyeglasses upside down. The odd costume astonishes me, and I ask Sabartés the reason for it.

SABARTÉS: It was my idea. It was a whim. I had always dreamed of being painted by Picasso as a sixteenth-century nobleman—the period of Philip II, and the way he would have dressed at the Escorial . . . And when you mention that sort of whim to Picasso, it's not as if you were talking to a deaf man . . . He made some sketches first—in 1938, at the rue La Boétie—and that collar with the starched ruff amused him. He was planning to paint a full-length, life-size portrait, in this costume of a grandee of Spain . . . I thought he had forgotten about it, though, and then one day in Royan he surprised me with this. Did you notice that he has used the colorings of the Spanish paintings of that period?

I could scarcely believe my ears: I had never dreamt that a Spanish *hidalgo* slumbered beneath the surface of this dedicated republican.

MYSELF: You must have a whole collection of Picasso portraits of you by now. And there is one in Moscow, isn't there? The one that's called *The Glass of Bock*, where you are leaning on a table.

SABARTÉS: Yes, it was in the Schukin collection. It's the oldest of his portraits of me—from the very beginning of the blue period, 1901.

MYSELF: The thing that surprised me about it is that Picasso painted you without your glasses . . . But you always wore them, didn't you?

SABARTÉS: Always. I am very, very nearsighted, and at that time I used to wear a pince-nez. But on that particular day I had taken it off. It was my first trip to Paris. I was living in the Latin Quarter, in a little hotel on the rue Champollion. My wife and I had gotten into the habit of meeting Picasso and some other friends every night in the upstairs room of the Café Le Lorrain. And that night he surprised me sitting with a glass of beer on the table and without my pince-nez, lost in my thoughts and with my myopic eyes just staring out at nothing. It must have been this unaccustomed appearance that intrigued him. A few days later, he showed me the portrait. He had done it from memory; I never posed for it.

MYSELF: How many portraits of you has he painted?

SABARTÉS: Four in all . . . Another one in that same year, 1901, with my hair as long as an art student's, falling around my shoulders. And a third a few years later. Then this one, the latest . . . Who knows? Perhaps he'll finish my full-length portrait as a grandee of Spain. And some day you will read the whole history of my portraits. I'm writing it now . . .

I walk with Sabartés to the Métro station at Sèvres-Babylone. He asks if there are still many of the sculptures to be photographed.

MYSELF: I've almost finished at the studio. But for the rest of them, how am I to know? Does Picasso himself remember all of his sculptures? And I know that I've missed some of his wire "constructions." I saw them at the rue La Boétie. But I'll have to go back there. Picasso promised to take me someday.

SABARTÉS, *with the bitter-sweet smile which crosses his face whenever someone mentions Picasso's promises:* Promised? Get it through your head, once and for all: promise and fulfillment are two things which rarely coincide in him. I know something about it. Generally speaking, I'm the one who suffers from his unfulfilled promises. His promises . . . Listen—he made me a present of the second portrait he painted in 1901. But every time I wanted to take it home with me in Paris, he said, "I'll give it to you in Barcelona." Well, in Barcelona he gave it to the cabaret we used to go to. That picture was sold, and passed from hand to hand until one day he was able to buy it back. It came back to the rue La Boétie. But he has never given it to me. Even though he told me that it was *my* picture.

MYSELF: Do you think he'll never go to the rue La Boétie with me?

SABARTÉS: Don't count on it! He has no desire to go there. That place revives too many painful memories for him—he is reluctant even to cross the threshold of the building. He was too unhappy there. Every time he makes a break of that kind, it's a definitive break, irrevocable. That's his strength! . . . the key to his youth . . . He's like a serpent when it sheds its skin—he leaves the old trappings behind and begins a new existence somewhere else. After a break like that with Olga, he would never turn his head and look behind. His faculty for forgetting is more prodigious than his memory. Some day, perhaps for the same sort of reason, he may even leave the rue des Grands-Augustins.

I ask Sabartés if there are still many things that were left at the rue La Boétie.

SABARTÉS: Almost everything that was in the studio has been brought over here. In the apartment, there are still a few of his older works.

MYSELF: And what's in that studio next door to the Catalan? I was astonished to hear Picasso say that there were at least fifty sculptures there.

SABARTÉS: He is mistaken about that. There are only the cast iron pieces from Boisgeloup and a dozen or so plasters . . .

I ask him if he has had any news of Paul Rosenberg.

23. Picasso's *Faucheur*, bronze

*Even though the hat is nothing but an impression in clay of a little dented pastry mold, it somehow evokes Van Gogh, Provence, the sky of the Midi . . .*

24. Jaime Sabartés, December 1943

*. . . his mouth has acquired the habit of curling inward at the corners of the lips, forming a smile that is at once disabused, ironic, mephistophelian . . .*

25. Picasso's rue des Grands-Augustins apartment, with a preliminary study for *L'Homme à l' Agneau*, December 1943

PICASSO: *That will be an amusing picture, but it won't be a "document" . . . Because you have moved my slippers. I never put them down that way.*

26. Picasso's maid, April 1944

PICASSO: *Isn't Inés beautiful? Have you noticed the color of her eyes?*

27. Picasso's *Chat Assis*, plaster

*. . . the secret of its birth is always present now, between myself and the cat. I can no longer look at it without seeing the woman.*

SABARTÉS: They took everything from him: house, gallery, furnishings, silver. Fortunately he got away in time himself. He has begun a whole new existence in New York. He was very close to Picasso, but only in the sense that he sold his pictures. That's all. It wasn't possible to have a really friendly relationship with him—he was too arrogant, and treated artists with contempt . . . But he could never impose on Picasso. In that case the roles were reversed . . .

I would like to invite Sabartés to dinner.

SABARTÉS: You are very kind, but my eyes are too bad; I'm afraid of the darkness. I always want to be at home by nightfall. And especially now, with the black-out . . .

### *Monday, December 6, 1943*

Picasso went out early this morning. While I wait for him to come back and open the cabinet, I make a portrait of Marcel, the chauffeur, and then one of Sabartés. Through the view finder of the camera, I study the parchment-hued face, the slender nose, the weak eyes behind glasses as thick as portholes. The look with which he surveys the world around him seems to emanate from an "abyss of sadness," and would give his entire face a melancholy appearance if it were not for the fact that his mouth has acquired the habit of curling inward at the corners of the lips, forming a smile that is at once disabused, ironic, mephistophelian . . .[24] It is undoubtedly his sense of humor, his sarcastic turn of mind, that has enabled Sabartés to overcome his native pessimism and look at things—and primarily at Picasso, his friend, his god, since earliest childhood—with philosophy and detachment . . .

I also study his curious headgear. It was his fear of cold, of drafts, of the wind, that caused him to adopt it: a sort of helmet, whose sidepieces can be pulled down over the ears and joined beneath the chin, lifted to the top of the head and fastened there with a snap, or left to float freely, like the two little wings on the helmet of Hermes. And it is Hermes—who was also called Mercury, the god of public relations—I always think of when I see Sabartés leading people in or out, eternally at his post as mediator between Picasso and the world . . .

I take a few photographs of some corners of the vestibule,

where a portrait of Inés, Picasso's maid, has replaced the Renoir drawing on the easel. Standing near the easel, an old chair seems about to collapse beneath the weight of a pile of papers and books, topped by another portrait—one of the many preparatory studies for *L'Homme à l'Agneau.* Picasso's bedroom slippers are on the floor at the foot of the chair. The portrait, the chair, and the slippers form a sort of personage, holding in his arms the mass of books and papers. Since the slippers are barely visible, I move them slightly, and am preparing to take a photo of my "seated man" when Picasso comes in. He glances briefly at what I am doing.

PICASSO: That will be an amusing picture, but it won't be a "document." And do you know why? Because you have moved my slippers. I never put them down that way.[25] It's your arrangement, not mine. And the manner in which an artist uses the objects around him is as revealing as his works. I like your photographs precisely because they are truthful. The ones you took at the rue La Boétie were like a blood sample that would permit an analysis, a diagnosis of what I was at that time . . . Why do you think I date everything I do? Because it is not sufficient to know an artist's works—it is also necessary to know when he did them, why, how, under what circumstances . . . Some day there will undoubtedly be a science—it may be called the science of man—which will seek to learn more about man in general through the study of the creative man. I often think about such a science, and I want to leave to posterity a documentation that will be as complete as possible. That's why I put a date on everything I do . . .

One day, when I was talking with Sabartés about this habit of Picasso's of dating even the least important of his writings or sketches—and indicating not just the year, the month, and the day, but sometimes even the hour—Sabartés had lifted his shoulders. "What sense does it make?" he said. "It's pure fantasy, a mania. Of what interest could it be to anyone else that Picasso did such and such a drawing at ten o'clock at night or at eleven?" From what Picasso has just told me, however, it is clear that the precision of his dating is neither a caprice nor a mania, but a considered, premeditated act. He wants to confer on all of his actions and works their proper place in his personal history of creative man; to insert them himself—before others undertake the task—in the overall annals of his prodigious life.

*Tuesday, December 7, 1943*

When I arrive at the rue des Grands-Augustins, I encounter Françoise Gilot. As usual, she is carrying great rolls of paper in her arms. Her fingers are purple, her hands swollen with frostbite, but in spite of the cold and the biting north wind in the street, she unfolds several recent gouaches to show them to me—still lifes, most of them done with a highly colored palette, revealing a certain gift for painting. "I'm going to show them to Picasso," she tells me, and smiles conspiratorially . . .

I have known her for three years, having met her for the first time in the Montparnasse studio of a Hungarian artist who was initiating her into the mysteries of the profession. Very young—seventeen or eighteen—mad about painting, eager for advice, impatient to display her talent, she often told me about her quarrels with her Parisian family, which she described as too bourgeois to admit that anyone could prefer the study of art to normal university studies, and the company of artists to the comfort of the house in Neuilly to which she invited me to dinner one night. I was struck by this girl's vitality, and her determination to triumph over obstacles. Her whole personality breathed an impression of freshness and restless vitality. Her childlike exaltation, linking art and artists in a single admiration, made me think of Bettina Brentano, who was equally dazzled by poetry and poets, irresistibly carried along in the wake of genius and seized with a violent passion for Goethe at the age of eighteen. Bettina had a devil in the flesh . . . For a long time now, Françoise has been consumed with the desire to show her paintings to Picasso. A few months ago—in May of this year—she met him for the first time, in a restaurant. She comes here often now, and waits in the vestibule until her idol calls . . .

For his part, he makes no attempt to conceal that a new passion has come into his life. Too flattered, too proud of his good fortune as a man, he flaunts it openly . . . But I do not agree with Max Jacob's theory that he would have preferred fame as a Don Juan to that of a great artist. Like his renowned compatriot, he is constantly avid for new conquests and constantly wearying of them, but he permits himself to be subjugated by women only so that he may free himself of them through his art.

To him the amorous adventure is not an end in itself, but the indispensable stimulant to his creative power, and therefore too serious for him to accept it as a furtive and clandestine affair. Far better to have tears and drama than to have a modest veil thrown across the name and face of the woman he loves. With the smallest encouragement he would shout his happiness from the rooftops. But even if he were to conceal his love, his painting, his drawings, his lithographs, his prints would betray the secret at once. The features of the newest love will immediately replace those of the last . . .

Fascinated and conquered by the small, somewhat sulky mouth, the straight line of the nose, the little beauty mark on the cheek, the long chestnut hair falling free around the face, the green eyes, very wide and asymmetric, the adolescent, slim-waisted body, already rounding into the forms of a woman, Picasso is in love with Françoise and offers himself for her adoration. His love for her is the same love he gave to the first woman in his life.

As a witness to the idyl which is taking form, and to the raw state of Picasso's nerves—a condition with him which is always the herald of a creative renewal—I cannot help but wonder in what form the irruption of this new feminine presence will be reflected in his art. Each amorous experience releases a new and original form of expression, and it often bears the name of a woman . . . And I am also apprehensive of the inevitable upheavals . . .

When I see Picasso, looking a little upset, shy as a college boy in love for the first time, he gestures slightly toward Françoise, and says, "Isn't she pretty? Don't you think that she is beautiful? Take a photograph of her some day, will you? But be careful; her hair must be a little uncombed, a little disordered. Above everything, don't take it when she has just come from the hairdresser. I have a horror of those applied hair-dos."

It is not the first time I have come in contact with Picasso's aversion to *belles coiffures*. He feels about a woman's hair just as he does about cats; it should be left wild and free. If the matter depended on him, every woman in the world would wear her hair loose, falling freely around her face and neck and breasts. It was thus that he usually painted Dora Maar, and it is thus that he is already painting Françoise.

*Wednesday, December 8, 1943*

*On a cold December morning toward the end of the year 1612, a young man whose apparel seemed extremely thin was walking back and forth in front of the door of a house on the rue des Grands-Augustins* . . . It was this prefatory phrase of Balzac's *Le Chef-d'Oeuvre Inconnu* that came to my mind this morning as I arrived, rigid with cold, at No. 7 of this same street.

The studio is glacial. My fingers are so numb that I cannot work. And in any case I have an appointment with Georges Bataille at the Café de Flore. For a long time now he has been trying to persuade me to provide photographs to illustrate two of his books: *Histoire de l'Oeil* and one which he plans to call *La Tombe.* A curious person, Georges Bataille! A true scholar in knowledge, background, and the scope of his intellect; a child in his sensitivity and freshness of vision; a libertine, a descendant of the Marquis de Sade, but clothed in the flesh of an anchorite, prey to all the remorses of sin, the wounds and mortifications of conscience; torn between eroticism and a profound feeling for the essential tragedy of life . . .

When I arrive at the Flore, I see Jacques Prévert. "Picasso has told me everything," he says. "His *L'Homme à l'Agneau* is now known as *L'Homme à l'Agneau sans Patte.*" He also gives me the details of the mysterious murder in his hotel on the rue des Beaux-Arts. And it was not he who committed it. The murdered woman had been a collaborator and it was a group of Resistance men who had shot her, with a blast from a submachine gun . . . We speak then of Henri Michaux. "A man of great depths," Prévert says. "He navigates among us like a fish . . ."

Which reminds me that I must telephone Michaux. It is Marie-Louise who answers: "We are both ill. I still have that awful grippe, and he has an abscess." She puts Michaux on the line. I ask him if at least they are properly heated.

HENRI MICHAUX, *in a strangled voice:* I try to get the fire going. It won't catch. It smokes. I cough, I suffocate . . . I have to open windows. And then we freeze. I'm in a very bad humor. I have an abscess which is giving me terrible pain. And you, how are you?

I don't dare tell him that I am perfectly well. It would be too unkind, so I invent some ache or pain.

*Friday, December 10, 1943*

Worked late into the night. I cannot bring myself to get out of bed. It is as cold in my apartment as it is in the street, and in the street it is seventeen degrees below freezing. The other night the water froze in the fishbowl, and Alfred is dead. Even a cold-blooded batrachian must succumb in the polar climate of this apartment.

I was very fond of Alfred. In his sublime ugliness—a dragon's tail, viscous skin, a flaccid, colorless belly, bulging, myopic eyes, a flattened head and an enormous mouth—my triton was the very image of our times . . . I bought him in a fish and bird shop on the Quai de la Mégisserie. He was a difficult, stubborn beast, who would swallow nothing but live flies whose feet and wings he could see moving on the surface of the water. I finally had the idea of stirring dead flies about with the point of a pencil. And Alfred allowed himself to be deceived. Gradually he arrived at the stage where he would swallow anything at all, provided only that it moved. I stirred up the surface of the water and murmured, "Alfred, come on, come on!" And he came. "There it is! Go get it!" And he would hurl himself at the tip of the pencil, trying to swallow it . . . I had a trained triton—an unheard-of side-show. My friends never ceased to be astonished.

In an attempt to avoid his fate, I have constructed a kind of shed at the center of my apartment, sacrificing for the purpose many of the enormous mounted enlargements which had been used in my exhibitions. I have a few chairs inside these improvised walls, a typewriter, a coffee pot, and a little portable stove. The whole area is well lit. No sooner have I entered it than a welcome warmth floods through me; the warmth of my own body, reflected, accumulated, as it might be inside a thermos bottle. If I am able to write these notes, it is because of my shed . . .

PICASSO, *bantering:* Well, Brassaï, so you finally got out of bed? It's very kind of you to give a little thought to me . . .

SABARTÉS: He comes later and later these days, and less and less often . . . I don't have the pleasure of seeing him any more. He always arrives just as I'm going out to lunch.

MYSELF: Picasso, would you take some of the figurines from the case for me? Would that be too much trouble?

PICASSO: Yes, it is too much trouble. I have a mass of people to see this morning . . . But the devil with that; let's go . . .

So he takes four or five of the statuettes from the "museum." I close myself with them in the glacial studio, and set to work. Suddenly the sound of a bugle crashes around me. It is obviously coming from the vestibule. It leaves the instrument in a distorted, laughable burst, and assaults the eardrums: *Ta-ta-ti, ta-ta-ti, ti-ta-ta, ti-ta-ta* . . . I hear scattered bursts of laughter, and then a whole chorus, dominated by one deep, throaty sound, spasmodically contracting to a sob, a laugh that would be recognizable in a thousand: the inimitable laughter of Raymond Queneau . . .

The door to the studio swings abruptly open. At the head of the marching platoon is Picasso, bundled into his overcoat, the brim of his hat pulled down over his eyes, brandishing his trumpet, his face still flushed with exertion. Behind him, Queneau, Oscar Dominguez, Georges Hugnet, and several other cronies, including a woman with the countenance of a young boy and a scarf knotted around her head: Valentine Hugo. Picasso wanted to surprise me.

He puts the bugle to his lips again. It had really been he who extracted those bastard sounds from it. He draws himself up until he resembles all of the cocks he has drawn and painted and sculpted. He fills his lungs with air. His cheeks puff out. The muscles of his neck grow taut. And again he wrenches those piercing, strident sounds from the instrument: *Ta-ta-ti, ta-ta-ti, ti-ta-ta, ti-ta-ta* . . . followed by another explosion of laughter.

VALENTINE HUGO: That was a surprise! I had no idea that you were also an excellent bugler! Every day we learn about some new talent of yours.

PICASSO: But how could you possibly not have known that I was a bugler? I've been a master of the art for years! And my bugle has been very useful. When I lived on the rue La Boétie, Albert Skira's office was in the next house. Brassaï knows it very well. We worked together at *Minotaure* . . . I did the *Metamorphoses* of Ovid for Skira. As soon as I had finished with one of the plates, instead of reaching for the telephone I reached for my bugle, went to the window and sounded those notes you just heard. In no time at all, Skira was there . . .

I am left alone with Picasso. As a rule, at about one o'clock, after the visitors have left, he telephones Dora Maar. She lives nearby, in an old house on the rue de Savoie. She never comes to the studio in the morning anymore. But as soon as he telephones, she comes down to meet him and they lunch together at the Catalan. Today, as on those other days, Picasso picks up the telephone. He has scarcely begun to dial the number when Kazbek, who had been lying motionless as a fur rug, stands up and starts toward the door.

PICASSO: Did you see how he jumped? He knew that it was Dora I was telephoning. God knows how. It's easy enough to understand that his stomach could tell him it was lunchtime. But I often telephone other people at about this same time, and he doesn't budge. How do you explain the fact that he can scent Dora from the other end of the line?

## *Monday, December 13, 1943*

A freezing cold again. And since I got up too late, I missed Picasso again. I go to Montparnasse, in the hope of getting warm. On the Boulevard Raspail, in front of the pharmacy, I meet Henri Michaux. His complexion has a pale green hue, translucid as alabaster, but the metallic glint of his eyes sparks it with a startling light. The more bloodless his face, the more intense the focus of his eyes becomes . . . I inquire how things are going.

HENRI MICHAUX: We have exactly twenty pounds of coal left for the rest of the winter. It's a frightful state of affairs. My wife has an incurable cough and I'm still suffering with that abscess. My arm is paralyzed, and I can't move my fingers . . . It's a rebellion—half of my body disobeys me. And the extraordinary thing is that I can feel the pulsing of the blood through all of that part of my body. Unless there is illness or pain, we're never conscious of that, are we?

MYSELF: In that case I suppose you haven't been able to work.

HENRI MICHAUX: No—scarcely at all! To work well, I have to be alone, absolutely alone. And at this moment I'm shut up with Marie-Louise in a single room which we can't even keep warm. I can only write by talking to myself, aloud. It's a kind of incantation for me. I have to be able to hear my thought expressed . . . For lack of anything better, I sometimes go to a little café across from the Gare Montparnasse. It's warm there, of course, but I'm not alone. And I have to remain quiet. I can't very well sit there and talk to myself. They would think I was a madman or a drunk and throw me out . . . But I can't work in a café in any event.

MYSELF: Jacques Prévert is the same way—he can only write by talking aloud. But in his case it's a crowd of people, a knowledge of human presence, that he needs.

HENRI MICHAUX: He produces very little. Or at least he publishes very little. A few poems here and there, some infrequent texts . . .

MYSELF: He prefers talking to "scribbling." He's primarily a talker. When he goes into one of his interminable monologues, no one can stop him. His words seem to provide an unfair competition to his writing. But I think that's often true of brilliant talkers.

HENRI MICHAUX: It's too bad. Because Prévert is a poet. Nowadays, someone turns up a new great poet every day. But among the many who have been suggested, I have seen none who is really original. And Prévert has written several poems whose quality of innovation is indisputable. I like the *Dîner de Têtes* very much, and also the one about the Pope . . . I can't remember its title . . .

Hoping to get warm, we go into the Rotonde and sit down at a table. Michaux pulls a letter from his pocket. It had been there for several days and he had forgotten to open it. "I hope it isn't an appointment for this morning," he says. No. It is an invitation from Jean Paulhan to the opening of an exhibition of paintings. The artist's name is Fautrier. The cards are printed individually in the name of each person to whom an invitation was sent, and there is a reproduction in colors. But Michaux has received an original drawing of this artist he does not know . . . He can't get over it . . .

*Tuesday, December 14, 1943*

It is hideously cold. I simply cannot get warm . . .

SABARTÉS: We've just been talking about you. We were wondering if you would come in this weather . . . You're courageous. Picasso is waiting for you—he's impatient to see the new photos . . .

PICASSO: Do you really intend to work? The studio is Siberian. It's madness even to go into it. I wouldn't advise it. We can easily bring the little bronzes in here, where it's warm.

MYSELF: I couldn't very easily take photographs in this room, because of the birds.

PICASSO: The birds? They disturb you? I don't understand . . .

MYSELF: I would disturb them. My explosions would frighten them.

PICASSO, *laughing:* Your explosions? Are you sure of that? These canaries and turtledoves have never been hunted. They don't know what a gunshot is. But even if they really were frightened, would we know it? They have no way of telling us . . . Don't concern yourself with all this poultry! Go ahead and set off your bombs!

The offer is tempting. The stove gives a pleasant warmth. But then I glance around me: not a nook or corner where I can set up the statues. Every available space is occupied. And asking Picasso to move all of this . . .

MYSELF: I think not—I'll go to the studio. It's more convenient for me. And I'm not afraid of the cold. When you're working, you're less conscious of it.

PICASSO: That's true enough. And I have suffered from cold in my life, more than a lot of other people. In Barcelona I used to burn my drawings to keep warm. And in Madrid, what a winter! The cold in my attic on the Calle Zurbano . . . No fire, and no light . . . I have never been so cold. And at the Bateau-Lavoir! A furnace in summer, an icebox in winter . . . The water froze . . .

SABARTÉS: And on the Boulevard de Clichy! We wore our overcoats, wrapped blankets around us, used anything we could lay our hands on. I'll never forget the cold of those nights.

PICASSO: Even at Boisgeloup—that unheatable barn, riddled with drafts . . . That's where I got my sciatica, in fact. But I can tell you one thing—cold stimulates you; it keeps the mind alert. It compels you to movement. You work to keep warm, and you keep warm by working. But a comfortable warmth makes you sleepy. So go ahead and get to work. Have courage.

## *Wednesday, December 22, 1943*

Last Friday I gave Sabartés his portrait. Picasso at once exclaimed, "You have never had a portrait like that."

And Sabartés said to me, "I don't like my face. I detest looking at myself in a mirror. And I have a horror of seeing myself in a photograph . . . I'm not really photogenic . . . But I'm pleased with this."

Then he showed the photo to the others who were there, quite proudly. "Look, Brassaï has photographed me on my 'throne.'"

And Picasso added: "You're only lacking the scepter and the crown."

Today Sabartés mentions it to me again.

SABARTÉS: It has had a great deal of success. My wife looked at it and said, "At last, a portrait in which I can recognize you!" And I have another piece of good news for you: we got some coal, and the studio has been heated since yesterday. You won't be shivering anymore!

Although central heating had been installed in all of the rooms in 1939, only the vestibule has been heated recently, because of the lack of coal. Now, for the first time, I can work without wearing a hat, scarf, and overcoat. A beautiful day of warmth. Even the pale sun of winter joins in the spirit of festivity . . .

Today I am photographing the little panels of compressed sand—Picasso did five or six of them at Cannes in 1933—composed of palm leaves sprinkled over with sand. In one of them a long glove of Olga's which he had stuffed with sawdust stands out against the background; in others there are little boxes and bits of cut-out pasteboard, sewn together and painted with the skill and patience of a dressmaker; and lastly a head whose neck is a simple roll of pasteboard . . .

This book of sculptures presents me with a problem on a material level. I am not very well remunerated for it—Picasso has reserved all of the rights to himself—and in addition to the proofs I give to the publisher I feel obliged to offer them, by the dozens, to Picasso . . . And my financial situation is extremely precarious. I confide the problem to Sabartés. He estimates that Picasso could pay me for the proofs and volunteers to "arrange" that.

He rejoins Picasso in the next room. I can hear snatches of their conversation. They are speaking in Catalan. They do it whenever they have private things to discuss and do not want others to understand. They are undoubtedly talking about my photographs. They go on for a long time. Occasionally Picasso raises his voice . . . Then his friend comes back to me.

SABARTÉS: Well, I wasn't able to arrange it . . . But I did a good job of pleading your case. Picasso will have absolutely nothing to do with paying for the photos. I know him. He can be generous, but he can never be confronted directly with a request for money. He gets his back up. It's become an instinct with him. It probably stems from those years of poverty . . . Banknotes, cash in hand—he still has enormous respect for them. He has always preferred paying for things with paintings or drawings, rather than cash—even when the work in question was worth more than the sum he owed . . . I am sure he will make it up to you some day when you may not even be thinking about it any longer. I would advise you to go on offering him the proofs.

I tell Sabartés that I have always offered the photos to Picasso without the slightest thought of asking anything in exchange, and only my present situation had obliged me to do it now. A little later, Picasso joins me in the studio.

PICASSO: I hope you will understand my point of view. Zervos, who photographs and publishes all of my paintings and drawings, always gives me a proof. The other publishers have done the same thing, even when it wasn't stipulated in the contract. It's not up to you to offer me the photos, that's for the publisher to do. Since

I have authorized him to publish this book he will make a good deal of money from it, and it is perfectly natural that he should offer me these proofs of my sculptures. You should settle the thing with him . . .*

*Friday, December 24, 1943*

Yesterday I worked at Picasso's all morning, and watched the delivery of a consignment of raw materials. The doors to the main staircase were opened, and for two hours after that Marcel and the delivery men brought up virgin canvases; I don't know how many dozens of them . . . The temple of art momentarily took on the appearance of a factory. I amused myself with the thought that, within a few weeks, Picasso would have multiplied the "net price" of the canvases by a hundred, a thousand times . . .

Today, Picasso opens the "museum" for me, and takes out his little statuettes. Among them, there is a standing nude, in a wheat-color bronze, quite realist in manner, the hair blowing free. On one of the three copies of it he has taken a chisel to the bronze itself: the breast and the little torso are as highly polished as the feet on the statue of a saint worshiped by pilgrims.

PICASSO: How do you like this little bit of a woman? Don't you think she is alive? I don't know how many times I've reworked it.

And his fingers lovingly caress the breasts of the little Venus . . . Left alone with Sabartés, I have a long conversation with him on the subject of *L'Homme à l'Agneau.* I ask him if Picasso had made use of a model.

SABARTÉS: A model? What an idea! He said he had seen a lamb at the Catalan . . . But can he really control his memories? It's probable that the lamb he saw at the Catalan simply revived memories of other lambs he had seen in his childhood. His memory for forms is prodigious . . . When he was very young, he

* The publisher—Les Éditions du Chêne—went bankrupt. *The Sculptures of Picasso* was published in France in 1949, and later in England, with a text by D.-H. Kahnweiler and more than two hundred of my photographs.

grasped them so completely, in all their detail, and remembered them with such exactitude that, later on, he no longer had any need to record objects on the spot.

MYSELF: But he still occasionally makes meticulous sketches "from life."

SABARTÉS: Occasionally, perhaps, but more to distract himself and exercise his fingers than to refresh his memory. He doesn't need to. He can reinvent the real in all its variety, in all its truth, without recourse to models . . . Men, women, animals, plants; he knows them all by heart—their contours, their singularities, everything that makes them unique. In some way they have all become his private property. He is always at the very heart of creation.

MYSELF: Doesn't the nature of his memory remind you of Balzac? He too was so impregnated with forms and observations that it was never necessary for him to "document himself" to create his characters. He carried them within him. He once said—speaking of Louis Lambert—that he possessed all the forms of memory, that for places, that for names, for words, for objects, for shapes . . . But basically he was never able to clarify the nature of this prodigious gift. He spoke of a kind of second nature. But I have the feeling that this man who wanted to clarify everything did not dare touch his own mysterious faculty for imitation and invention. Perhaps he was afraid of it.

SABARTÉS: Yes, your comparison with Balzac seems right to me. With Picasso too, it's a matter of an extraordinary impregnation. At any instant all the forms of the real are at his disposition. What he has seen once, he retains forever. But he himself does not know when and how it may take form again. So when he places the point of a pen or a pencil on the paper, he never knows what will appear . . .

I ask Sabartés then how *L'Homme à l'Agneau* was born.

SABARTÉS: Picasso began a large etching . . .

MYSELF: The one that's on the easel, a bearded figure? I was struck by his resemblance to the shepherd. But I thought he did it after the sculpture.

SABARTÉS: No, that print preceded it; it was its origin. You saw all the figures that surround the bearded man, offering him gifts.

Among these gifts, there is a lamb. The man with the beard is just taking it up. It was this that produced the idea of the statue. Subsequently, to clarify it in his mind, Picasso made a great number of drawings, a hundred or more.

MYSELF: I photographed about twenty of them the other day, set on an easel in the sequence of their execution. The sculpture is surprisingly fresh.

SABARTÉS: And do you know why? After months and months of preparation, he modeled it in a single session, in a few hours. Ask him about it some day. He'll tell you all of this . . .

I was not thinking of it at the time, but—curious coincidence —we were talking about the good shepherd and his lamb today . . . Today, Christmas Eve of this sinister year of 1943 . . .

*Friday, April 9, 1944*

Yesterday, as I was leaving a restaurant in Montparnasse, I met Henri Michaux. He was wearing a handsome new mackintosh.

"The exterior signs of wealth!"

"It was my watercolors that got it for me."

I had been on my way to do some drawing at the Académie de la Grande Chaumière, and Michaux suggested that he come along. But, as we approached the entrance, he became reticent about it, and began asking all sorts of questions:

"Don't they ask you anything when you go in? Do they watch what you do? Do you have to talk to teachers?"

I tried to reassure him:

"Why, no, of course not. You're entirely free. You do whatever you like. You sit down wherever you can find a place. The majority of people come here to get warm, and not to draw. And since it's quite cold tonight . . ."

The classroom was filled, and it was very warm. The generous form of Victoria, one of the Grande Chaumière's best-known models, was on display on the harshly lit platform. Perched on a high stool, with his back to the wall, Michaux became a trifle more calm. Once his first emotion had passed, he whispered in my ear: "I could never do any drawing here. This crowd makes it impossible. But I'll act as if I were drawing—otherwise they might suspect me of something." Then he turned away from me, to stare at these men and women of all ages, hunched over their drawing blocks and portfolios, surrounding a nude figure petrified on the platform in an unimaginable pose, her buttocks blue with gooseflesh, her limbs stiff with cramp. There is no sound but the grating of pen or pencil on paper, so he whispers to me: "This would be a terrifying spectacle to anyone who didn't know what was going on."

PICASSO: What a surprise! Just the other day Sabartés said, "We don't see Brassaï anymore. What do you suppose has happened? Could he be one of Doctor Petiot's victims?" Seriously, we were beginning to be worried . . . Strange things are happening . . .*

It is quite true that I was seized with a sudden desire to do some drawing again, and I have not been to Picasso's studio for three months. And I understand his anxiety . . . In occupied Paris, any long separation may signify a permanent farewell.

PICASSO: Did you know that Robert Desnos has been arrested?

MYSELF: Yes, I heard of it. A tragedy. And a friend had telephoned to warn him, just at dawn. It seems she was well informed; she knew the Gestapo was coming.

PICASSO: He could have gotten away in his pajamas. But he had begun to dress. He hadn't finished when they arrived.

MYSELF: I'm sure he did it deliberately. He didn't want them to arrest Youki in his place. So he didn't want to get away. Is he still at Fresnes?

PICASSO: They have already transferred him to Compiègne.

We talk for a long time about Robert Desnos. Picasso is very fond of him. Just a few weeks ago he did some marvelous etchings for him, for *Contrée* . . .

I first knew Desnos about 1927, at the time when he was living in the same house with André Masson and Joan Miró; 45, rue Blomet, the street of the famous Negro dance hall, enlivened by all the children of Guadeloupe and Martinique. At that time he was still a part of the surrealist group. In a sense, in fact, his gift of poetic prophecy had made him its incarnation. He led the life of the constantly needy, moving from one profession to an-

* Doctor Petiot was the Landru of the occupation. On pretext of getting them passage to America, he had gained the confidence of many people, both men and women, and brought them, with all of their fortune, to the rue Lesueur, where he burned them in a crematory oven.

other: real estate agent, broker, journalist. I used to meet him late at night in the cafés and bars of Montparnasse, after he had spent an exhausting day of work in the editorial rooms. He was friendship, brotherhood, generosity personified. Solitude, destitution, fatigue had never erased the smile from his lips nor fettered his eagerness for life. And at last the siren of *Siramour,* the vampire of *Nuits sans Amour,* the phantom of *Journal d'une Apparition,* had become flesh. Youki, the ex-wife of Foujita, joined Elsa, Nush, and Gala as one of the stars in the firmament of surrealist love. Then there was work on the radio, the period of slogans, jingles, publicity devices. Far from seeing it as a disgrace, a "moral suicide," Desnos, who was both a searcher and a singer, who loved the songs of the sailors and the laments of the streets, greeted these new forms as a return to the popular sources of poetry. Affluence came at last, and with it the apartment in the old house at No. 19, rue Mazarine, very near Picasso. This center of friendship and love, hung with abstract and naïve paintings, cluttered with phonograph records—where an enormous provincial table was constantly laden with food and drink—never ceased to welcome visitors, never emptied altogether. The pinard flowed *à gogo,* even during the occupation. But during these last months Desnos had become almost unrecognizable. The plump, unlined, and rosy face had melted away. Nothing remained of it but a shadow behind the big smoked glasses which now hid the eager blue eyes, once so childlike, so candid . . .*

Picasso is elegant today; a rare occurrence—dark blue suit, white shirt, red checked tie. Jean Marais is there, accompanied, as always, by his white Samoyed. Among the other visitors I am delighted to see Pierre Reverdy. I like his masculine voice, his grape-black eyes—closely related to Picasso's—the lofty tilt of his head, and even his fits of temper, the lightning bolts of a stormy mind. He questions me about myself. I tell him that I have been forced to flee from my apartment, take refuge with friends and live with a false identity card. As an ex-officer in the Rumanian army, I have been mobilized by the Germans, but I preferred desertion . . . Reverdy is a man who saw death everywhere, when it was more discreet than it is today, and even though he is not directly

* For two years Desnos had been a member of a Resistance network. He was also a member of the clandestine publishing house *Éditions de Minuit.* From Compiègne he was deported to Buchenwald, and then began the exhausting exodus of prisoners—largely on foot—to Czechoslovakia. He died there, on June 8, 1945, at the very moment when the nightmare was ending for almost everyone else. His ashes were returned to Paris for burial.

threatened by the war he is shattered by it. He asks me if I can see any end to all of this. I repeat what Léon-Paul Fargue said to me one day at the Brasserie Lipp, shortly before his stroke: "What an age we are living in, dear friend! The skin of a rabbit is worth more than the skin of a man!"

Is it possible that we are on the eve of an Allied landing? Everyone is talking about it, citing the destructive, murderous bombing raids which are becoming more and more frequent. Picasso tells some strange stories. Jean Marais adds some of his own: tragic, comic, magical in their horror. ". . . as a result of the decompression from the fire, she flew out of a sixth-floor window and landed safe and sound. The thickened air had carried her as if she were floating on a cushion . . ."

PICASSO: I heard a story about a young girl who was hurled against a wall by the explosion of a bomb. She hung there, flattened against the wall, like a bas-relief on a background of blood. All these scenes of horror remind me of the carnage and atrocities of the Spanish Civil War . . . Guernica . . . The Spaniards are alone in their love of violence and cruelty—they love to see it flow, to run; the blood of horses, the blood of bulls, the blood of men. Whether they are "whites" or "reds," whether it is priests or communists who are tortured and burned, there is always the same pleasure in seeing the flow of blood. In that particular realm, there is no one who can top the Spaniards . . .

A publisher of art books comes in.

PICASSO: Here is the only publisher who pays me! Wonderful—I need his advice on how to make the others pay! You should draw up a sample form of a contract for me. And do it right! Put in all of the conditions that are best for me . . . Publishers are curious people. Look here, just this morning, in the mail, there is a letter from a German publisher about an album of my paintings. At the end of the letter—now listen to this!—he has the brazen gall to write: "I hope, Monsieur Picasso, that you will sell a great many of your paintings, thanks to my book." And he is the one who will sell his books, thanks to my paintings.

The publisher explains that he is preparing a book on the Douanier Rousseau, and would like to reproduce all of Rousseau's canvases in Picasso's collection.

Picasso throws up his arms.

"As if I didn't have enough to do with my own work!"

The publisher says, "You can't just think of yourself! Why are you a great collector? Why have you gathered together all of these beautiful things?"

As a matter of fact, a new album of the Douanier's paintings has just been published. Since it is the most recent arrival, it is still visible in the pile of books. Picasso takes it out, begins leafing through it, and suddenly cries:

"But that's a fake!"

Then, calling on us to witness his findings, he continues to look through the book.

PICASSO: Just look at this! That one is a fake too. And here's a third one, a fourth . . . All of those heads nodding sentimentally on the shoulders . . . Rousseau would never have painted that! The heads of his people were always planted solidly on the body, and the expression on their faces was downright bad-tempered, even his children. But the faces painted by this counterfeiter are completely soft and gentle. Tricks like this are becoming everyday occurrences. Someone makes up an album which appears to be a serious work, tacks the name of some chic art critic to it, and the thing is done. The fakes included in the book have been authenticated. It's incredible! And there are always imbeciles who will be fooled by it.

Picasso also talks about the false El Grecos in Chicago—a story I have never entirely understood. Someone else remarks: "It's the painter __________ who is doing these fake Rousseaus." And another voice adds: "I met him not long ago. He was complaining that Picasso had accused him of painting false Rousseaus, and said, 'The next thing you know he'll be accusing me of having painted *The Sleeping Gypsy!*'" Picasso bursts out laughing and everyone joins in.

The publisher announces that he has just come across an early Picasso self-portrait and has bought it.

PICASSO: You did well to buy it! Portraits of myself are very rare. I have never been too concerned with my own face.

He asks me if I have anything to show him; this is almost always his first question. If my response is negative, he is disappointed. But if I tell him, "Yes, I brought you some photos," his face lights up and he wants to see them at once. Since I hesitate to take all of the proofs—there are fifteen or so—from my briefcase at once, he says:

"Show them to me—all of them. It's curious, isn't it, but it's through your photographs that I can judge my sculptures. When I look at the pictures, I see the work with new eyes."

Since he can only glance at them briefly now, he wanders around the room, clutching the package in his hand, searching for a "safe" corner. Unable to find one, he goes upstairs, to leave the photographs in his bedroom, his Noah's ark, where he rescues from the deluge everything that is important to him at the moment: a letter, a book, photographs . . . Up there he can look at them or read them peacefully, at night, in bed . . .

At about twelve-thirty I am left alone with him. Suddenly the door opens and Inés comes in, carrying springtime in her arms: a great cluster of lavender and white lilacs.

PICASSO: Isn't Inés beautiful? Have you noticed the color of her eyes?[26] You'll have to take a photograph of her some day . . .

The smiling young girl goes to work distributing her flowers around the room. In the past years she has often opened the door for me. With her flowered dresses, her dark complexion, her long black hair and constantly smiling expression, she might easily be taken for a Polynesian *vahine.*

PICASSO: Do you know Mougins? It's a village in the hills behind Cannes. I spent the summer of 1936 there, with Dora, at the Hôtel du Vaste Horizon.

MYSELF: I know the hotel; I've even stayed there myself. They showed me some splashes of paint you left on a door. They guard them religiously, as a souvenir of your visit.

PICASSO: It was in that hotel that Dora discovered Inés. She and her older sister were working there. Inés was a chambermaid, and her sister was a cook. She was pretty, and she was very nice. So we stole her and brought her back to Paris with us.

We are just preparing to leave when the manufacturer of paints arrives. He proposes a barter to Picasso: a house he owns in the country, in exchange for the still life he has wanted for so long. As an enticement, he brings out a series of photographs of the house and its gardens. I have the impression that Picasso is not indifferent to the proposal. When I leave the studio, the discussion is still being briskly pursued.*

* I believe this man was the director of Couleurs Linel, which was the supplier preferred by Braque and Matisse, as well as Picasso.

*Tuesday, April 27, 1944*

I leave home early this morning. But what rotten luck! Two air raid alarms in half an hour. The Allied bombings are going on night and day now. Recently some bombs dropped by British planes, supposedly on the railroad yards at La Chapelle, fell at the foot of the hill of Montmartre. In the Lecourière studio, where Picasso does his etchings, his canvas *Nature Morte à la Lanterne Chinoise* was damaged by flying glass . . . I was stalled in the Métro for a long time, but finally arrive at the rue des Grands-Augustins. I ring the bell, and then wait for a long period. It is Picasso himself who opens at last, hastily dressed, neither shaved nor combed. Sabartés and the chauffeur have doubtless been stalled somewhere, just as I was.

PICASSO: You've come at a good time. I've been thinking about photography this morning. When I woke up, and saw myself in the mirror with my hair in this wild disorder, do you know what went through my mind? I regretted that I was not a photographer! It's entirely different—the way other people see you and the way you see yourself at certain moments in a mirror. Several times in my life I have surprised an expression on my face that I have never been able to find in any of the portraits of me. And they may have been the most truthful of my expressions. We should arrange to put a hole in the mirror, with a lens behind it, so it could capture your most intimate expressions when you weren't even thinking of it . . .

Could Picasso have been thinking of the horrified expression on his face on that sad day in November 1918 when he was told about the death of Guillaume Apollinaire? He was in the midst of shaving, at the Hotel Lutetia . . . It was after this that he developed his hatred of mirrors—all mirrors—whose cold reflective cruelty throws back in our faces the lines, the wrinkles, the circles that time engraves there from one day to the next. Having seen the shadow of death pass across his own face that morning, he ceased completely to paint or draw it . . .

Jean Marais comes in with his dog, carrying an enormous broom handle under his arm . . . He is putting on a production of Racine's *Andromaque* at the Théâtre Edouard VII. The majority of the roles have been given to stars of the films. Marais is fascinated by the chain-reaction vengeance of Hermione, and it is his plan to restore the character of Pyrrhus to its place at the center of the drama, instead of relegating it to one of secondary importance, as is generally done. He wants to give full scope to the Greek sense of fatality, and to the bitterness, the vengeance, the duplicity of wars. "It's a barbaric play," he tells us. And he plans to emphasize all of its savagery. He will play Pyrrhus himself. He wants to appear almost nude, wearing only a leopard skin. In his slightly raucous voice, he says to Picasso:

"I'll just be carrying a scepter in my hand to indicate my rank."

And to be worthy of his father, Achilles, and his grandfather, Peleus, the King of the Myrmidons, Jean Marais explains, "I would like the scepter to be something that is both sumptuous and barbaric. Picasso, would you make it for me?"

Picasso studies the broom handle, turning it around and around in his hand.

"Leave it with me," he says. "I might have an idea . . . But how am I to find time? Are you in a hurry for it?"

"A great hurry, alas," the actor answers. "I need it for tomorrow."

There are some new arrivals at this moment—Françoise Gilot, Pierre Reverdy, and the Catalan sculptor Fenosa, whose little bronzes Picasso admires. And also another actor, Alain Cuny.

When I leave the group and go into the sculpture studio, I notice that the tail of the plaster *Chat Assis* is broken. One day, some time ago, Picasso had confided the secret of this cat's history to me. He had modeled it first as a figure of a standing woman but had not been satisfied with it. Then he had the idea of transforming the woman into a cat. Her breast had become the cat's head, and her legs the cat's two forelegs. Then he had added the rest of the body and the tail. No one else knows of this metamorphosis. But the secret of its birth is always present now, between myself and the cat. I can no longer look at it without seeing the woman.[27] It is the woman-cat or the cat-woman . . . And who has broken its long tail? It had stood so proudly erect! Now it lies broken on the pedestal. Not without a certain mischievous pleasure I say to Picasso: "At least I'm not the only one who demolishes your sculptures."

PICASSO: But it's your fault! The other day there was a mob of people here. And everyone was amazed at the sight of the broken foot on the lamb. "It's Brassaï who broke it," I told them. "When he comes into the studio, he breaks everything! He wanted to turn *L'Homme à l'Agneau* around—and you know how heavy it is—so he took it by that fragile hoof. Naturally it came away in his hand. It's just as if I were to try and lift this cat by the tail!" I wanted to show them how you went around breaking my statues, and I broke the tail of the cat myself. It's your fault, it's all your fault!

Since my last visit, three weeks ago, there is a new canvas on display. An enormous canvas in a gilded frame. A nude, voluptuously stretched on a couch. It is so well painted that from a distance—but only from a considerable distance—it might be mistaken for a Courbet.

SABARTÉS: It belonged to Aubry, the antique dealer . . . Picasso is afraid of running out of canvases and brushes. He has always been haunted by that thought. But since the war it has become a regular obsession with him. So he decided to build up a stock of old canvases, in case there should be a shortage of new ones. He told all the antique dealers to be on the lookout for them. But when Aubry showed him this one it was love at first sight. This woman has completely enthralled him. He would never think of painting over it. He loves it too much.

And, in fact, he is so pleased and proud with his discovery that when friends and visitors come to see him he ignores his own works and takes them in to see this opulent figure of a woman.

"What do you think of it?" he asks me. "What if we were to take a photo of our new 'lady?' With all of us gathered around her?"

But almost before the words are spoken he has a new idea. "I know what we're going to do! I'll be in front of the canvas, portraying the 'artist in his studio.'"

He is so excited by this idea that he is incapable of remaining an instant in any one place. When this mercurial man is seized with a desire to create some kind of joke or farce, it is as imperious as the need to paint or sculpt. He has already taken down an old palette from its place on the wall—the palette he had used during his stay in Royan. He snatches up a handful of brushes, and begins posing in front of the nude. His caricature is made even more amusing by the fact that he himself has almost never painted with a palette in his hand. We are all aware of this, and laugh all the harder at the attitudes he strikes in the attempt to imitate the artist in his studio.

The "professional artist!" It oftens seems that nothing gives him greater pleasure than holding this concept up to ridicule. He lets himself go completely. His voice becomes mocking, his laughter almost shrill. There is nothing he abhors so much as the "artistic" attitude toward life, toward people and things. In his effort to communicate with reality—with all reality, the truest and most immediate, the most ordinary and the least picturesque—the "artistic" point of view seems a poor and shabby thing. How many times have I heard him say: "I do what I can do . . . I am not a professional artist . . ."; as if he were claiming innocence of a slander. And yet, when he comes across some view of a landscape or panorama of the sea, it frequently happens that he will say: "Ah, if I were an artist . . ." Sabartés has told me that sometimes, looking in the window of a gallery at paintings of sunsets, moonlight scenes, little cows or clumps of trees reflected in the mirror of a lake, Picasso will exclaim: "How it would amuse me to paint like that! You can't imagine how much it would amuse me!"

It is possible that a touch of envy is mingled with the irony here. Everyone, even Picasso, has his limits, milestones marking the frontiers of his ability and talent. The formless is outside the domain of this uncontested master of form. Rebellious against music, he does not have the soul of a landscape artist. In his work "the indeterminate regions of the forest" will always be determined. It is almost as if the clouds, the mists, the far-off glitter of the air which might appear for a moment on his canvas, are then crystallized into solid, tangible little blocks, sharp-angled and made part of a network of squares, triangles, and rectangles. One day Picasso was standing in front of a canvas on which he had sketched in some figures, talking with the painter Balthus, whose British stolidity he enjoys, and I heard him say: "I have done the figures; now you are going to paint the interior for me. You have the secret of creating an intimate atmosphere. I don't." It wasn't meant entirely as a joke. Didn't Rubens, who was also primarily a man of forms, often confide the landscape in his compositions to La Patellière?

"But we have forgotten the model!" Picasso suddenly exclaims. "I must have a model! What is an artist in his studio without a model?"

He then suggests to Jean Marais that he should play the role of the "lady." Marais requires no lengthy urging. He stretches out on the floor, brushing constantly at the dust that accumulates on his pale green corduroy suit, and twists his body around until he has duplicated the pose of the model, with his arms folded behind his head. Then I take a photograph, with "sets and direction" signed by Picasso.[29]

He wants to show us his most recent canvases, so we go upstairs. He doubtless feels some hesitation before unveiling works that are scarcely finished, but this slight apprehension is a far cry from the bashfulness of Braque, who sometimes waited months and even years before deciding to release a particular painting to the view of strangers. Picasso's "timidity" is rapidly dominated by a desire and a need to observe the reaction of "the public." I have seen him hovering over the rows of completed canvases, rummaging among them, pulling out one painting, eliminating another, spreading them out in a display, grouping them as he feels they should be, completely absorbed in a ritual of presentation—sometimes to people who have no feeling for his work—and I have asked myself why he went to so much trouble. I think it is because this very act of presentation constitutes an important moment of his creation. It is when it is seen by someone else that his work detaches itself from him, and his mind becomes fully conscious of what he has wanted to do, what he has succeeded in doing. From a painting submitted to this test, it sometimes happens that he receives the same initial shock as the spectator. I have heard him say of a canvas which he had just shown in public: "I am seeing it for the first time."

The ceremonial for this operation has doubtless remained unchanged since the days at the Bateau-Lavoir. It is basically a matter of building a sort of pyramidal construction with the paintings, of assembling them—generally around an easel which already holds one and possibly several—placing the smaller ones above the larger, showing them off to best effect, through either their affinity or their contrast. Picasso adores these improvised arrangements in which chance always plays its part; this final reunion of works of the same "generation," grouped as they might be for a family portrait rendered sentimental by the knowledge that they will shortly, irrevocably, be dispersed throughout the world.[28] He can thus embrace an entire period's work at a single glance, and often for the last time. There are several drawings and paintings that bear witness to the fact that Picasso has himself drawn inspiration from his presentations. I have photographed many of them at different periods of his life.

Today he sets out a series of "nocturnes" with a candlestick—which has been given a role of primary importance in all of our lives by the frequent breakdowns in electricity and the restrictions on the use of current—as a *leitmotiv,* and the composition built around the harsh shadows projected by the flame. The presentation is never halted by a lack of paintings, but only by the lack of space, when at last every corner is filled and there is no possibility of building higher.

A garret window in the ceiling of the studio throws the cold light of the sky across the canvases. There is an iron ladder that leads up to the window, and if he wished to do so Picasso could escape from his studio across the rooftops of Paris. Hung very high on the wall, near the window, I notice a sketch for a portrait of him. But it is not his work. I am told that it is Ortiz de Zarate, a Spanish artist and one of Picasso's oldest friends, who had begun the portrait, in this very studio.

I want to do a "group" of everyone present for the presentation. Picasso insists that I must be in it too. He wants to call Marcel, so that he can click the shutter. I tell him that this is unnecessary, since the automatic mechanism gives me ten seconds to join the group after having set it. Picasso is in the middle, with his dog at his feet, Pierre Reverdy, Jean Marais and Fenosa on his right, and Françoise Gilot and Sabartés on his right. The place for me, then, is beside Sabartés. I rehearse the obstacle-strewn course I must take; I will have to leap over several canvases to reach my place.

The light is bad, the exposure will have to be fairly long. I ask my friends not to move, and release the shutter. The little buzzing sound of the timing mechanism begins. I hurry to reach the group before the shutter clicks. I pass the first canvas without difficulty, and have successfully hurdled a second when my foot strikes against and turns over some object which must have been on the floor behind this canvas. A liquid spreads out across the red tiles of the flooring. Kazbek leaps to his feet, dripping wet, Picasso turns quickly to see what has happened. And the shutter clicks. Everyone laughs, and Picasso is triumphant: "I told you so! Brassaï breaks everything, turns everything upside down, causes floods . . . Tomorrow, he will probably start a fire in here."

The object I had turned over was Kazbek's big drinking bowl, filled with water. Since the photograph has been ruined, we decide to begin again. But can one ever remake a photograph? It is as impossible as bathing twice in the same river, as my friend Heraclitus said, a great many years ago. While Picasso, disturbed about the safety of his canvases, busies himself with rearranging them so that I will have a free path, even the group itself alters. Sabartés has been called away to the telephone. And another character has appeared: the stormy Catalan painter Ortiz de Zarate. A well-known figure for many years in Montparnasse, it was he who engraved Apollinaire's poem on Brancusi's tombstone for the Douanier Rousseau. And shortly after this the profile of Jean Cocteau, which seems to have been cut out with scissors, emerges from a frogged and fur-lined overcoat of the latest style, and he joins the group. I click the shutter again. And this time everything works properly. No one has moved except Kazbek, who appears in the photograph as only the ghost of a dog.

This is not the first time I have seen Cocteau at Picasso's. After having fled to Perpignan in the summer of 1940, and remained there long enough to finish *The Typewriter*, he was anxious to return to Paris. At the end of the year he settled in the Hotel Beaujolais, at the edge of the Palais Royal gardens, and in 1942 he took an apartment at 36, rue Montpensier, on the side of the gardens that also houses Colette and the Grand Véfour restaurant. I have been to see him once or twice in this strange lodging, presided over by his faithful Madeleine, with her enormous cat and the prominent blackboard of her "duties." One window of the apartment looks out on the arcades, the grillwork, and the candelabra of this melancholy garden, deserted now by even the ghosts of the libertines and dandies of the Regency and the Revolution. Picasso and Cocteau have known each other for twenty-eight years. Their friendship has lost none of its ardor since the day in 1917, in the midst of a war, when the poet succeeded in wrenching the painter away from his studio in Montparnasse and dragging him to Rome to create *Parade* with Diaghilev and himself. Cocteau has often said that his meeting with Picasso was the *capital* event of his life. The audacity and clarity of vision of the artist have doubtless stimulated his quicksilver mind, and so too have Picasso's humor, his verbal comedies, his ellipses, his genius for breaking-off and for change, his piercing definitions, his "profound fantasy" . . . Since his return to Paris, Cocteau has come here often, to drink at this inexhaustible source. Sometimes they lunch together at the Catalan, with or without Jean Marais. And Cocteau is no longer apprehensive of finding himself face to face with Paul Éluard, since the two poets no longer mention the old and sometimes violent quarrels in which they were involved in the surrealist days. I study Cocteau: still young and slender—not a streak of silver in his short-cropped hair—built entirely of nerves and muscles, without a superfluous ounce of flesh. His long hands, with their bony wrists and unending fingers, accompany the dazzling flow of his words with a constant, hovering movement, admirably set off—staged, in fact—by sleeves so short and tapered that they seem almost shrunken. He is discussing films. After *Juliette ou la Clef des Songes* and *Le Baron Fantôme,* for which he wrote the dialogue, he has just finished shooting *L'Éternel Retour,* which was inspired by the legend of Tristan and Isolde. It is the first major film whose concept and scenario is entirely his work. "If poets were to take over the cinema," he says, "it could become the royal highway of poetry." Cocteau is full of new projects, and is already dreaming of a film he wants to do with Jean Marais and Christian Bérard: *La Belle et La Bête* . . .

When the visitors have left, I remain alone with Picasso. Suddenly my attention is attracted to a blackened sculpture in relief, hanging on the wall. I go over to it and discover that it is the carcass of a skinned rabbit, dry and dark as a mummy.

PICASSO: Isn't it marvelous? I found it in the Cour Carré of the Louvre.

I am amused at the thought that this miserable rabbit, tossed into the courtyard of the Louvre, may some day enter the Museum of the Louvre. It would only be necessary for Picasso to restore it, to give it dignity by incorporating it into a picture, as he did with the sackcloth of the bathroom at the rue La Boétie, when he employed it in *La Guitare.* Why shouldn't this skinned rabbit take part in the same kind of adventure?

PICASSO: You know, I pick up everything—especially the things other people throw away. Did you ever hear the nickname Cocteau gave me one day? King of the Ragpickers. Look here . . .

And he brings out a whole series of little boxes of white wood.

PICASSO: I took them out of a trash can last night, as I was coming home. It's an absolute marvel that anyone should make boxes so simply, with such ingenuity! Look how ingenious it is: the top opens and closes, with just two little nails in the place of hinges. A real work of art!

I share with Picasso this love for the most ordinary of objects and outcast bits of material, and I think of the remark of Leonardo da Vinci, whose head was so filled with wonderful ideas: ". . . I behave like a man whose poverty causes him to go last to the market and buy the things already seen and disdained by others . . ."

MYSELF: I love those big boxes of matches. I put them one on top of another and glue them together, making a skyscraper of them. Then each box becomes a little drawer holding matches, thumbtacks, paper clips, safety pins, spare fuses, butts of cigarettes, and cigarette papers. In these days of air raids, power failures, and shortages of tobacco, it's the most useful piece of furniture I have, and it's always within easy reach.

PICASSO: I never dare throw away a box of matches, or for that matter a box of cigarettes. I keep them, and pile them up. Do you remember the piles of them on the mantelpiece at the rue La Boétie? And matches! I've always wanted to make sculptures from them—constructions. After all, they're a miniature version of those metal tubes engineers assemble to make scaffoldings. Wait a minute, I'm going to show you something . . .

Picasso disappears for a moment, and when he returns he is holding a little piece of wood on which there stands a sturdy and astonishing construction, made entirely of matchsticks, each of them attached to the other with a tiny ball of putty. I would like very much to take a photograph of it. But Picasso tells me that there are still some elements missing from its composition, and that he plans to finish it someday. And it is already one o'clock and I have put away my camera. Too bad. I'll photograph it some other time.*

* Naturally this project was never carried out—like most of those that are not accomplished immediately. The fragile little construction has probably been destroyed.

*Wednesday, April 28, 1944*

It was understood that this morning I would go with Picasso to his "studio annex" next door to the Catalan. He is still in bed when I arrive and sends word for me to come up. A sign of friendship: only the members of the household and his closest friends are admitted to his bedroom . . .

The emptiness of this room contrasts sharply with the overflow in the studio. He is seated on the bed, smoking a Gauloise. He must have smoked a great many of them during the night—the ashtray is filled with butts. Marcel has just brought up the mail. Several letters have already been opened and read and are scattered around him on the bed. Last night's and this morning's newspapers are piled on a stool. And also a few books. No one has ever seen Picasso with a book in his hand, reading. And yet he has read everything, remembered everything. His conversation reveals that he is well acquainted with literary developments, and knows everything that is being published. He reads a great deal, but never during the day. Only in the late hours of the night, after he has put down his brushes, and until he falls asleep.

PICASSO: Many times when you have made an appointment with me you haven't come. You have preferred your bed, or a woman, to Picasso. Now, for once, I have the right to prefer my bed to you, don't I? We'll go to the studio some other day . . . Do you know why I'm still in bed? It's because of that damned broom handle of Jean Marais'. I worked on it almost the whole night . . . Do you want to see it? It's over there, in the corner. How do you like this royal scepter of Pyrrhus?

I pick up the staff. It is very beautiful. Picasso has burned into it a series of long spirals and circles in the geometric style of some reinvented archaic art. I am struck again by his infallible gift for giving life to whatever material he touches. It is as if the sources, the secrets, all of the age-old experiments and methods of the graphic and plastic arts had always been immediately available to him; so that, at first sight, he senses, invents, and reinvents the techniques best suited for treating it.

PICASSO: I wanted to paint it at first. But on the stage, black and white is more effective than color. Then the idea came to me to burn it. But with what? I have no tools here for that kind of work. And Jean Marais was in a hurry for it. That was when I thought of my little electric hot plate. All night long, I kept turning and re-turning that staff across the hot coils. It was slower and more difficult than I had imagined . . .

Sabartés comes upstairs and announces: "So-and-so wants to see you. He came about . . ."; "So-and-so just telephoned. He will be here in an hour . . ."

## *Wednesday, May 3, 1944*

I hope that this time we will be able to go to the studio annex.

SABARTÉS: You have come at a bad time. Picasso is absolutely swamped this morning. He'll never have the time to go to the storeroom with you . . .

I am preparing to leave when Picasso appears, beaming, in his most amiable mood. I show him the photo in which he is acting the part of the artist in his studio in front of the voluptuous nude. He is delighted with it. I also take from my briefcase the photos of the "group"; first, the one which had been spoiled. "I developed it anyway; I think it will amuse you."

PICASSO: I'm glad you did. What a document! We were all looking directly at the lens when "the event" occurred. And what do we see now? No one has moved. And yet, you had turned over the bowl and the water was spreading over the floor . . . Kazbek and I are the only ones who reacted at once. Why? Because I have quicker reflexes—as quick as those of a dog.[30]

MYSELF, *laughing:* The others didn't move because they didn't want to spoil a photograph of themselves with Picasso. And you—you were worried that I might have ruined your paintings. That's my version of it.

Picasso laughs, but he knows that I am joking. He does possess rapid reflexes, to an eminent degree. In the quickness of his movements and his eyes, in his constant air of vigilance, his instantaneous reactions, I always see the concentration, the presence of mind of the torero, for whom the slightest distraction or inattention would be punished by death . . . I give him a proof of the second photo of the "group."*

PICASSO: Look at this photograph. What is it that catches the eye, the very first thing? It's the crease in Jean Cocteau's trousers! Like the edge of a razor, like a plumb line! Ever since I have known him, that crease has always been just as sharp, just as perfect. Cocteau was born with a crease in his trousers,[31] he was born well pressed . . . And look at how elegant Jean Marais is. I am very well framed! Between those two, with my trousers that can't even remember when they had a crease, I look like a tramp . . . I have a great many appointments this morning, including one with a beautiful South American. I'm sorry, but we can't go to the annex. And I still have to go and make myself handsome . . . But you stay here. You can photograph whatever you like, even the South American, if she pleases you . . . You won't disturb me . . .

The light is wonderful today. It shimmers across the rooftops, the chimneys, the bare walls which are always in Picasso's view while he is painting[32]: a discreet background in a whole range of watery grays and reds and browns. The rays of the sun filter into the room through the big window; revealing little clouds of dust dancing around the old beams; rippling across the hexagonal red tiles of the floor, and breaking on its uneven surface into patterns of light and shade; illuminating the little metal table, stained with paint and littered with brushes and tubes, vestiges of a night of struggle. On a fragment of carpet beneath the window, Picasso's dog stretches out luxuriously, warming his skeletal frame in the sunlight.

I take a few photos. During this time the vestibule never once empties of visitors. I can hear the murmur of their conversation beneath me, an occasional voice louder than the others, the sharp laughter of Picasso. He brings up the South American woman for a moment, to show her his canvases. It is noon. The visitors have left.

SABARTÉS: I'm leaving too. I can smell an air raid coming. And if there's an alarm they'll cut off the gas before I get home

*In November 1963 Peinado told me this story of Picasso's reactions: "I was with him the other day when the telephone rang. A voice said, 'Is that you, Pablo? This is Van Gogh.' Without the slightest surprise or hesitation Picasso said, 'Yes, but which one? Vincent or Theo?'"

and I won't be able to prepare my lunch. It's happened to me several times already . . .

Picasso comes upstairs and sits down. "Ouf! Alone at last!" Then, quite suddenly, he flings his eternal question at me: "And the drawing? Have you begun to draw again?"

Since the beginning of the year, I have gone back to it, and as it happens I have brought a folder of my recent drawings with me. He wants to see them.

PICASSO: I like them even better than your youthful drawings. I have no reason to flatter you, or to tell you a lot of stories. You should have an exhibition. What sense does it make to hide these things? You should show them, sell them . . .

I tell him that since I decided on photography I have not wanted to spread myself too thin, and for the past twenty years I have never touched a drawing pencil. Without his persuasion, I would probably never have gone back to it . . .

PICASSO, *almost angrily:* Frankly I don't understand you! You have a gift, and you make no use of it. It is impossible—do you hear me?—impossible that you are completely satisfied by photography. It is forcing you into a total abnegation!

MYSELF: That self-denial pleases me. One has an eye, but not a hand; you are separate from objects, can no longer touch them . . . A man withdraws into photography as if it were a monastery. In the cubist period, you yourself became a member of an order. Your canvases no longer bore your signature.

PICASSO: True. But it lasted only a very short time. When you have something to say, to express, any form of submission becomes unbearable in the long run. You have to have the courage of your vocation and the courage to live by that vocation. The "second profession" is a trap! I was often penniless myself, but I always resisted any temptation to live by any means other than my painting. I could have followed the example of Van Dongen, Villon, and Juan Gris, and done drawings for some of the satiric periodicals. *L'Assiette au Beurre* offered me eight hundred francs a drawing, but I stuck to earning a living with my painting. At the beginning my paintings didn't sell for very much, but they did sell. My drawings, my canvases, they all left me, and that's what counts . . .

I tell Picasso that I did not choose photography as a second profession, or just as a means of earning a living, but because I considered it one of the means of expression of our times.

MYSELF: Few artists have your gift for imposing a painting such as the *Demoiselles d'Avignon.* They would die of starvation. Matisse told me one day: "One must be stronger than his gifts, in order to protect them . . ." And you had that gift: at the age of twenty-five you were famous, you had already known success.

PICASSO: But success is an important thing! It has often been said that an artist should work for himself, for the love of art, and scorn success. It's a false idea. An artist needs success. Not only in order to live, but primarily so that he can *realize* his work. Even a rich painter should know success. Few people understand much about art, and not everyone is sensitive to painting. The majority judges a work of art in relation to its success. So why leave success to "successful painters?" Each generation has them. But where is it written that success must always go to those who flatter the public taste? For myself, I wanted to prove that success can be obtained without compromise, even in opposition to all of the prevailing doctrines. Do you want me to tell you something? It is the success of my youth that has become my protective wall. The blue period, the rose period—they were the screens that sheltered me . . .

MYSELF: "The best hiding place is a precocious glory," as Nietzsche said.

PICASSO: Perfectly correct. It was in the shelter of my success that I was able to do what I wanted to do, everything I wanted to do . . .

Picasso spreads out my drawings. He arranges them against the walls, against the furniture, even on the floor. He studies them and endlessly repeats: "You have to exhibit them, sell them . . . Let me take care of it . . . I'll do something about it . . ."

We have been talking for an hour or more. Someone rings. Picasso introduces me to a man whose name I cannot catch.

"Who did these beautiful drawings?" he asks.

PICASSO: Would you like to exhibit them? You were precisely the person I was thinking of.

"I would like nothing better," the unknown man replies. "I like them."

Picasso gestures toward me and says: "Here is the man who did them. All you have to do is arrange it with Brassaï."

When the visitor has left, Picasso tells me: "You couldn't have done better. And it happened even quicker than I had thought. You'll be in good hands. Do you know the gallery Renou et Colle, on the Faubourg Saint-Honoré? It's a very good gallery. I had an exhibition of my drawings there myself, before the war, in 1936 I think. The man you just saw is Pierre Colle. I am sure you will be successful . . .

We leave the studio together, and he continues to give me advice:

"Don't ask too much for them. The important thing is to sell as many as possible. Then your drawings will travel all over the world, and that's what counts."

## *Thursday, May 4, 1944*

Sabartés, wearing his helmet-cap, is with Marcel and another young man, Robert Marion, the brother-in-law of Christian Zervos. In front of them is an enormous pile of portfolios, tied up with string and stuffed with drawings and gouaches. Each of them carries an inscription and a date. On one I read: *Boisgeloup, 1936*. In another I can see some of Picasso's oldest Parisian drawings, gathered together into several sketchbooks in which every page is numbered and annotated as if it were already the property of a museum.

I ask Sabartés if Picasso possesses many such portfolios.

SABARTÉS: He must have about sixty of them. But there are many stored away in trunks or closets somewhere. How many, I don't know. Some of them have been sorted out, and contain only his own works, but others are a collection of old prints, posters, catalogues of exhibitions, and drawings and lithographs by other artists—all mixed in with his. To try and make any order out of that; what a job!

The three men set to work making up an inventory of all these treasures, which is destined for a new volume in the *Cahiers d'Art*, a monumental publication which is planned to include all of Picasso's work—an unprecedented thing in the lifetime of an artist. It will doubtless never be completely up to date. Countless times, over a period of the next hundred years, someone will discover a drawing, a gouache, a piece of sculpture that has somehow escaped all cataloguing, all investigation . . .

I am surprised to see Marcel, the "chauffeur"—who has had no car to drive for four years—armed with a ruler and directing the inventory. It is he who files each sheet of paper in its respective category, and announces in an authoritative tone: "Number 2735, black lead, 30 centimetres by 36, Boisgeloup, March 16, 1936"; thus awarding its proper status to each of Picasso's works. To my great astonishment this "man of the people" is perfectly familiar with Picasso's different periods, and makes liberal use of technical terms. I mention my surprise to Sabartés.

SABARTÉS: Marcel is a good example of the extent to which Picasso's most revolutionary developments become naturally classical. None of his work, no matter how enigmatic or daring it may be, irritates Marcel or provokes his laughter or censure. Marcel no longer sees anything subversive or aggressive in it. At the beginning, this painting must have baffled him completely. But twenty years of intimate and daily contact with it have taught him how to read a language which is still incomprehensible to many people.[33] The evolution of this chauffeur proves that, in always addressing himself to a public which does not yet exist, Picasso both creates that public and imposes on it the criteria by which his work must be judged. If Marcel is in advance of his class, it is because his period of apprenticeship has been considerably reduced, as a result of that everyday familiarity with Picasso's work.

As I watch all of these drawings paraded in front of my eyes, I am surprised to see among them some portraits so meticulously drawn that the lashes on the eyes can be counted. These almost "naturalist" and sometimes even conventional drawings appear in every one of Picasso's periods and seem to be independent of the context of his style of the moment. I pick up one of these drawings, which represents Dora Maar sleeping . . .

SABARTÉS: Good God, what are you doing! You're holding that drawing with one hand! If Picasso were here, he would kill you. There is nothing in the world he is so particular about as the ground for his drawings. He wants it to be impeccable, perfectly smooth, without a single wrinkle. On that subject he is totally uncompromising. No degree of friendship could alter it! The other day, there was a publisher here who was imprudent enough to pick up a drawing and hold it in one hand, and at the center, instead of with two hands, by the borders . . . He threw him out of the house.

*Friday, May 5, 1944*

This morning—at last!—I go with Picasso and the publisher of the book to the studio annex. The first pieces of sculpture I see there are the figures in wrought iron from the park at Boisgeloup.

PICASSO: They were badly damaged. The château was occupied by the French army in the first months of the war, and then by the Wehrmacht. The Germans didn't do any damage. It was the French soldiers of that pre-Blitzkrieg period who amused themselves by balancing my statues on windowsills. I've redone them, as best I could.

Then he begins opening the cases. I am anxious to see all of these works which are still unknown to me. Because of the lack of bronze, they are all still in plaster: birds, doves, personages, a great many heads in bas-relief, sometimes modeled in negative. Others are curious forms of imprints. I have a picture of Picasso amusing himself, but with the gravity that children and gods apply to their games, by imprinting in the plaster all sorts of forms, structures, and materials. He will use the tops of a box, an orange, the bark of a tree. And why not a leaf, living or dead? The earliest of these experiments go back to 1934, at Boisgeloup . . . I can see him trying the effect of a pastry mold, and of those little sand molds which are the delight of children on a beach; surprised to find that the casting of a simple piece of pasteboard, folded and refolded, can give a result as monumental as the Great Wall of China[34]; that the imprint of a crumpled piece of newspaper can assume the aspect of a rocky mountain . . .[35] The round bottoms of the pastry or sand molds,[36] the rectangle of boxtops, pierced with two, three, or four holes to serve as eyes, nose, and mouth, then gave birth to primitive countenances similar to those of neolithic idols or the graffiti scratched into the walls of Paris.[37] In many cases, several of these imprints are assembled into a single sculpture. One of the most beautiful is a figure born of a corrugated carton, with a rectangular head and a casting of real leaves in her arms: a goddess of barbaric extravagance emerging from mythology.[38]

I am struck by the novelty of these plastic experiments. All that Picasso has done here is to arrange for a meeting between familiar structures and materials, and to assign them a new sense and a new destination. The hand of the artist—the thumb of the sculptor—modeling the clay and leaving his own imprint there is totally absent. Without intervening directly, he has allowed his figures to model themselves, renouncing the use of his own hand, normally the most eager, the most patient—and the most impatient—to draw, to engrave, to paint, to model, to sculpt.

But curiously enough I find this hand, which has been eliminated, prohibited, in the experiments, figuring as subject and object in a great many other casts and imprints, as if Picasso were then focusing on his hands the attention he had once given to his face.[39] Twenty years earlier he had made a whole series of charcoal drawings, gouaches, and pastels of his left hand, working from life. Now he has imprinted another such series in fresh plaster and made castings of the closed fist and the strong wristbone, as though he wanted to seize all of their concentrated strength.[40] I also see a casting of his right hand, which I think must have been done by someone else. It stands as a monolithic whole, a monument to a sovereign force and balance: a fleshy palm, the hill of Venus bursting with sensuality, a headstrong thumb, fingers so tightly matched against each other that not the smallest ray of light could pass between them.[41] And what clarity, what precision in the deeply etched lines that rib this artisan's palm and dominate the line of fortune, climbing straight as an explosive fuse to the base of the middle finger.

Sabartés was wrong; Picasso was right: there are easily fifty or more sculptures in the cases we unpack. Picasso says to me: "You see, you still have bread in the oven!"

The publisher, a trifle terrified at the thought of the scope the book will assume if all of these modelings are included, gestures toward some of the "imprints" and murmurs to me: "You can discard those; they don't seem very important to me." Picasso, hearing him, protests: "Oh, yes—on the contrary, they are very important! And I insist ab-so-lutely that they appear in your book . . ."

Picasso can have lunch at the Catalan again. After four weeks of forced closure, his favorite restaurant is opening its doors again today.

### *Tuesday, June 14, 1944*

Just as I am ringing the bell, I hear a thunderous outburst of voices: "I will never step foot in here again! Tell that to Picasso! He may be Picasso, but I am Ortiz de Zarate! I want my painting—I want to take it with me!"

When the door opens I see a passionate man, a man so enraged that not even the calm and diplomacy of Sabartés can soothe him. This Spanish friend had wanted to do a portrait of Picasso, and Picasso had said: "Come here whenever you like, and I will pose for you. I want a portrait of myself, done by you." And Ortiz de Zarate had gone to work. Picasso had granted him a first sitting, very graciously, and others were scheduled. "You can leave the canvas and the paints right here; you'll go on with it tomorrow." The sketched-out portrait was hung on a wall, in the spot where I had seen it a few weeks before. Ortiz de Zarate came back the next day, and Sabartés said: "He is very busy, but wait a while . . ." He waited one hour, two hours, the whole morning. "Come back tomorrow—there won't be so many people . . ." And the artist came back the next day, the day after that, the entire week, several weeks . . . Finally, this morning, this man's wounded sensibilities had exploded. He was shouting, he was arguing. His arms flayed the air, he beat his breast: "I have my pride too; I have my vanity! If Picasso wants a portrait by Ortiz de Zarate he can come to me; he knows my address! This comedy has gone on long enough!" He demands his canvas, his paints, his brushes. He takes them, slams the door behind him, and leaves, racing down the stairs like a madman.

Sabartés says: "That was a narrow escape . . ."

The manufacturer of paints comes in, beaming. He has been successful in his exchange of the country estate for the still life. "I'm in seventh heaven!" he tells me. "I love that still life. It is unquestionably the most beautiful of all of those Picasso has painted recently."

SABARTÉS, *speaking to the manufacturer of paints:* You lucky—! Do you know that your famous "château" has just been demolished by a bomb? And just a few days after the agreement. Obviously you couldn't care less; it's no concern of yours anymore! You have the still life.

I am not sure whether Sabartés is joking or not. With this mephistophelian man, one never knows. The story may be simply an invention. He loves taking people in. Mystification has become his second nature. With the same imperturbable countenance, he may tell an anecdote or announce a catastrophe . . .

P. Berès, the publisher of art books, arrives, and six others at the same time. Among them, I am delighted to see my old friend Raymond Queneau. Picasso goes through the ritual display of his canvases, but the latest news of the war is too exciting to permit calm discussion of art and painting. Events have been happening too rapidly, and everyone has his own opinion of them. The French army under General Juin has taken Rome, but the most stunning fact of all is the Allied landing in Normandy. We don't know exactly what is happening. The German communiqués are hesitant; the BBC broadcasts exultant. But, through the fog of news, we have learned that Bayeux, Isigny, and Carentan have been liberated. The Allies certainly do not seem to have gained much ground, but we have the feeling that the bridgehead will hold. The "impregnable" Atlantic wall has obviously been broached.

## *Friday, June 16, 1944*

Madame M.M. has been bothering me for several days. She has an El Greco for sale. And I am supposed to tell "Pablo" about it. He will unquestionably be happy to buy it. The other day, when I was alone with him at the end of the morning, I spoke to him about it.

PICASSO: Yes, it interests me; I'd like very much to see this Greco. And if I don't buy it myself, I may be able to find a buyer. There's only one trouble: there are a lot of stolen pictures on the market right now. Unless you know exactly where something comes from, you run the risk of serious trouble. If the picture has been stolen, you'll be obliged to restore it to its proper owner, and with the present inflation the price you are paid for it may be worth nothing at all. And that's if you're not considered a partner in the thing. In that case, you can even go to prison. I hope the papers for this Greco are authentic. The best thing would be to have it brought here, to the studio. But let me know beforehand . . .

Madame M.M. telephoned again yesterday. The Greco is to be loaned to her this morning. And she has found a man who will bring it to Picasso's studio on his cart. It will take him about two hours to tow the cart from the Étoile to the rue des Grands-Augustins. So I will have to find out at what time Picasso wants it to arrive. She will wait for a call from me before telling the man to leave . . .

Picasso is in the midst of his morning ablutions when I arrive, and sends word for me to come up. When I first glimpse him through the open door to the bathroom, he is shaving. Naked, broad-shouldered, hunched in front of the mirror, he resembles a not-quite-so-fat Japanese wrestler. I tell him about the El Greco, and he waves his arms at the heavens.

PICASSO: Today, of all days! What a day! All of the actors in *Desire Caught by the Tail* are coming here this morning. And a lot of other people too. It will be a madhouse. Really, it would be better another day . . .

I tell him that Madame M.M. has only a two-day option. But the Greco can be left with him for forty-eight hours—until Monday morning.

PICASSO: That's very kind, but I want no part of it! Suppose a bomb falls on my studio tonight? Suppose you start a fire? The picture would be destroyed, and I would be the one who would have to pay. But come to think of it, why not have it brought over this morning? I'm dying to see it. And it certainly should be interesting for the others. An El Greco—they're not all that common . . .

I telephone Madame M.M. "Picasso agrees. You can send the package . . ."

In the meantime he has finished shaving. He has, in fact, shaved so close, because of the reception and the presence of pretty women, that he proudly invites me to feel his skin, which is soft as a baby's. He often shaves at night, before going to bed, thinking to save time in the morning. Then he does nothing the next day but cover his beard with shaving soap and wipe it off. "You shouldn't wash too often," he has said to me. "It's unhealthy."

MYSELF: Do you know Doctor Besançon's book *The Days of Man*? He describes the bathroom, and the mania for soaking in hot water every day, as the saddest and most unhealthy inventions of civilization.

Picasso, fascinated, wants to hear more.

MYSELF: He's a curious kind of doctor. He has taken the opposite point of view to everything taught by medicine. And his book has stirred up a storm. "You have hemorrhoids?" he asks. "Thank the Lord for them; you will have a long and happy life." He ridicules everything prescribed by doctors, and prescribes only one remedy himself: "Drink wine and make love." I've rarely read such an amusing book.

Picasso is instantly sympathetic to this doctor and his ideas, and as he dresses I tell him another anecdote from the book: "A man who claims to be a healer has just been arrested. He is interrogated for hours at the Préfecture de Police, and finally gives in and confesses. He is a *licensed* doctor. He begs the inspectors not to divulge his 'secret,' because he would lose his entire clientele . . ."

Picasso's preparations are almost completed. He hesitates between a white shirt and a shirt of deep beige wool. He chooses the latter and puts it on. Then comes the moment for choosing a tie. He has a great many, most of them either polka dots or checks, red and white, red and black, blue and white. All his life he has had a passionate attachment to ties, and Fernande has said that, even at the Bateau-Lavoir, he kept those he refused to part with in an old hatbox of hers. But I have noticed that the bow ties he preferred in his "worldly" period have almost all disappeared. And I wonder if others have noticed that these *motifs*—polka dots, squares, checks—often crop up in his painting; that the composition of colors in his tie, his shirt, his vest, frequently recall a fragment of one of his canvases. Today being a reception day he selects a sumptuous pale blue tie with large white polka dots, and after some hesitation decides on an informal woolen vest. After all, he will be in his own home . . .

By this time the vestibule must be filled with visitors. Marcel has come up several times to announce them. Picasso goes down, and I remain upstairs to take some photographs. A new *motif* has appeared in the studio: two potted tomato plants, doubtless a gift. The angular stalks are clearly visible through the leaves, and a few tomatoes are beginning to ripen, their tender green brightening into orange. The studio is already filled with drawings and sketchy gouaches representing these plants . . .*

When I rejoin Picasso, I find him surrounded by people, and engaged in animated discussion. Once he has embarked on a speech whose subject is important to him, no one can interrupt him.

PICASSO: . . . but all the documents of all the periods are false! They all represent life "as seen by the artists." Every image we have of nature we owe to the painters. It is through their eyes that we see it. That alone would be enough to make it suspect . . . You speak of "objective reality." But what is objective reality? It has no value for the costumes, for the individual types, for anything . . . Just this morning, as I was shaving, a phrase occurred to me, and I'll pass it on to you: objective reality should be carefully folded up, just as one folds a sheet, and tucked away in a cupboard, once and for all . . .

Marcel informs me that "the Greco" is waiting in its cart, in front of the house. The man who had towed it down the length of the Champs-Élysées, across the Place de la Concorde, and along the quais of the Seine to Number 7 of this street, is bathed in sweat, mopping his forehead with a handkerchief. Madame M.M., who has not left him for an instant, is completely exhausted. The painting sits in the cart, shrouded in several layers of coverings, enormous. Impossible for it to be brought up by the little spiral staircase. Picasso decrees that it will enter through the big door and arrive by the central staircase, as befits a guest of honor. At last it is set down in the center of the studio. The man who has brought it here, Madame M.M., and Marcel set to work to remove its cords and wrappings. The dozen or so people gathered in the studio watch the operation with undisguised interest. The final veil falls away.

My first impression is one of a disaster. It is a great religious poster: Christ, wearing the crown of thorns, and bending beneath the weight of the cross. The head itself recalls El Greco, but

* Between the third and the tenth of August, as the Allied armies were advancing on Paris, Picasso painted several canvases of them.

the hands and the folds of the materials are too labored; the sky and the cross too mannered. There is a profound silence in the room, due more to amazement than to emotion. No one moves, or dares say a word. Picasso puts on his glasses and walks over to the canvas. And in the midst of this silence we suddenly hear the stentorian voice of Madame M.M.

"You see before you, ladies and gentlemen, one of the most beautiful El Grecos in the world. Its owner was asking eight million francs for it—a bagatelle for such a masterpiece. He had planned on selling it to a German museum. But the Germans don't like El Greco and detest Christ. So he is prepared to let it go for four million. Four million! It is almost a gift . . ."

She was talking with the disarming assurance of a guide reciting a prepared speech to a group of ignorant tourists. Picasso listens to her, amused—in spite of what people may think, he *listens* willingly to the opinion of others—and he would doubtless not have interrupted her so brutally if she had not committed the imprudence of saying:

"One of the most beautiful El Grecos, gentlemen, and it is not just I who say it—it is the opinion of the director of the Prado Museum—"

That phrase brings an abrupt reaction.

PICASSO: *Pardon, madame!* I am the director of the Prado Museum! And I am thoroughly qualified. Yes, it's true! I was appointed by the government, the republican government. And I still hold the position; I've never been sacked. I've had to read piles of reports, I've been bombarded with letters from my "subordinates." They all wanted to express their admiration, their devotion to me. And the safety of all those masterpieces! It has caused me enormous worry, enormous difficulty! And I have never received so much as a franc of my "salary," which doesn't amount to very much anyway. After all, I was the director of a museum that was only a phantom, a Prado whose masterpieces had all taken refuge in Valencia.

Picasso looks directly at Madame M.M.:

"If you want the opinion of the director of the Prado Museum, madame, I will give it to you: yes, it is an El Greco, the most beautiful perhaps of all of those he painted on commission from certain convents and churches. If the good sisters of Sainte-Thérèse, or the orphans of Sainte-Ursule asked for a few more tears, he was happy to add them, at so many pesetas per tear. One has to live. But this El Greco of the good sisters is of no interest to me! Believe me, the conservators of the German museums are not as stupid as all that! If it had been a good El Greco, they would have bought it, in spite of the cross, the tears, and Christ."

He then asks Marcel to stand the Matisse still life with oranges and bananas beside the El Greco. He looks at them closely, comparing the two paintings.

PICASSO: Decidedly I prefer my Matisse! The subject is of little importance. I judge them as examples of painting. And this Matisse is quite a different matter from this El Greco!

Sabartés, who is standing next to me, says:

"I don't share Picasso's infatuation with this Matisse. How can he find it so beautiful? Matisse exasperates me. I have never had, I never will have, the slightest feeling for him . . .

Picasso had telephoned Fabiani, Vollard's successor, to tell him that there was an El Greco for sale, and he arrives, having run all the way from the rue de Martignac. But, after having studied the painting, he too declines.

"No one wants to buy it?" Picasso demands. "Then wrap it up!"

While the painting is being reclothed in all of its coverings, tied up again in all of its cords, carried down to its cart through the main staircase and the main door, Picasso, with his harsh, rather joking little laugh, says to the people in the room:

"Poor Greco! He is going on just as he began. No one wants him. I remember an incident that took place at the end of the last century, when he had just been rediscovered. A Spanish collector bought two of his paintings, which happened to be in France. They were brought back to Spain on foot, towed in a wheelbarrow by two artists from Barcelona. I was only twelve years old at the time, but the two men became good friends of mine later, and they told me about that strange pilgrimage . . .

Someone asks Picasso how he discovered El Greco himself.

PICASSO: I had seen some of his paintings, and was very much impressed by them. So I decided to make a trip to Toledo, where most of his work was. I was even more deeply impressed then. It's probably as a result of his influence that the figures in my paintings of the blue period are elongated as they are . . .

It is almost noon. A new wave of visitors arrives. The upper strata of Paris' intelligentsia is gathered here. Among others, I notice Michel Leiris and his wife, Louise, who is Kahnweiler's sister-in-law and now directs his gallery. Even in the darkest days at the rue La Boétie—when Picasso was completely despondent and wanted to see no one—the Leiris were among the few who were always welcome.

It was in their new apartment, almost next door to Picasso's studio, on the fourth floor of a building on the Quai des Grands-Augustins where almost all of the windows look out on the Seine, that the "première" of Picasso's play *Desire Caught by the Tail* took place a few days ago. Picasso wrote this little *divertissement* in Royan in four days—from the fourteenth to the seventeenth of January 1941—in a schoolboy's composition book. He had simply allowed his mind to wander, following the dictum of "automatic writing," a verbal trance that gives full rein to dreams, obsessions, unconfessed desires, odd confrontations of ideas and words, absurd and everyday banalities. Picasso's sense of humor and inexhaustible spirit of invention are revealed in it in their purest form. Everything that preoccupied him in those days of uniformity at Royan: the harsh winter, the German occupation, privations, isolation, the pleasures of bed and table are the motors animating the characters of his burlesque: Bigfoot, Onion, Tart, etc.*

The six acts of the tragic farce take place against backgrounds as varied as they are rich in color. The setting for the second act represents one of the corridors of "Sordid's Hotel." In this scene—perhaps the most successful of the play—a half dozen feet, two in front of each of the doors, writhe in pain, weep, moan, and shout: "My chilblains! My chilblains!" Then, there is the undertaker who drags these heroes away from a great meal they are preparing, in order to thrust them into coffins where a crocodile devours a policeman.

The idea for this presentation—or, more accurately, this reading—of the play came from Michel Leiris, I believe. He confided the direction to a man of the theater: Albert Camus. It was also Camus' task to describe the settings, announce the sequence of events, and introduce the protagonists. Leiris played the role of Bigfoot; Raymond Queneau was Onion; Jean-Paul Sartre,

* In an essay on the subject, Raymond Queneau has shown the extent to which the play is imbued with the preoccupations of the war and occupation: cold, hunger, etc.

Roundbutt; Georges Hugnet, Fatty Agony; Jean Aubier, the Curtains; and Jacques-Laurent Bost, Silence. The beautiful actress Zanie de Campan, Louise Leiris, Dora Maar, and Simone de Beauvoir shared the feminine roles: Tart, the two Bow-wows, Skinny Agony and her Cousin. There were several afternoons of rehearsal in the Leiris apartment, and Picasso sometimes attended these—worried, but also intrigued and moved.

On the day of the reading, a considerable audience crowded into the apartment. Braque was among the many artists and writers present. And there were also Señor and Señora Anchorena, a fabulously wealthy Argentine couple for whom Picasso had promised to paint a door—but in spite of their millions they had never obtained it.

In the role of Tart, Zanie de Campan achieved a considerable personal success, even though she did not follow Picasso's stage directions to the letter: "Everyone leaves the bathtub fully dressed and covered with soapsuds, except for Tart, who is naked . . ."

The play was enthusiastically applauded, and the author congratulated. Some members of the audience professed to find in it no more than a trivial amusement, a tall story, a belated reflection of Apollinaire's *Les Mamelles de Tirésias;* others discovered in it the truculence of Rabelais, the verve of Alfred Jarry. Picasso had wanted to thank his "actors" personally, by inviting them to his studio.

Among those who accepted his invitation for this morning were Albert Camus, Jean-Paul Sartre, Pierre Reverdy, and several of the ladies, who had obviously done their best to triumph over wartime restrictions in the matter of apparel: Zanie de Campan, in private life the wife of the publisher Jean Aubier, was wearing a dizzying turban-like construction of silk; Simone de Beauvoir, who generally dresses very soberly, had added an elaborate brooch to her black suit and another tier to the high crown of her hair-do; and as for Valentine Hugo, she must have hesitated for some time before the coffer of family jewels before selecting the enormous brooch she was wearing—a coat of arms surmounted by a crown and angels of silver, incrusted with enamel and semiprecious stones. It attracts everyone's attention, and primarily Picasso's.

VALENTINE HUGO: Are you looking at my brooch? It belonged to Madame Victor Hugo. It was made by the great jeweler of the period, Froment-Meurice, the "Cartier" of the Second Empire.

How do you like it? It's a little elaborate for my taste, but it's a family treasure and I only take it out for exceptional occasions.

Then she asks Picasso to show her his recent engravings. They are on display in a corner of the studio: heads and nudes. "How beautiful they are!" Valentine exclaims, "and you haven't even trimmed them . . . I can't work at it anymore, alas! The doctors have forbidden it. It seems I would go blind if I kept it up."

Picasso conducts a guided tour of his sculptures. But he has also planned a surprise for us. From one of his secret cupboards he extracts a faded manuscript of Alfred Jarry, part of the cycle of *Ubu Roi.* This particular cupboard is stuffed with rare books and manuscripts, almost all of them annotated and illustrated by Picasso himself. He might just as easily have taken out manuscripts of Paul Éluard, Louis Aragon, André Breton, or of Pierre Reverdy or Max Jacob. One day he showed me the manuscript of Apollinaire's *Bestiaires,* which he had covered with drawings of animals of all kinds. He also uses this cupboard to store the majority of the letters he has received from the poets who are his friends . . . The manuscript of Jarry's he shows us today is either *Ubu Coou* or *Ubu Enchainé,* I am not certain which. Picasso recites several passages from it—he knows them by heart —and then says to Albert Camus: "That should be put on a stage!" Camus appears sincerely interested.

Some of those present are discussing the banning by the Vichy authorities of Jean Marais' *Andromaque* at the Théâtre Edouard VII. Admiral Darlan's militia has halted the production and closed the theater. Since 1941 a real cabala has been formed, with Cocteau and Marais as its chosen victims. Ever since that time they have been subjected to an avalanche of insults, and the press never stops printing diatribes against them. The revival of *Les Parents Terribles,* in 1941, was constantly plagued by violent demonstrations by the militia. *The Typewriter,* which was given at the Théâtre Hébertot in the same year, was banned almost immediately. A series of incidents disrupted the performances of *Britannicus.* Marais himself was involved in a fight with Alain Laubreaux, one of the most venomous of the occupation critics; and Cocteau was attacked and quite badly hurt on the Champs-Élysées . . . The régime of the "new order" has attributed the defeat to a decline in morals and multiplied the number of arbitrary arrests and trials . . . André Gide and Jean

Cocteau, "corruptors of French youth," were ready-made scapegoats, as much by reason of their work as by their personalities.

Some people feel that the hostile environment surrounding the hero of *Andromaque* was not improved by the play itself: "It was badly acted . . ."; "It was a mistake to give the roles of classic tragedians to film stars . . ." As for Jean Marais himself, leaping about the stage half-naked, his back gleaming with sweat and grease, his chest and loins girded into a panther skin, brandishing the staff Picasso had decorated for him, he seemed more a dancer than an actor. Others say that when it is actually played on a stage, the excesses of this tragedy inevitably border on the comic.

PIERRE REVERDY: I saw Jean Marais just recently. He is desperate. His letters of protest to the newspapers have had no effect whatever. It is all right to criticize a play, to say anything you like about it, but it is inexcusable to attack a man's private life. Marais can do nothing about these slanderers. The censors have strictly forbidden publication of his answers. What is happening to us? A person can be publicly dragged through the mud and not even have the right to defend himself . . .

Valentine Hugo asks Reverdy what he is working on.

PIERRE REVERDY: Working on? On nothing, Valentine. I think the events going on around us surpass anything in literature.

VALENTINE HUGO: You surely don't mean to say that the war communiqués are more interesting than poetry?

PIERRE REVERDY: Why, yes, that's exactly what I mean . . . the only literature worth reading at the moment. And I can assure you that it fascinates me.

"And yet," I remark to Reverdy, "1870 and 1871 were also war years, and disastrous ones, but it was a fertile period for the arts, particularly for painting and poetry. It was as if the war had actually stimulated the artists."

PIERRE REVERDY: That's entirely possible, my friend. All I can tell you is that, for myself, I have been paralyzed by what is happening, incapable of writing a single line so long as the frightful period we are living through goes on . . .

I suggest to Picasso that it would be a good idea to take a photograph of the assembled group. Unfortunately, several people have already left. But the rest of us go up to the painting studio.

Picasso stands at the center. On his right are Zanie de Campan, Louise Leiris, Pierre Reverdy, Cécile Éluard (Gala's daughter), and Doctor Lacan; on his left, Valentine Hugo and Simone de Beauvoir. Jean-Paul Sartre, Michel Leiris, and Jean Aubier sit on the floor, and Albert Camus squats on his heels between them. At the last minute, with his back turned to the camera, Kazbek decides to join the group.[42]

I leave the studio with Reverdy. We walk toward Saint-Germain-des-Prés, discussing the latest events. As we are about to part company, he turns to me and says emphatically:

"I hope you still have the portraits you took of me. I like them. But don't publish them so long as I am alive, my friend. Let them bear witness to what I was, after my death.

*Saturday, May 12, 1945*

I wonder if things have changed here.

My last visit dates back to June 21, 1944, almost a year ago! Two months after that, on August 25, Paris was liberated, and from one day to the next Picasso's studio was invaded. His courageous attitude had made him into a kind of standard-bearer, and the entire world was anxious to salute in him the symbol of liberty restored. Poets, painters, critics, museum directors, and writers, all wearing the uniform of the Allied armies, officers and ordinary soldiers, thronged up the narrow staircase in a compact mass. The vestibule was constantly jammed with people. He had become as popular in China and Soviet Russia as he had been for some years in the United States. During these months Picasso had tasted a universal glory and accepted it with pleasure and good grace, making himself readily available to journalists, photographers, and even to the curious who simply want to see him "in the flesh" . . .

I meet Inés in the courtyard, Marcel at the door, and Sabartés in the vestibule. Everyone is at his usual post . . .

"What a surprise!" Sabarté exclaims. "Why don't we ever see you anymore?"

"I was waiting for the storm to pass. It's been a madhouse since the Liberation, hasn't it?"

PICASSO, *embracing me:* Brassaï, what's become of you? Yes, it was an invasion! Paris was liberated, but I was besieged, and I still am. Visitors come by the dozens, every day. Just yesterday there was a real mob here. People treat me as if I had nothing better to do than to receive them. Mind you, I adore doing nothing myself. I find it very agreeable. But then, I am naturally lazy . . . Come with me, I want to show you something . . .

Picasso leads me into his little apartment. The something he wanted to show me is a first edition of a book of poems of Stéphane Mallarmé. He has just bought it. And no sooner had he acquired it than he embellished it with a striking portrait of the poet. He smiles at me and says: "I paid a great deal for this book, and I wanted to insure my money."

He then opens a copy of a book of Edgar Allan Poe's, to which he has also added a portrait of the author. Buying rare books, and then making them truly unique by adding the work of his own pen, has become a habit with him. He has done it with almost all of the books and manuscripts in this cupboard.

It seems, however, that he had another reason for showing me the Mallarmé. Beneath the portrait he has scrawled three words, in his spasmodic, unpredictable handwriting. Three words that mark a historic event in his life:

NO MORE FORELOCK! *Paris, May 12, 1945*

The famous black lock of hair that escaped from beneath Picasso's broad-brimmed hat and frightened his family; the raven's wing that was so often drawn, caricatured, even sculpted, departing abruptly from the extreme right of his forehead and sweeping across it until its point brushed his left eyebrow . . . In reality it had been gone for a long time. There was nothing left of it but a few sparse, symbolic hairs, powerless to mask his baldness, but he continued to groom and nurture them carefully, as emblems of his youth . . . It was only this morning that he had had the courage to break at last with the past and solemnly inter the dead forelock in this volume of poetry.

PICASSO: One cannot both be and have been. So . . . when are you going to photograph me without my forelock?

I notice then that his hair actually is cut short. The end of an epoch.

PICASSO: When will the book come out? I'm looking forward to it, very much. It's always a pleasure to see a reunion of works that have been dispersed, lost from sight for a long time, even forgotten. Just the other day I came across a group of your photos. Dora was here, and some others, and we looked through them together.

MYSELF: At the moment the publisher has no paper . . . and I am still missing several of your early sculptures. The only one I've been able to photograph was the *Fou au Bonnet,* in a private collection.

PICASSO: What can we do? Fabiani still doesn't want them to be reproduced. I have some of them myself, but they're at the rue La Boétie. But I do have *La Femme Assise* here now—my very first piece of sculpture! I did it in 1899.

MYSELF: She is exactly as old as I am . . .

Picasso is turning the little bronze statue around, looking for the best lighting, when Paul Éluard comes in. Ever since Éluard's 1926 poem *To Pablo Picasso* the ties of affection between the two men have become constantly stronger and closer, aided, in the early days, by the association of the surrealists with Picasso, who illustrated several collections of Éluard's work. In 1936 the poet delivered a lecture on Picasso in Barcelona, to accompany a retrospective exposition of his painting. But poet and painter became active partners only after the outbreak of the Spanish Civil War, which stirred up their consciences and brought about a mutation of their art. Together they took up an unshakable position in the face of those climactic events. The great stanzas written by Éluard at the time form an echo to Picasso's *Guernica.* Their taste for life, their intrinsic force, their will to transform pain and hardship into the joy of creation are the common denominators of their friendship. To the most realist of painters and the most visual of poets—neither of whom can imagine life without love—art is the act of living and seeing and not of imagining and dreaming. Based on the physical, it demands the support of the real, and flees from anything gratuitous . . .*

Éluard, who had just returned from London, has a great many

* A dozen or so portraits of Éluard and numerous drawings and canvases of his wife, Nush, bear witness to their friendship. In 1944 Éluard published a book on Picasso which contained most of the poems and texts he had devoted to him. In 1947 he wrote a long prose poem on *The Man who held in his hand the fragile key to the problem of reality.*

things to tell us. He has bought some statuettes from the Cyclades islands and is still excited about them. I remark that if I had to choose among all the sculpture of the world I would unhesitatingly select one of these goddesses of the Cyclades. To me these sculptures from the Aegean Sea—so pure, so stripped of nonessentials—represent the quintessence of the plastic art . . .

ÉLUARD: The market for works of art is almost nonexistent in London. And the taxes are staggering. People have little money. They can't allow themselves such "follies." So a foreigner can easily find some very interesting things, and at a reasonable price. I came across a very beautiful drawing from the blue period, only eighty pounds, but I didn't have any more money. Roland Penrose offered to lend it to me. In the end he bought the drawing himself, and I got a Paul Klee water color in its place.

A publisher of art books comes in, and Picasso shows us the series of engravings he has made for him.

ÉLUARD, *to the publisher:* You should be happy! Picasso has done wonders for you. As a rule you have to urge him on, over and over again, use all the words at your command and wear out your shoes, before you have everything . . . You know that yourself . . . But this book is complete: everything is there—the etchings, the tailpieces, everything!

The publisher says to Picasso: "There is still one thing we have to settle. How much do I owe you?"

PICASSO: Really—are you serious? You want me to go into money matters? Very well, come on!

He conducts the publisher into an adjoining room. A few minutes later, they reappear.

PICASSO: That's done.

ÉLUARD: But no one heard the sound of a cash register.

PICASSO: You will hear it, very soon. I'm going to install one with a bell. And I hope it will ring often . . .

I was pleased to have seen Paul Éluard again. Our relationship has been a friendly one, ever since the period of our collaboration on *Minotaure*. He habitually sent me inscribed copies of his books.* But I rarely saw him during the occupation. The last time had been in the month of November 1943, when he was preparing to leave for the Unoccupied Zone. I had seen some of the mimeographed poems which were circulated clandestinely, and also *Poetry and Truth,* but I knew nothing of the courageous, though prudent part he had played in the Resistance. Like Picasso, Éluard had not wanted to leave Paris.

A few weeks ago I happened to go into a café on the Boulevard Saint-Germain, and he and his wife were there. Nush's face was paler than I had known it, and Éluard's hair was grayer and his hands trembled more than they had before. He told me delightedly that he had at last been able to return to his own apartment, after having spent the last months of the occupation in one on the rue du Bac, loaned to him by friends. Why did I not come to see them? We made an appointment for the next day. Éluard lives in one of the most desolate quarters of Paris, a region of warehouses, freight-car marshaling yards, pyramids of slag and coal: La Chapelle. Born in Saint-Denis—the sepulcher of the Kings of France, now become a city of communists and factories—it is almost with pride that he intones: "I was born behind a hideous façade." And it is a fragment of the climate of his childhood that Éluard has found in La Chapelle—"beautiful, in a sinister sort of way," as Prévert would say. The Canal Saint-Martin, which also passes through his native quarter, is not far from him here. And Léon-Paul Fargue, the "pedestrian of Paris" is almost his neighbor . . .

An apartment building just like all the others, on the rue Marx-Dormoy, a three-room apartment on the third floor, this is where Paul Éluard lives: a chapel of art and poetry in the heart of La Chapelle.[47] The trinity dear to Éluard is named: Max Ernst-Giorgio de Chirico-Pablo Picasso. Ernst, whom Éluard first met in Cologne in 1920, is represented here by *L'Homme aux Yeux Bandés* and by a portrait of Gala. A tall figure of a mannequin, set against a stark and lonely architecture, represents Chirico, the artist of unmoving forms, of deserted, dream-filled places, absorbed in silence. The fascination Chirico exercised for

* In his last little book, *Le Phénix,* of 1952—illustrated with the beautiful engravings of Valentine Hugo—the dedication traced out in his studied handwriting and signed with his curious little flourish of crossed swords, was a reproach that was both amiable and sybilline: "For Brassaï, more close to him than he thinks. Paul Éluard." It was his last message. He died a few weeks later.

so long over the surrealists can be compared only with that of Lautréamont, the other "fixed point" of their movement. Mystery, dreams, the unexpected, the attraction of an unknown universe, charged with anxiety—everything they loved they found in his enigmatic works; surrealist before surrealism. Their cult of Chirico dates from the day, during the 1914 war, when André Breton saw the *Cerveau de l'Enfant* in Paul Guillaume's display window as he was passing the shop in a bus. He leaped from the bus, bought the canvas, and from that point on it became a focal point for the admiration of disciples who visited him at home. Éluard, at one time, had also owned the celebrated *Mannequins de la Tour Rose* and the *Départ du Poète.* But when Chirico, after a mental transformation rare in the annals of art, disowned his "metaphysical" painting, the initial confusion of the surrealists rapidly turned to anger. They took his about-face as a blot on the movement, an infamous treason.

Since my last visit here, however, it is the Picassos that now dominate the walls. Among them, there is a portrait of Nush dated August 1941; a masterpiece. Picasso has painted this ethereal creature with all the gentleness, all the delicacy of which his brush is capable, as if he had wanted to put aside the terrible and rest in the gracious. Nush's head and shoulders—the frail body of an adolescent, the slender neck, the rebellious hair, the long lashes shadowing the eyes, the childlike mouth, with a little smile on the lips—seem to have been breathed onto the canvas by a quality of light. Emerging from a background of pearl gray, Éluard's wife appears as a disincarnate, incorporeal creature.*

Éluard has many other paintings. He shows me a curious series of youthful drawings by Salvador Dali, and a very unusual still life by Chagall, in reds and blues, dating from 1912: *Table avec une Bouteille.* A canvas by the English art critic Roland Penrose, ambassador in England of the surrealist movement, testifies that he was himself an artist before crossing to the other side. Both Picasso and Éluard have been guests at his home in Sussex. Penrose married Lee Miller, the beautiful American girl who was a student and a model of Man Ray in those wonderful postwar years in Montparnasse. Picasso had painted a portrait of her in 1937, a picture flooded with humor and fantasy.

A sculpture known as the *Roi Fou*—carved from wood by a madman wielding a knife—presides over this apartment, seated

* After Nush's death, Éluard gave this painting to the Museum of Modern Art in Paris.

on his throne in a corner, his legs sheathed in boots, his enormous head surmounted by a crown. He is surrounded by little pre-Columbian terra cottas, fetishes from Easter Island, British Columbia, and New Mexico. Éluard's favorite object here is a bronze death's-head in which the top of the skull opens when a button is pressed and reveals a watch: the ticking timepiece is lodged in the brain like a worm in an apple . . .

Éluard opens his great Directoire bookcase for me and takes out Balzac's *Le Chef-d'Oeuvre Inconnu,* illustrated by Picasso, and also containing several of Picasso's original drawings. Then he shows me an extraordinary relic: the only existing manuscript of Isidore Ducasse, Comte de Lautréamont. All of the books in Éluard's possession have been lovingly stuffed with letters, autographs, drawings, and photographs; and this is particularly true of Dali's *La Femme Visible* and André Breton's *Nadja.* There are several letters and drawings from *Nadja,* Breton's annotations about the strange heroine of surrealism, and a great many photos, including one of the *Dame au Gant* and one of the Hôtel des Grands Hommes, just across from the Panthéon, where Breton lived at the time. Éluard also showed me some of his own manuscripts, and I was surprised by the number of changes and corrections he had made. His poems are so simple, so clear, in the reading, that one would think they had been written in a single burst of inspiration. Éluard shatters this illusion. Not one of them has been born of the tip of the pen. He writes them laboriously, sometimes struggling with them for a long time. "There is just as much of the conscious will as of spontaneity in a poem," he tells me. "Few fortuitous images can take their place in a poem, just as they occur. They must be clarified, mastered, according to the feeling that dominates the poem. Intoxication demands to be carefully written out, verbal frenzy to be controlled by the sensitivity of the poet."

During the luncheon which Nush had prepared for us, I was struck with what Éluard told me of the influences that had played a part in his own development. Before citing Baudelaire, Rimbaud, Lautréamont, Shelley, Hölderlin, or Goethe, he spoke of Walt Whitman. It is possible that, ten years earlier, before his conversion to militant communism, Éluard might not so categorically have pronounced this name as being that of his immediate ancestor. "Had he lived in our time," he tells me, "the great American poet would have chosen the same path as I."

*Tuesday, May 15, 1945*

A radiant sky, happier faces . . . Paris is visibly recovering from her long illness, beginning to live again. The streets are filled with beautiful young girls on bicycles, their skirts blowing in the wind like the multicolored petals of flowers —one wonders where they have been through all these dreary months. I am going to meet her at ten o'clock at the Café Danton, the habitual base for my expeditions to Picasso's studio. Will she come? She would undoubtedly like to meet him. But just yesterday she was still very reticent about it.

As I approach the café, I can see her sitting on the terrace, drinking a glass of muscadet, her hair wild as usual, her eyes smiling. We have known each other for four weeks now . . . A magazine had asked me for a photograph of the *Femme à l'Orange*, to illustrate an article on Picasso's sculpture. "Our messenger will be there in an hour, to pick it up . . ." After this telephone call a young girl had arrived, instead of the regular messenger. She had explained it to me: "The messenger had an urgent call from the maternity hospital. His wife had just given birth. So I volunteered to come in his place." We exchanged a few words. She began to look at my photographs, my drawings. Time passed. I gave her the photograph, but I made a mistake: it was the *Young Girl Playing with a Ball* instead of the *Woman with an Orange*. What a drama! The magazine was forced to publish the real *Woman with an Orange* in the next issue, and print a letter of apology to its readers. But, thanks to this blunder, I was permitted to see her again . . .

And she is here, in a white blouse, a pleated Scotch plaid skirt, Basque espadrilles, deep purple, from the Pyrénées, where she was born. She has come here only to tell me: "Nothing in the world could convince me to go to Picasso's. What would he think of it? Bringing someone he doesn't know to his home, without any reason . . ." How can I persuade her? I order two glasses of muscadet. She is still arguing: "But on what grounds? On what grounds?" "If you absolutely insist on having a function, before you'll go to Picasso's," I tell her, "I'll make you my secretary. He wants to buy some drawings from me, and you can show them to him." At long last the muscadet has its effect . . .

Marcel announces us. Picasso appears, wearing nothing but pale blue shorts.

"You are not alone? Forgive me . . . I am not presentable . . . Appearing naked, with a young girl . . ."

He speaks the words with a false kind of modesty, and makes a pretence of leaving. But he remains with us.

PICASSO: Good morning, mademoiselle, how are you? I greet you as if I had known you always—you'll agree with that, won't you? (*Turning toward me:*) But she is delightful, this girl . . . I'm going to get dressed. I'll have quite a few visitors today. Brassaï will guide you through the house. He knows every corner of it. I'll be with you in a few minutes . . .

When did Picasso acquire the habit of receiving guests in such rudimentary attire? A photograph taken in 1912 in his studio on the rue Schoelcher, just opposite the Montparnasse cemetery, shows him wearing only a pair of shorts and an old cap, pushed back on his head. So it must be a habit of long standing. Fernande has said that sometimes, in the heat of summer at the Bateau-Lavoir, he greeted visitors in his shorts and some of the more prudish among them had requested him to put on a pair of trousers . . .

Gilberte is delighted. "How simple he is. I hadn't pictured him like this." We are alone in the studio, and she is looking around her at the sculptures assembled here when her glance falls on the *Femme à l'Orange*. "Look there," she remarks to me, "without that statue we might never have met, never have known each other." "You're forgetting the messenger's wife," I answer, laughing. "We have to be grateful to her too—and to her baby . . ."

Picasso reappears, as naked as he had been before. Instead of getting dressed, he has been looking for a box of chocolates for Gilberte.

PICASSO: Here, take them. They're very good. The Americans gave me a whole carload of them.

A quarter of an hour later he joins us again, dressed this time. I tell him that a date has now been set for my exhibition at the Renou and Colle gallery.

PICASSO: That's wonderful! For once, someone has listened to me. As a rule, whenever it happens that I praise someone's work everyone else gets suspicious. You wouldn't believe it, would you? But it often happens.

MYSELF: I brought you some of my drawings, as you asked. But the best ones aren't here. I kept them for the exhibition. What you really should do is choose from among those.

PICASSO: I'm not in the least bit worried about that. Your "best drawings" are surely in this portfolio . . . among the ones you decided not to show. Artists always select the works for an exhibition very badly. And I am no exception to the rule. We should leave that choice to others. You will be successful, and I hope you will continue. And why don't you try etching, or aquatint? It would suit your style very well. You draw just as usual, but with a needle and varnish, and you can obtain any effect you want. Burin engraving requires more concentration and experience.

An officer comes in. It is "Colonel Berger," the ex-colonel of the International Brigades in Spain, André Malraux. Picasso greets him joyfully.

ANDRÉ MALRAUX: What a pleasure it is to see you again! And in such good form! I was worried, knowing that you had stayed in Paris.

PICASSO: When was the last time we saw each other? Four years ago? A lot of things have happened since then. I thought of you often . . . What has become of André Malraux? I was afraid you might be one of those who wouldn't come back. You enjoy tempting fate. You chase after danger . . .

Malraux, who commanded the forces of the Maquis in Lot-et-Garonne and Corrèze, tells us how he had managed to survive through the years of the Resistance, and how he was captured and then freed by the Gestapo, because they did not realize who he was. "The greatest enemy of the Secret Army," he says, "was not the Wehrmacht, but the Gestapo." He also tells us about the "Iron Plan," the plan for sabotage of the German communications system, which had succeeded beyond anyone's hopes or expectations.

ANDRÉ MALRAUX: I shall never forget that night in June, listening to the BBC. There were fifty warning messages before at last we were given a green light . . .

A few months ago Malraux had lost his wife, the novelist Josette Clotys, in a tragic accident: she fell from a train in the station at Brive-la-Gaillarde, at the very moment when she was on her way to rejoin him. He does not talk about it now. Instead he tells us about his experiences at the head of his brigade in Alsace; the capture of Strasbourg, and the dramatic struggle to avoid evacuation of the city during the German offensive in the Ardennes last December . . .

ANDRÉ MALRAUX: Everyone in Germany regrets that the Army plot against Hitler was a failure. The war was already virtually lost. There wasn't the slightest hope of victory. How many German cities might have been spared . . . I've traveled through all of them: Berlin, Hamburg, Frankfurt, Munich . . . All in ruins . . . It's something you have to see for yourself—unimaginable! I've just come back from Nürnberg. That city where Hitler held his famous parades is no more than a sinister skeleton . . .

PICASSO: It must be fantastic . . .

ANDRÉ MALRAUX: It is fantastic . . . An apocalyptic spectacle! No streets at all. Nothing but wreckage, and enormous bulldozers fighting to open a passage. They look like snowplows moving through piles of houses reduced to dust. I remember the Museum of Natural History—there were just a few corners of the walls still standing. The bombs had hurled animal and human skeletons everywhere. You came across them in the most unexpected spots, staring at you, sometimes through the shattered glass of the windows. It was a house of horror . . . The house of the dead . . . Do you know what it evoked for me? Goya.

PICASSO: And the Nazi leaders?

ANDRÉ MALRAUX: Each of them ended in a manner befitting his character: Hitler, cremated in the fire and steel of the battle for Berlin. A Wagnerian death, like something out of *Götterdämmerung*, with an accompaniment by Stalin's organs . . .* Her suicide with Hitler gives even that insignificant Eva Braun some of the stature of a heroine of the *Nibelungen* . . . Goebbels, that vicious, fanatical clubfoot—another suicide, after he had murdered his wife and five children . . . And as for fat Goering, the *bon vivant*, the eternally smiling Goering—well, he goes on: he eats

* In the last months of the war, the vast concentrations of Soviet artillery were referred to by the Germans as "Stalin's organs." *Translator's note.*

and drinks, changes costumes, gives interviews, struts around and has his photograph taken from every angle . . .

PICASSO: And Mussolini! What a grisly end he had. Hung by the heels, like a side of beef in a butcher shop . . . Every time I saw him bellowing at the crowds, puffing up his chest and tossing his head back, I had the impression that someone was kicking him in the behind . . .

I ask Malraux if there have been attempts on the lives of the Allied "occupants" of Germany . . .

ANDRÉ MALRAUX: I've traveled everywhere in a jeep, with just my orderly and a noncommissioned officer. Do you think I could have done that if there had been any real resistance? No, in reality, there is no resistance any longer. The Germans are relieved. And content to be occupied by us and not by the Soviet armies. They are emerging from a nightmare . . . Even the most fanatical Nazis—although they might not admit it—are glad that it is over, done with.

MYSELF: Then why is there so much talk about a "German maquis?" Is it just a legend?

ANDRÉ MALRAUX: It is a legend . . . but a legend that has been carefully nourished by the "occupants" themselves. It's in their interest to keep it alive. On the pretext that there is still resistance, they can do a great many things which could not be justified otherwise. For example, on almost any night you can see a detachment of men armed to the teeth leaving on an expedition against the "maquis." In the morning they return from the forests with the captured enemy: hare, wild boar, deer, and other game. With the "maquis" as a pretext, they have gone hunting . . . and the commanders close their eyes to it. After all, they enjoy eating the enemy as much as anyone else . . .

Picasso introduces Malraux to Nush Éluard, who has just come in. The author of *Man's Hope* and *Man's Fate* has quickened to his subject. Tapping nervously at his temples, he addresses us now as if we were a vast audience.

ANDRÉ MALRAUX: The most serious problem, you understand, is that the Allies have no clear-cut policy for Germany. The Russian system is completely different from that of the English, the French, or the Americans. And the Americans sometimes act in an incoherent, even self-contradictory manner. Would you like an example? They decided to conduct an intense propaganda effort over the radio. And that might be an excellent idea. But at the same time they rigorously confiscated all the radios. You can see them everywhere, piled up by the hundreds, the thousands. There isn't a German in their zone who can hear their propaganda.

NUSH ÉLUARD: Is it possible to buy anything at all in Germany?

ANDRÉ MALRAUX: Yes, hogs. The number of hogs is unbelievable. Anyone would think that only the hogs had escaped all the destruction and massacre. You begin to wonder whether they aren't French hogs, whole trainloads of them that have somehow wandered into Germany. And they may be. I never saw their identity cards. . . .

We go into the studio. Malraux is immediately fascinated by *L'Homme à l'Agneau,* whose damaged foot Picasso has now repaired.

PICASSO: I did this statue in a single afternoon, but not until after months of reflection and I don't know how many sketches. Paul Éluard was here. Marcel helped me. I set up the armature first. But it's rare when you can calculate that correctly. And I made a mistake with this one. It was much too weak; it wouldn't hold. The statue began to stagger under the weight of the clay. It was dreadful! It was threatening to collapse at any moment. I had to do something, quickly. I enlisted Paul Éluard, to help Marcel. We took lengths of cord and lashed *L'Homme à l'Agneau* to the beams. I decided to cast it in plaster immediately. And it was done that same afternoon. What a job! I'll never forget it . . . I had intended to go back to it, to work on it again. You see those long, thin legs, and the feet, just indicated, scarcely separate from the ground? I would have liked to model them, in keeping with the rest. I didn't have the time. In the end, I left it as it was. Now it's too late. He is what he is. If I were to touch it now, I would risk ruining it completely.*

We go upstairs, and Picasso sets out his latest canvases: the quais of the Seine, the bridges, the Île de la Cité, the statue of Henri IV . . . very small, sometimes tiny paintings.

* In 1950, when Picasso was made an honorary citizen of Vallauris, he presented this town of potters and ceramic workers with a bronze replica of *L'Homme à l'Agneau.* It was set up in the square in front of the church.

PICASSO, *speaking to Malraux:* It surprises you, doesn't it? I have never been considered a landscape artist. And, in a way, it's true. I haven't painted many landscapes in my life. But it just happened. Since I couldn't travel during the occupation, I often walked along the Seine with Kazbek, and I drank in all the images of the trees along the quais, the Pont Neuf, the Pont Saint-Michel. Then one day all of these things which had become part of me without my even knowing it began to come out. I've tried to render a synthesis of them, more than anything else. None of them is a "slice of nature." None of them was painted from sketches, or with the "motif" in view. What do you think?

Malraux studies all of these variations on the same theme. He is especially impressed by their colorings: symphonies of tone in grays and beige, ranging from deep to cool, with skies of gray-mauve-blue. Picasso has painted the banks of Paris' river in all of their different lights: dawn, daylight, dusk, night; flooded with sunlight and beneath a starry sky. He shows us one picture in which the equestrian statue of Henri IV can be glimpsed between the arches of the Pont Neuf and the great trees on the quais. Painted in 1943, this landscape is the first of this whole series. In another canvas the white silhouette of Sacré-Coeur looms above the rooftops—a souvenir of youth . . .

Malraux leaves us. Picasso then groups all of the canvases in which Notre-Dame appears, and turns to me.

"Have you photographed Notre-Dame from the rear? I find it more beautiful from the back than from the front.

MYSELF: Yes, I have photographed it. From that angle the cathedral is more of a surprise, more unexpected. But what bothers me is that great metallic spire Viollet-le-Duc constructed at the very center of the whole architecture. It seems to me that it's completely arbitrary.

PICASSO: I was surprised by that spire too. But it doesn't bother me. On the contrary. It's like a banderilla planted in the *morillo* of Notre-Dame.

MYSELF: What intrigues me in your landscapes is that they have an extraordinary resemblance to the quais we know, even though one can't really situate anything at all.

PICASSO: I always aim at the resemblance. An artist should observe nature but never confuse it with painting. It is only translatable into painting by signs. But such signs are not invented. To arrive at the sign, you have to concentrate hard on the resemblance. To me, surreality is nothing, and has never been anything but this profound resemblance, something deeper than the forms and the colors in which objects present themselves.

Paul Éluard comes in, with a bibliophile friend who has brought a book bound by Bonet for Picasso to see. Whereupon Picasso buys a rare book illustrated by Picasso . . . Next to arrive is a young American soldier: the photographer Francis Lee. And then Baron Mollet. Nush Éluard asks Picasso if he has done much recent work.

PICASSO: I can't work well right now. Too many visitors, too many reunions, delegations, invitations . . .

Picasso's latest canvas is a large nude reclining on a bed, almost monochrome, with touches of gray and blue. Even though the various parts of the body have been completely rearranged, the breasts seeming to form a part of the buttocks, it exudes an air of great sensuality.

PAUL ÉLUARD *leans toward me and says:* If I had a choice among all these canvases, I would take that nude. I admire the still lifes, of course, but candlesticks and leeks don't really mean a great deal to me. But this nude *moves me* . . .

Picasso leads Paul Éluard and me into his little adjoining apartment, and tells us, with an enigmatic smile:

"I am going to show you something."

And he takes his private notebook from a drawer. It is this book to which he confides his very first sparks of inspiration, and also—primarily, in fact—his sexual obsessions. All of his work that can be placed under the sign of Eros undoubtedly stems from these masculine preoccupations. And an astonishing anthology could be made from all of those female bodies in which the sex is underlined, the points of the breasts aggressive, the line of the buttocks opulent and quivering. Even *Les Demoiselles d'Avignon*—the painting that gave birth to cubism and long since a classic—would be a part of it. Was the painting itself not born of an erotic dream, and originally titled *Le Bordel d'Avignon*? And yet, in all these images of desire, a light veil of modesty disguises and transposes his obsessions into the symbolic, the magical, the mythological . . . It is only in his intimate notebooks that Picasso gives free reign to his eroticism. Like the majority of great masters, he has a stock of works that are kept "under the counter" and completely apart from the main body of his work. There is a little notebook always within reach, to receive his most immediate and intimate confidences. "Art is never chaste," he told me one day as he was showing me some erotic woodcuts of Utamaro—prints of a rare beauty in which the organs of sex figured prominently but were stripped of all crudity and emerged as so many strange vegetable forms, part of a strange landscape, shaken by a strange wind of emotion . . .

The notebook he shows us now is undoubtedly just a sample. Paul Éluard and I leaf through it. Among the erotic images I notice a sketch Picasso had done just recently, on his return from one of his daily walks along the Seine with Kazbek. Unquestionably inspired by the swarms of amateur artists who are always there, with their easels focused on the *motif,* Picasso has peopled the quais with monkeys, brushes in hand—some of them are even perched in the branches of the trees—busily painting Notre-Dame.

Picasso suggests that we all have lunch together at the Catalan. We are seated together at one big table: Baron Mollet, Picasso, Gilberte, Francis Lee, Paul Éluard, Nush, the bibliophile, and myself. A ninth place is reserved for Dora Maar, warned of our departure by telephone, just before we left the studio. Picasso is dying of hunger and orders a Chateaubriand. But he is also courteous and thoughtful—he is almost in his own home in this restaurant—and busies himself with taking orders for the others. He is in particularly good spirits today. Only at a table, during a meal, surrounded by friends, does his conversation attain its full heights of fantasy and humor. At such times he is an unquenchable source of maliciously witty stories, of gossip and souvenirs, good and bad puns . . . A born talker and juggler of words, with an inimitable gift of improvisation . . . Today, finding himself in an agreeable climate for talk, he permits his taste for amusement to run free and never stops telling—miming, really—his stories. He is talking now about a woman seated at a nearby table. In the general hubbub, only snatches of phrases reach my ears:

"She was really very beautiful . . . She had splendid breasts . . . As a rule, she drove her car completely naked . . . One day she invited me to go for a drive . . . We had a breakdown . . . I plugged it up . . . Then we ran out of gas . . . She didn't have any money with her, so I was obliged to lend her a hundred francs . . ."

Dora Maar comes in. She is in a somber mood. She clasps her hands together, clenches her teeth, says nothing to anyone, does not even smile. She sits down in the empty chair. Two minutes have not passed when she stands up again and says: "I've had enough, I can't stay. I'm going." And she leaves the room.

Picasso, who has not yet had his Chateaubriand, leaps to his feet and runs after his friend. Dora's departure had been so abrupt that he could not have restrained her. We go on with our own talk, but now the meal is troubled. Those two empty places spoil our appetite. Nush Éluard leans toward me and says, with that lovely smile of hers: "Let's not get upset! It's one of those women's things."

An hour later Picasso reappears at the Catalan, distraught, his hair in wild disarray. I have never seen such distress on his face. "Paul, come quickly, I need you," he says to Éluard. The poet gets up and follows Picasso. The rest of us no longer dare leave the table. It is four o'clock and we are still waiting for them. An eternity. Neither of them comes back. At five o'clock we leave. Francis Lee drives Gilberte and me to Montparnasse in his jeep, of which he is very proud.

*Thursday, May 17, 1945*

Met the English painter M.C. He told me this story: "The other day, on the Quai Montebello, for the first time in my life I felt I wanted to paint a landscape, with Notre-Dame. I was really struggling with the canvas. Everything was going wrong. I've rarely been so dissatisfied with anything I was doing. The mere thought that any curious passer-by could see what I was painting was enough to deprive me of any ability at all. Suddenly I sensed that there was someone standing behind me. I turned around. It was Picasso! I felt as if the breath had been knocked completely out of me. I have never felt so miserable in my life. For years I've dreamed of meeting him, of showing him my work. And now he was there, behind me, looking at that frightful thing. I hoped he would go away. But he didn't even move, and his dog was lying at his feet. He said, "Don't worry about me—just go ahead." Do you think I would watch Picasso paint? But I couldn't even have stood up, my legs wouldn't have held me. I was so ashamed I wanted to throw myself in the Seine."

I was very careful not to tell M.C.—since I had no wish to urge him on to suicide—that his canvas must have made a profound impression on Picasso. It was probably one of those that inspired the drawing of all those monkeys in the notebook.

## *Friday, May 18, 1945*

Appointment with Jacques Prévert at the Café de Flore. Pierre Tisné is going to publish an album of my drawings in a limited edition, accompanied by a poem of Prévert. But the poem is late in arriving. The printers are at work on the drawings, and some of the sheets of the album are scheduled for display at my exhibition. The poem is coming along, or so it seems. As for royalties, Jacques tells me: "I don't want money. Let the publisher pay for a suit from my tailor . . ."

At about noon we go to see Picasso. He introduces us to an elderly man whose name I cannot remember. He was doubtless a friend of Pierre MacOrlan's, since he spoke a great deal about the author of *Quai des Brumes*. After he had left, Picasso says:

"I like Pierre MacOrlan very much."

"I'm delighted to hear it," says Prévert.

PICASSO: I knew him in Montmartre. He lived at the Bateau-Lavoir, in fact, in the same studio that Max Jacob once had, and then André Salmon, and then Reverdy, I think . . . MacOrlan was thin! And he wore an enormous hat pulled down over his eyes . . . Since he has been living away from Paris, almost like a hermit, I don't see him anymore. But we are still good friends . . . A rather secret man, unreachable . . .

MYSELF: About ten years ago I was working on a book on the "lower depths" of Paris, a sort of document on customs and morals. MacOrlan was to write the text for it. He likes photography, especially when he finds in it his beloved *fantastique social*. He told me a great many things:

"Montmartre, the Bateau-Lavoir, the Lapin Agile—what is all that to me? Souvenirs of '*La Vie de Bohème*'? That's a lot of crap! For me it means the landlords who took the key to my room because I was late with the rent. It was a horrible period: privations, misery, humiliation . . . There is nothing so terrible as youth spent like that. In Montmartre—happily, I only lived there for a year—I never had enough money to pay for a room in a hotel, a proper suit of clothes, a real meal. I was literally starving. If I went to see my friends, it was to try and borrow money. But most of the time they were just as broke as I was."

He retained only bitterness about his adolescence, about the picturesque life of Montmartre.

PICASSO: That's right. Very often it was black poverty. But in spite of his troubles MacOrlan was always gay and irresistibly amusing. He was always telling the wildest stories. A mind filled with paradoxes and hidden corners . . . To make some money he often used to write little articles for the humorous or satirical journals, or even licentious novels, just like Guillaume Apollinaire. They should be collected. *Le Sourire* has been published often. He signed them Dumarchais or Dumarchey, his real name. One day when he was very, very broke and his publisher wouldn't agree to advance him any more money, we thought up a wonderful plan. I took some little empty bottles and disguised them as pharmaceutical bottles, with labels and colored seals I made myself. Then we stretched MacOrlan out on the bed, closed the windows and drew the curtains. As soon as the room was thoroughly transformed into a sickroom, a couple of us went to see his publisher, put on our most desolate faces and shattered voices, and announced that our dear friend was . . . dying. He followed us to the bedside of the dying man. Then, with his eyes filled with tears and his mouth filled with sighs, he left twenty francs. Twenty francs! It was a fortune at that time. He would never have given them to a healthy MacOrlan, so that he could eat his fill, for once, and get on with the business of writing!

JACQUES PRÉVERT: *Le Chant de l'Équipage, Sous la Lumière Froide,* what beautiful books! MacOrlan is something more than just a master of the adventure story. Other people have written stories of corsairs and mountebanks, pretty girls and bad men . . . But he does better than that. He gives life to his characters, a spirit of—I don't know just what—of the tragic, the poetic, the mystical. If he enjoys danger and violence, it's because he feels that this is the way to put his finger on destiny. An odd sort of bloke, MacOrlan. I like him . . .

The conversation veers to the colorful figure of Baron Mollet.

PICASSO: I'm very fond of Mollet; he's staunch and faithful as a dog. He came to see me earlier this morning. As always, he was broke. And as always, I helped him out a little.

JACQUES PRÉVERT: The Baron Mollet! What an adorable man! He never takes offense . . . Right now I'm working with Paul Grimauld on a full-length animated cartoon, *The Shepherdess and the Chimney Sweep,* from one of the Grimm tales. I imagined a bird as the animator of all the action . . . I don't like to conjure up the characters in my films from whole cloth. I prefer to pattern them on people I know. Pierre Brasseur, Michel Simon, Arletty have often played themselves in my films. While I was looking for the character of The Bird, I told myself: "But, of course, The Bird, my bird, is Baron Mollet! It fits him like a glove." So I built my bird around him. Then, the other day, I saw him again. "I know everything," he told me, "there's no point in your denying it." I pretended not to know what he was talking about. But someone must have said something, and he had learned about it. I was afraid he would be offended. "So, then, I am The Bird?" he asked me. But he wasn't annoyed. Flattered, in fact. He found it very funny.

MYSELF: And what energy, at his age. No one I know is so restless. You meet him on the Left Bank, the Right Bank, Montparnasse, Saint-Germain-des-Prés, Passy, everywhere . . . He goes to bed the last, and gets up the first.

PICASSO: He has always been like that. Ever since I've known him, he has trotted from one café to another, from one studio to another, relaying the latest news about everyone, always up-to-date on everything that is happening. As a matter of fact, it was through him that I met Guillaume Apollinaire. He took me to a bar near the Gare Saint-Lazare one day—Ausin's, on the rue d'Amsterdam—knowing that Apollinaire went there often. And it was in that same bar that I, in turn, introduced Max Jacob to Guillaume Apollinaire . . . Mollet is a regular matrimonial agency. He loves bringing people together.

MYSELF: Was he rich once?

PICASSO: He has always been penniless . . . looking for a job . . . and always afraid he might find one. The only role that really suits him is that of "confidant." It was because of this that he became Apollinaire's secretary, his primary claim to fame.

MYSELF: Was he his secretary? He denies it.

PICASSO: Too proud and too modest to admit it. But it is a fact that he performed all kinds of services for Apollinaire; he proofread, filed his papers, even took dictation of *Le Poète Assassiné, Le Roi-lune,* and several other texts. And he turned away the people who were constantly besieging Apollinaire. So he was actually his secretary. Mollet has done a great many things in his life, but he doesn't like to work, to exercise a profession—he's even embarrassed by that word. And yet, you know, this man who has always lived at someone else's expense is the soul of generosity. That must be said for him! If, by some miracle, he has a little money, the first thing he thinks of is his friends. His greatest pleasure derives from rendering a service, from giving pleasure. In the worst circumstances, the darkest days, he brought me gifts. Oh! nothing important: a little tobacco, a Havana cigar, a book, things like that . . . Things that warm the heart . . .

MYSELF: Is he really a baron?

PICASSO: No more than I am. It was Apollinaire who conferred the title on him. And it suits him admirably. By imagining and playing the role, he has become a baron. I know a young girl who went through a violent period of depression, a nervous breakdown. She imagined herself a queen. And not just any queen, but the Queen of Tibet. So she began to behave like a queen. She no longer wore shoes: a queen always walks barefoot. She no longer wanted to eat: everyone knows that a queen is above such things. And she was constantly talking about a duke. "The duke did this . . ." "The duke did that . . ." But when someone spoke to her about this duke, she answered, "He is no longer a duke, he has been named a count."

JACQUES PRÉVERT: That's marvelous! A duke who has been named a count.

PICASSO: It's marvelous, and it's disturbing. We are in a world of magic and in the midst of a nightmare. Where is the frontier between imagination and madness? But, speaking of grades and titles, do you know this story? Napoleon, wanting to reward one of his officers, told him: "I name you marshal of France!" "But, sire," the officer replied, "I am already a marshal." "Good," Napoleon said, "in that case, I name you colonel!"

As we are about to leave Picasso, Prévert tells us this little story:

"This happened to the son of my cleaning woman. His mother scolded him for something or other, and then went off to her various jobs. When she came home, she found the boy sitting on the threshold of the door, with a little pack on his shoulder. He had gathered together everything he owned, and was about to leave. "What are you doing?" his mother asked. "I'm running away. Give me my ration tickets."

PICASSO: "Give me my ration tickets . . ." That's what the children of today must think about when they decide to run away.

JACQUES PRÉVERT: "And where do you plan to go?" his mother asked. "To Monsieur Jacques!"—Monsieur Jacques, that's me—"He is a good man, Monsieur Jacques, he will let me stay!" Then his mother said: "To Monsieur Jacques? But he is away; he is off on a trip." With that the child became very pale. Without saying a word, he unpacked his belongings and put them back in their proper places.

## *Friday, May 25, 1945*

Jacques Prévert and Roland Petit, a young dancer consumed with ambition and a fugitive from the Opéra, came to see me recently. A new troupe has been formed and plans to present three ballets at the Théâtre Sarah Bernhardt. They asked me to do the sets for *Rendez-vous,* written by Prévert. Kosma will do the music, and Mayo the costumes. I am to do three sets made up of giant photographs, and I have already made a model.

Today I go with Prévert to the rue Casimir-Delavigne, the apartment of the director of the new ballet troupe. I have learned in the meantime that this man is none other than the "Boris" I met in Picasso's studio—Boris Kochno, an ex-collaborator and friend of Serge Diaghilev. I saw him again the other day, when he came to Picasso's to ask about the curtain Picasso had promised to do for the ballet. Naturally he had not yet begun work on it. Basically Picasso has a horror of all "commissions." He is not really at ease except when he can work in complete freedom. For his books he generally manages to arrange things by allowing the publisher to choose from his abundant graphic work the prints or lithographs best adapted to the text.

28. Picasso arranged several of his recently completed paintings in this presentation to his friends, April 1944

*Picasso adores these improvised arrangements . . . this final reunion of works of the same "generation," grouped as they might be for a family portrait rendered sentimental by the knowledge that they will shortly, irrevocably, be dispersed throughout the world.*

29. FOLLOWING PAGE Picasso plays the professional artist before a painting he bought from an antique dealer, the model: Jean Marais, April 1944

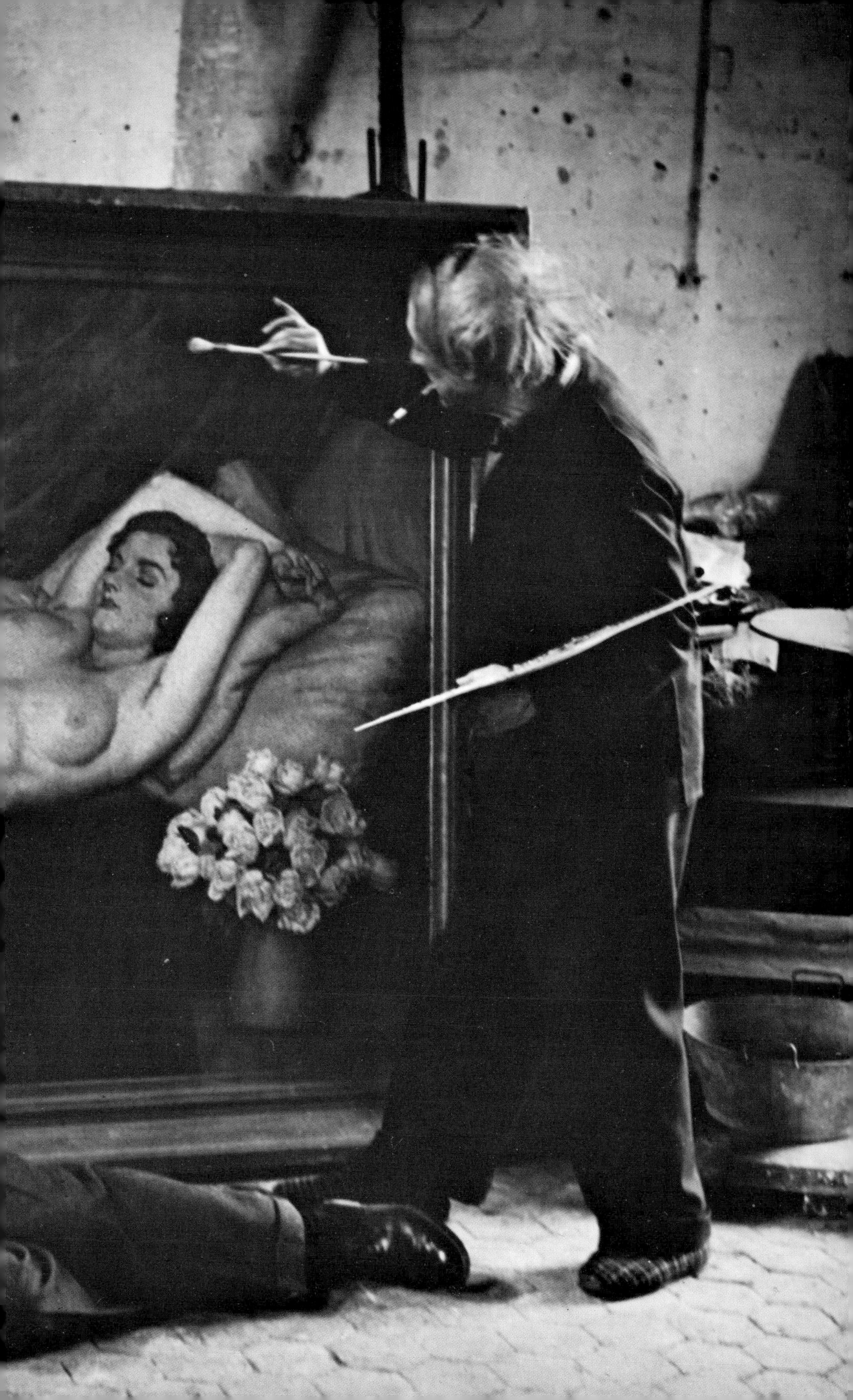

30. (left to right) Fenosa, Jean Marais, Pierre Reverdy, Picasso, Picasso's dog Kazbek, Françoise Gilot, Sabartés, and Brassaï in Picasso's studio, April 1944

PICASSO: *. . . water was spreading over the floor . . . Kazbek and I are the only ones who reacted at once. Why? Because I have quicker reflexes—as quick as those of a dog.*

31. (left to right) Ortiz de Zarate, Françoise Gilot, Fenosa, Jean Marais, Pierre Reverdy, Picasso, Jean Cocteau, and Brassaï in Picasso's studio, April 1944

PICASSO: *Look at this photograph. What is it that catches the eye . . . ? It's the crease in Jean Cocteau's trousers . . . like a plumb line! . . . Cocteau was born with a crease in his trousers . . .*

Even the aquatints for Vollard's edition of Buffon were selected in this manner, and Vollard then had to go through Buffon's writings and pick out fragments of text that would correspond—at least, relatively—with the illustrations. Boris' urgings on the matter of the curtain for *Rendez-vous* are equally vain; it is still no more than a project . . .

PICASSO: Listen, Boris, I have an idea. Since you are pressed for time with this curtain, why don't you go through my latest gouaches and select the one that conforms best to the spirit of *Rendez-vous?* There are some with candlesticks, skulls, mirrors . . . That would express the idea of destiny . . . It would be simple to enlarge whichever one you prefer . . .

Boris finally takes a gouache of a black velvet mask and a lighted candle. The curtain for our ballet has at last been born . . .

The impresario's apartment is a curious collection of rooms with large terraces looking out on the dissection rooms of the School of Medicine, perched high among the rooftops of the Latin Quarter. Kochno shares it with Christian Bérard. Cluttered with souvenirs of the great years of the ballet—Picasso drawings, portraits of Diaghilev, Nijinsky, Stravinsky, the great Russian ballerinas—all grouped around a bronze horse of the Italian Renaissance, Kochno's part of the apartment is shining, polished, smelling of floor wax and lavender water; but when you pass through the door that links it with Bérard's apartment you enter a realm of dust, of a nonchalant let-well-enough-alone, of the odor of tobacco and opium . . . This is where Christian Bérard—"Bébé" to his friends—lives and works. His gift for fashion design is as great as his gift for drawing, and for fifteen years he has dressed the stages of theaters as if they were so many pretty women, employing all the sobriety, the elegance, and the ingenuity of Parisian *haute couture.* Since he has become the darling of Paris society, his ink-stained fingernails, his rumpled shirts and down-at-heel shoes are the delight of snobs, and the smartest salons of Paris are invariably jammed when this dandy in reverse is expected. And he never goes without Jacinthe, his inseparable white terrier, snuggled in his arms . . .

I look at Boris, trying to find in this man, still handsome but now completely bald, the seductive young man portrayed in a beautiful drawing of Picasso's—a young man with great dark eyes and a high, clear forehead. There is a curious alliance of masculine and childlike traits, of energy and indolence, candor and affectation . . .

We discuss *Rendez-vous* and my sets. A young Russian dancer has just come in: Marina de Berg. She is to be the heroine of our ballet—"The Most Beautiful Girl in the World." When Prévert and I leave, Boris is discussing the terms of a contract with her. We can hear his deep voice, with its guttural Russian accent, even through the door.

### *Saturday, May 26, 1945*

At the Café de Flore, with Jacques Prévert, the painter Mayo, and the decorator Trauner. We are again discussing the ballet *Rendez-vous*. Ribemont-Dessaignes is at a nearby table. Beneath the enormous dome of his skull—he has been bald since the cradle—his blue eyes sparkle wickedly through their hooded lids. First a dadaist, then surrealist, poet and novelist, I have known him since he was editor-in-chief of *Bifur*, a new kind of literary review at the time, sumptuously printed and illustrated. One day—I think it was in 1930—in his tiny office on the Boulevard Saint-Germain, he handed me a manuscript entitled: *Family Souvenirs, or The Warder Angel.*

"Read that," he told me, "and remember the name of the author. He brings a new sound to French poetry."

I began to read it right there: "We lived in a little house in Saintes-Maries-de-la-Mer, where my father was a maker of trusses . . ."

"Even when he writes," Ribemont-Dessaignes had said, "you would think that he was talking. He comes from the street, and not from "literature." A very special case. He loves life and despises "proper people." There's a simplicity about him, a taste for happiness, a corrosive humor that escapes all classification . . ."

I asked the author's name, and for the first time in my life I heard of Jacques Prévert. It was through Ribemont-Dessaignes, as a matter of fact, that I made his acquaintance shortly afterward . . .

An hour later I am at Picasso's. He is with Oscar Dominguez, a strapping Spaniard from Tenerife who is as passionate an *aficionado* of bullfighting as Picasso himself. He comes here more and more often these days. A gifted painter, with a staggering mastery of technique, he has learned a great deal from Picasso—too much, in fact. Some of his canvases seem to be painted "in the manner of . . ." Picasso has a weakness for this wild bear of a man (he even wears a heavy coat of shaggy cotton, increasing the resemblance): despite the uncut edges of his manners he is filled with a robust vitality, reflected in the enormous, disproportionate hidalgo's head, with its fine black mustaches. He likes his mercurial mind, his black humor, and perhaps he also likes the quality of violence and unrest that stems from his Spanish blood. This great, apparently peaceful body is inhabited by a demon, and no one is safe when alcohol releases it. I have seen Dominguez brandishing a switchblade knife or a revolver, creating panic around him, sending everyone present scurrying for safety. It was he, in fact, who put out the eye of the surrealist painter Victor Brauner, one night of drunkenness and anger in Montparnasse. He hurled a glass at Brauner's face, thus fulfilling—as if this were a Greek tragedy—a premonitory dream. For years past, Brauner had seen himself as a one-eyed man, and was so obsessed with this vision that in all of his painting and sculpture he had begun to represent the human face as having only one eye . . .

Dominguez praises the freshness of Picasso's most recent still lifes.

PICASSO: I am pushing them less and less. If I go beyond a certain stage, it would no longer be what it is. I would lose in spontaneity what I might gain in solidity. And I am using less and less color, and allowing the virgin canvas to play its part more and more. If this goes on, I will soon arrive at this: I will put my signature and the date on absolutely virgin canvases. An untouched canvas is a beautiful thing, isn't it?

A group of young painters arrives. The only one of them I know is Gischia. Close-up and from a distance they sniff, test, scrutinize Picasso's newest canvases, compare them, dissect them, trying to probe a path into his secret. Sometimes their voices are raised and they argue violently among themselves.

Then they begin to talk about the suffering of the deportees who are now returning home, still garbed in the uniforms of the camps, their heads shaved, their eyes haggard, almost mad, the visions of horror they have seen still graven in their minds. And there are those who did not return, who remained forever in Auschwitz, in Dachau, in all the other camps . . . Picasso is beginning to boil. He is silent for a long time, but his face betrays his emotion and his anger. Then this man who had never concerned himself with politics until the Spanish Civil War—as a good Spaniard, he was basically a monarchist—but who is now engaged in it body and soul, suddenly explodes.

PICASSO: Fascism must be fought, wherever it appears. We should fight against the tribunals now—they are much too indulgent with "collaborators." The Marshal himself—hasn't he escaped punishment, because of his age? If the Germans—God help us!—should come back and occupy France again, I'll tell you right now I would be the first to "collaborate" with them. Yes, I would do business with them, I would make friends with them. And why not? There doesn't seem to be any reward for having resisted them. They are just passing a sponge over all the crimes, all the dealings. Understand it, if you want to . . .

And he continues in the same bitter and violent tone. In the diatribe, I hear an echo of his almost daily discussions of this burning subject with Paul Éluard—it dominates all of their feelings at the moment. "I can still see those pitiable, stupid women," Éluard will say, "trembling with fear, while the crowd laughs at them. It was only themselves they sold, not France . . . And at least they don't reproach others. But the bandits with the faces of apostles have gone. And there are even some of them who are sufficiently aware of their power to remain calmly at home, hoping to begin again tomorrow . . ." Picasso's phrase *Understand it, if you want to* . . . formed the title of one of the poems in which Éluard lashed back at the judges who convicted indiscriminately and acquitted with revolting indulgence . . .

The exhibition of my drawings is to open in a few days at the Renou and Colle gallery. As I am about to leave, I ask Picasso if it is true that he has broken with Pierre Colle.

PICASSO: Broken? No. There has just been a little difficulty between us—nothing that will prevent me from coming to see your exhibition. But don't count on me for the opening. Openings bore me . . .

As we are talking, a group of Spanish painters has come in. They often come to see him. Manuel Angeles Ortiz, Hernando Viñes, Pedro Flores, Castanyer, and Joaquin Peinado are part of the old guard. Picasso has known them for twenty years or more. Among the younger ones I have met Antoni Clavé, the sculptor

La Torre, and Xavier Vilato, Picasso's nephew. In a sense, every Spanish republican artist is almost a part of his family; he considers himself their spiritual father. But never, to any one of them, has he given advice in the matters of painting or sculpture. In this domain he feels that everyone should find his own way, as best he can. I leave with Peinado. He has known Picasso since 1924.

PEINADO: Picasso went to the Salon d'Automne that year, and I had a painting there. He stopped in front of it, and said to Ortiz who was with him: "This picture is certainly the work of a Spanish painter." Ortiz told him that I had done it, and that he knew me. "Bring him to see me," Picasso said. That was how I first met him. I saw a great deal of him after that, until Sabartés came into his life. Not so often since then. I know Sabartés very well, but that makes no difference; he carries his devotion to Picasso to the point of preventing his friends from seeing him . . . One day I wanted to take some American friends to the rue des Grands-Augustins, so I telephoned him. "Come, if you want to," he told me, "and bring your friends. But you will only see me." "And why won't I see Picasso?" I asked. "He's working at Lacourière's just now, and goes out every morning . . ." The next day I went to the studio with my friends. And Picasso was, in fact, invisible. On the stroke of noon Sabartés disappeared. I heard a discussion going on, in guarded tones. Then suddenly, very loud, Picasso's voice: "But yes, yes, I want to see my friend Peinado." He came in and joined us, and embraced me just as he always had. And he was delightful to my friends . . .

We go on talking about Sabartés, and about the thankless role he has agreed to play for Picasso—watching over his most precious possession: his *time,* performing it joyfully and devotedly, without concern for the jealousies and bitterness he may provoke. It is to protect the genius of his friend that he has become his guardian angel, and in a way his jailer. In such a role it is difficult for him to distinguish between sincerity and flattery. Is the friendship someone might express intended for him or for the "intermediary"? It is this that has caused his suspicious air, his mistrust, even of his own friends . . .

Tonight I go out in search of some photographic elements I need for the sets of the ballet. Gilberte and André Virel, a young colonel in the Resistance, accompany me. What I am looking for is a dance hall whose marquee carries only the word *B A L.*

But they are all Bal à Jo, Bal des Quatre Saisons, etc. I can find nothing at all on the Left Bank. It is midnight when at last I unearth the *B A L* I need, near the Place de la Bastille, in the sordid Passage Thiéré, behind the rue de Lappe. But I am still lacking a set for the murder scene in *Rendez-vous*. Very late, we are in La Villette. The unexpected silhouette of the drawbridge on the rue de Crimée, crossing the putrid waters of the Ourcq canal, will supply me with this final set. The sinister black wheels and pulleys of the bridge stand out like instruments of torture . . .

### *Tuesday, May 29, 1945*

The day of my opening is drawing near. This morning I sent off two cartloads of drawings to the gallery on the Faubourg Saint-Honoré. Then I decided to make a quick stop at Picasso's. I wanted to say a word of thanks. After all, it was he who "organized" this exhibition. But he is still in bed. Sabartés is confronting one of his eternal, delicate problems. Skipper after God of Picasso's ark—the Bateau-Lavoir number two—he is giving orders from the bridge to Marcel and Inés:

"If Baron Mollet arrives, tell him that Picasso has gone out . . . If the American woman arrives, shut her up in the studio so that she won't see him . . . But if B., the publisher, arrives, announce him right away. Picasso wants to see him . . ."

And Sabartés tells me: "There is an American woman who wants to see Picasso. Lady Abdy is the chaperon and Baron Mollet the guide . . . She is coming here, like a great many others of her kind, so that she can announce to her friends in New York: "I'm just back from Europe. I saw the Pope, Pompeii, the Escorial, Versailles, and Pablo Picasso . . ."

In the afternoon, at the gallery, I am arranging my drawings for hanging. An unknown man comes in. He is wearing a light topcoat, a light felt hat pulled down over his eyes, and has a hint of a mustache. He wanders around among the drawings, spread out everywhere, even on the floor, and then says to the young salesgirl: "I want to buy that one . . ." Pierre Colle introduces me, and murmurs the visitor's name: Dunoyer de Segonzac. Shortly after this, someone else comes in and buys two of my drawings. Before the exhibition has opened, I have three little red stars on the corners of my frames.

*Wednesday, June 6, 1945*

A brilliantly sunny day. When I go to the rue des Grands-Augustins at about noon, Sabartés tells me:

"Picasso is busy. He is with a collector, but he told me to ask you to wait, if by chance you came by."

I wait in the vestibule and read Sabartés some passages from *Bistro-Tabac*, a collection of thoughts and observations I had jotted down in a café during the summer of 1943, at the time when Kharkov was retaken by the Red Army.

Picasso comes down, with the collector. It is Roger Dutilleul. I am delighted to see him again . . .

DUTILLEUL: We have just been talking about you. Picasso showed me your drawings. It looks as if you were having an exhibition right here.

PICASSO: A permanent exhibition! I like them, so I show them to everyone. I want you to leave them with me for a few days longer . . . so that I can choose the ones I want without being rushed. How much are you selling them for?

For some time now Picasso has been using the familiar "tu" when he speaks to me. Should I begin doing the same, and say, "*Pablo, tu sais* . . ."? It is not the difference in our ages—about twenty years—that holds me back, but the example of those who use the familiar form in addressing him in order to advertise a friendship which is often precarious. Picasso and Kahnweiler, who have been friends for forty years, still use the formal "vous" in all their conversations. And very few of even his closest friends call him "Pablo." Sabartés himself always says "Picasso" . . .

*Friday, June 15, 1945*

Tonight, at the Théâtre Sarah Bernhardt, the first great première of a ballet since the war. Liberated Paris is becoming herself again. We are emerging from a four-year night, and in a sense this evening was a festival of liberty restored. Just over a month ago Hitler committed suicide and the Wehrmacht surrendered . . . The balletomanes and the snobs are there, as well as all the celebrities of Paris, from Comte Étienne de Beaumont to Marlene Dietrich, from Jean Cocteau to Picasso. Only the presence of a few men in uniform reminds us that the war is still going on in the Far East . . .

Seated next to Picasso in the orchestra—with Gilberte on my right, and Dora Maar beside Picasso—I glance through the elaborate program. There are reproductions of Picasso's curtain; drawings by Bérard, Valentine Hugo, Mayo, and Lucien Coutaud; photographs of my sets and of the male and female dancers of the troupe. All through these recent weeks, I have been plunged in this word of smiles and tears, of *entrechats* and *crocs-en-jambe;* the fascinating, hysterical world of the ballet. I have followed rehearsals in a dance studio on the Boulevard de Clichy, and then on the stage of the theater, in the glare of footlights and the paroxysm of nerves and excitement in the last hours before the "creation." For hours on end, sometimes throughout the night, I have watched Boris and Bébé arguing, losing their tempers, bursting into tears, and then happily being reconciled; Roland Petit, tireless, his muscles straining, whipping a young and undisciplined troupe into shape, his enthusiasm infecting the others, Marina de Berg, Ludmilla Tcherina, and Zizi Jeanmaire—beautiful and fragile as a Tanagra figurine . . . *Only the ashes of the unforgettable phoenix of Serge de Diaghilev remained to us,* I read in Jean Cocteau's introduction to the program. *But we know the myth and the truth of the myth. This phoenix died to live again* . . . The shade of Diaghilev hovers over this crowded hall and its elegant, turbulent audience. The atmosphere, the shiver of impatience that is evident everywhere, recalls the Ballets Russe of years ago. Is it possible that the miraculous synthesis of music, dance, and the pictorial arts will happen again?

This agitation about a revival of the ballet, the collaboration with his friends, the visits from Boris, have awakened Picasso's old passion for the dance. Every time I have seen him in the past days, he has questioned me exhaustively on the progress of rehearsals, the quality of the dancers, my sets . . . He watched over every step of the execution of his curtain, remembering the things he had created for other ballets: the Chinese conjurer, the jugglers of *Parade;* the curtain peopled with bareback riders, harlequins, and guitarists of his rose-period world; the Goya-like curtain for *Tricorne,* on which he had brushed a panorama of the bull ring, with women in mantillas and men in capes and sombreros; the curtains and sets for the *Pulcinella* he did at the Paris Opéra with Stravinsky; and those for Manuel de Falla's *Quadro Flamenco,* depicting the red, gold, and black loges of a nineteenth-century theater; the curtain for *Mercure,* with its great white Harlequin and red Pierrot . . . Perhaps he is also thinking of that spring of 1925, when he and Olga were in Monte Carlo, and he devoted almost all of his time to the dancers and the ballet . . .

Very belatedly, in an atmosphere charged with excitement and tension, the evening begins—*Les Foraines,* by Kochno, Bérard, and Sauguet. The "blue period" lives again. The emaciated figures of the street players weave through the languorous music of Sauguet.

And then, *Rendez-vous.* The red house curtain rises, revealing the blue-mauve-beige curtain of Picasso. The candlestick, the velvet mask, concealing fate . . . For a long moment the curtain with the word *Suntuchia* painted on it hangs motionless in the air. There is applause. And then there are whistles and shouts . . . Since Picasso joined the Communist Party, his painting, no matter what its subject, causes the same fury in some people as a muleta does in a bull . . . At this year's Salon d'Automne, in which Picasso—deviating, for once, from his rule of never participating in group exhibitions—displayed seventy-four canvases and five of his bronzes, there were noisy outbursts and some visitors went to the extent of removing paintings from the walls . . .

A smattering of boos and jeers, but there is also applause. Beyond a slight tightening around his eyebrows, Picasso shows no reaction whatever. He has seen other demonstrations of the sort. During the intermission he told me that tonight's display was no more than a tempest in a teacup compared with the scandal provoked by *Parade* in this same theater twenty-eight years ago. The ballet fans of that time expected a successor to *Schéhérazade* or *Spectre de la Rose,* but what they saw was a cubist ballet that trampled on all convention and shattered their eardrums. "Picasso, Satie, and myself," remarked Cocteau, who had joined our group, "couldn't even get backstage. The crowd had recognized us and was threatening us. The women had their hatpins out and would probably have stabbed us to death if it hadn't been for the presence of Apollinaire, who was in uniform, with a great bandage around his head from his wound . . ."

Picasso's curtain rises, to reveal my first set. To the left, my

Place de la Bastille dance hall, with a red spotlight focused on the word *BAL;* in the center, a tall panel of a street light, lit in blue; on the right, a decaying fragment of a wall, with a hotel sign A LA BELLE ÉTOILE which the projectors have bathed in yellow.

I am reassured. Constructing a set for a ballet from photographs for the first time was a gamble, but the atmosphere is there. It is the proper framework for this marvelous and horrifying adventure imagined by Prévert; this idyll born in hovels and ending in blood, mingling love and death—the inescapable encounter with destiny. There is applause. Picasso nudges me with his elbow and smiles and the orchestra takes up the first measures of Kosma's music, nostalgic and moving as the plaintive laments of the streets . . .

Second set: a night view of one of the pillars on an elevated station of the Métro. The black shadow projected by a street light on a wall resembles the profile of one of those giant statues from Easter Island. Destiny looms up here. Third set: the drawbridge of the rue de Crimée. Crime, Crimée . . . It is here that Marina de Berg—in Mayo's costume of black stockings, a short mauve skirt, and a tight-fitting yellow blouse—kills the young man who is so madly in love with her, after an audaciously sensual *pas de deux* . . . The bitter, direct, and disturbing poetry of *Rendez-vous* conquered its audience. Picasso says to me: "It's a very beautiful thing. And I like your sets. I had never thought that photography could do that."[48]

## *Tuesday, July 10, 1945*

Appointment with Marina de Berg, the young Russian dancer, at eleven-thirty. Yesterday morning we wandered through Les Halles, among the piles of vegetables. I bought her a little case of peaches. She told me that her greatest desire was to meet Picasso. I promised to take her to see him.

By some miracle she is on time, but so excited, so agitated that she cannot even swallow her coffee. "It's madness," she says. "How will he receive me? What can I say to him? I've been told he can be very, very difficult." I try to reassure her: "There's nothing to be afraid of, Marina. The worst that can possibly happen is that we might miss him or arrive at a bad time. Just now the studio is often jammed with people. The last time I went there, there was such a crowd that I turned around and left without having seen him . . ."

Marina is fortunate. Picasso is there, stripped to the waist, in blue shorts. And there is no crowd; just two or three other people. I introduce her to him: "You saw her dance the other night at the Théâtre Sarah Bernhardt."

PICASSO: I remember it very well. You were remarkable in *Rendezvous*. You danced "The Most Beautiful Girl in the World." But you were dangerous with that dagger . . . I saw how you kill a man you are holding in your arms. The ballet is a success, isn't it? I hope so; we all worked on it together . . .

Since his visitors are still there, he tells me:

"You play the guide, Brassaï. Show Marina the studio, and my sculptures. And be sure not to forget the "museum." I'll be tied up for about five minutes, and then we'll go upstairs.

But, before leaving us, he whispers in my ear:

"She is charming!"

Marina is enchanted:

"He's really a love, your Picasso! So simple! So kind! I'm having a wonderful time."

I show her all of the scupltures. Her face crinkles up in dismay. Apart from the cats and the cocks, nothing pleases her:

"There are only monsters here! Horrors!"

Picasso, freed of his other guests, takes us up to the painting studio and shows us his latest still lifes.

"I painted them yesterday, beginning at six o'clock in the evening."

I study the paintings. Three variations on the same still life with a mirror. On each canvas, the cold tones of the objects placed before the mirror form a kind of counterpoint to the highly colored tones reflected there. Picasso's facility, his marvelous agility in the handling of canvas, can be disconcerting. Three paintings, done in a few hours . . . But don't we arrive at a false concept of "a painting" when we think of all those that have required years of work and effort? Delacroix said, "We should paint drafts of paintings, conserving the liberty and freedom of a sketch . . ." Picasso, more and more, is employing canvases as sheets of paper, and oil paint in place of water color

. . . It still happens, however—and more often than is thought—that he will let a painting develop over a period of weeks, months, even years. Speaking of an enormous canvas, *The Charnel House*—a sort of echo to *Guernica*—which had been sketched out in charcoal and then remained for weeks in the same state, until a day when I saw a few timid areas of color appear, Picasso told me: "I'm treading very gently. I don't want to spoil the first freshness of my work. If it were possible, I would leave it as it is, while I began over and carried it to a more advanced state on another canvas. Then I would do the same thing with that one. There would never be a "finished" canvas, but just the different "states" of a single painting, which normally disappear in the course of work. To finish, to achieve—don't those words actually have a double meaning? To terminate, to execute, but also to put to death, to give the *coup de grâce*? If I paint as many canvases as I do, it is because I am searching for spontaneity, and when I have expressed a thing with a degree of happiness I no longer have the courage to add anything at all . . ."

Marina is looking at the three still lifes with the mirror. She is astounded:

"But these canvases of yours are shocking! They frighten me! Three paintings, since six o'clock yesterday afternoon . . . And what will you sell them for? Sincerely, do you like these, Brassaï? Do you find that beautiful? You just say it out of snobbishness, all of you . . ."

I am afraid that this young dancer's naïve frankness will annoy Picasso . . .

PICASSO: I like Marina! She is authentic, she is real. She says what she means. And I love that. Did you see the young American painter I was talking to just now? He had just told me: "I used to like your painting very much, Picasso; ten years ago I was mad about it . . . But now? Frankly it no longer says anything very much to me!" I listened to him, and I wasn't annoyed at all. His frankness delighted me . . . (*He turns to Marina, and adopts a mischievous tone:*) So, that is all you think of my painting? If I understand you correctly, none of my canvases pleases you.

MARINA, *a trifle embarrassed:* Why, yes. Yes . . . If you were to offer me one, I would choose this portrait.

And she points out a head of a woman of Arles, by André Marchand, the only canvas in the studio not done by Picasso.

We both burst out laughing. Marina is confused.

PICASSO: Don't be upset. You are not the first . . . One day at the Bateau-Lavoir, Paul Poiret, the great couturier, was looking at a little gouache. He was ecstatic about it: "It's extraordinary! It's wonderful! It's inspired!" Well, it wasn't one of mine. It was done by Fernande Olivier . . . A portrait of herself, as a matter of fact. Poiret was thoroughly done in when I told him.

MYSELF: I didn't know that Fernande Olivier painted.

PICASSO: Oh, yes. And she also drew. Some day I'll show you her drawings. I have a lot of them in my portfolios. Very beautiful drawings, you'll see . . . She was very gifted, but she didn't possess that sacred fire of work. Her work resembled Marie Laurencin's a little, but Fernande had a more vigorous line, less pretty-pretty.

Picasso looks at Marina. She is seated on a bench, her legs crossed, her head resting lightly in her cupped hands, the little nose upturned, her eyes sparkling with mischief beneath the reddish crown of hair; her face, the long neck, the arms all starred with freckles.

PICASSO: But she is very beautiful—Marina . . . This profile is adorable. If only I were an artist . . .

MARINA: You would do my portrait! No, thank you. I don't want it. You would reconstruct me just the way you have all those women over there—the eyes in the ears, the mouth in the nose.

PICASSO: Why, no, I wouldn't. I wouldn't treat you like other women. I would make you very beautiful. By the way, how old are you?

MARINA: How old do you think I am? I never tell my age.

PICASSO: But to me, you can tell it to me. Whisper it in my ear . . . an old man like me . . .

MARINA: But you are young. I had no idea that you were so young. What do you think of *Rendez-vous?*

PICASSO: It seems to be doing very well. I've heard a good deal of talk about it, and the critics all praised it. As an ensemble the corps de ballet is good. But it isn't yet disciplined enough. Ah, if you had seen Diaghilev. What a forceful man that was! He didn't joke about things. He always had a conductor's baton in his hand, and when someone didn't obey him—well, he hit them with it.

MARINA: Do you think that is a good system?

PICASSO: Of course I do. When you get hit across the rump with a baton, you're not likely to forget it very soon. For creating and maintaining discipline, he was unbeatable.

MARINA: What do you think of Boris? He's very capable and intelligent, isn't he? And he was practically raised by Diaghilev . . . He has very good taste . . .

PICASSO: But he is not Diaghilev—alas!

I pick up my briefcase and take out my most recent photographs of the graffiti inscribed in the walls of Paris. He snatches them away from me.

PICASSO: A wall is a wonderful thing, isn't it? I've always paid close attention to what happens on them. When I was young, I often used to copy the graffiti I saw . . . And the number of times I have stopped before a fine blank wall, and been tempted to engrave something on it! The thing that held me back is that . . .

MYSELF: . . . that you wouldn't be able to take it away with you.

PICASSO, *laughing:* Yes—that I would have to leave it there, abandon it to its fate. Graffiti belong to everyone and no one . . . But some day, why don't we go out together, for a long walk, and I'll carry a knife and you bring your camera? I'll scratch drawings in the walls, and you can photograph them.

MYSELF: You never have scratched anything on a wall?

PICASSO: Oh, yes. I left a lot of them on the walls of Montmartre. One day, in the center of the city, I was waiting for something in a bank. They were in the process of renovating the building. I saw a blank stretch of condemned wall between the scaffoldings, so I did a graffiti on it. When the work was finished, it had disappeared. A few years later, as a result of some kind of new alterations, my graffiti reappeared. Someone thought it was interesting, and then they learned that it was an original . . .

Picasso. The director of the bank halted the work and had my scratching cut out, as if it were a fresco, with the whole wall around it. He had it set into the wall of his apartment. I wish you could photograph that some day.

I ask Picasso if he has left many paintings on walls, now lost forever.

He tells me about the figures he painted on the landings of one of his studios in Barcelona, and also about the nude, the hanged man, and the couple making love with which he decorated Sabartés' garret room in the same city.

PICASSO: There was a round window in that room—an oeil-de-boeuf. I transformed it into a gigantic eye. I simply enclosed it between two big eyelids . . .

On the walls of Frédé's first cabaret in Montmartre he had left a nude girl, a hermit, a bat, and a portrait of Sabartés. All that has disappeared. There isn't even a reproduction of any of them. It hadn't occurred to anyone to detach them from the walls. Picasso was not yet Picasso. But a still life with a mandolin, a bottle of Pernod, and a sheet of music bearing the title *Ma Jolie* had a happier fate. Painted on the wall of a villa at Sorgues, where he spent the summer of 1912 with Eva, it was saved. Kahnweiler had it taken down, along with a whole section of the wall, and transported to Paris in a specially built packing case . . .

MYSELF: I would like to do a ballet entitled "Graffiti." The curtain would rise on a great wall covered with graffiti, and a small boy cutting out a new one. In front of the wall, on the sidewalk, three little girls would be dancing a game of hopscotch. Later, the graffiti would emerge from the wall: the "Arrow" pursuing the "Heart," the "Sickle," the "Hammer" . . . There would also be "Death," the "Masks," the "Sexes," and all sorts of other symbols . . .

PICASSO: Well, Marina, what are you waiting for? Why don't you dance a game of hopscotch for us?

MYSELF: But remember—it must be danced on just one foot, like a piece of music written for one hand. Those are the rules of hopscotch.

Marina de Berg poises on the red hexagons of the studio floor and, on the toe of one foot, balances, leaps, pirouettes between the Heaven and Hell of a child's game. I realize then that hopscotch and this "half-step" could really be the source of a quite original choreography.

We applaud. Picasso encourages Marina, shouting, "Encore! Encore!" I am almost surprised that he does not cry, "Olé! Olé!"

Breathless, she sits down again, and turns to me: "I'm having a good time! I'm having a wonderful time! He is really astonishing, your Picasso!"

PICASSO: You must come back and see me again, Marina . . . I can give you some helpful advice . . . For example, why do you wear high heels? That's not permissible . . .

MARINA: Because I was going to meet Picasso, and I wanted to look my best.

PICASSO: High heels destroy the feet. A dancer should never walk in anything but sandals. No one ever told you that? Let me see your slippers.

Marina extends one foot, so that he can see the laces. He is visibly moved.

PICASSO: That reminds me of a lot of things . . . My wife was a ballet dancer too . . . She had her slippers sent from Milan.

MYSELF: Don't you think that Marina resembles Olga?

PICASSO: I noticed it at once! My wife had that same profile, the same neck, the same look. And, like you, she was Russian . . .

The resemblance between the young dancer and Olga Kochlova had surprised me at the very moment I met her for the first time in Boris Kochno's apartment. And it pleases me that Picasso, forgetting his conjugal difficulties, the storm clouds of his separation, the seizure of his paintings, should have retained of his wife only the shining image of a young dancer he had met one winter day in Rome; forgetting the bruises of the past, he should be so moved at having rediscovered in Marina's roguish smile the face of the woman he once had adored. His fidelity to joyous things chases the bad memories from his thoughts and retains only the moments of happiness.

Dora Maar has just come in, and Picasso turns to her at once, and says, "This is the dancer, Marina de Berg. Look at her, Dora—wouldn't you say that it was Olga, Olga as a young girl?"

Then he continues his interrogation of Marina.

PICASSO: And how do you soften the points of your slippers? Do you crush them in a door? Yes, that's it, you can also do it with a door. But . . . your slippers don't really seem to be very solid . . . And the points are not well enough reinforced on the inside. That's nothing but pasteboard. They must get worn out quickly.

MARINA: I use them twice to soften them. But after I have danced once in them in public, they are no good anymore.

PICASSO: Well, I still have quite a few of my wife's slippers. I'll find them for you. There is good leather in those. I'll give them to you. And how do you fasten your waistband? That's very important. You don't fasten it? Well, the next time you come I'll show you how waistbands should be fastened . . .

André Bloch, the director of *Art d'Aujourd'hui*, comes in. He would like to reproduce the painting of Picasso that has recently been transposed into an entirely new form known as "gemmes"—multicolored bits of glass, resembling precious stones. The original canvas is easily recognizable, but three-dimensional, transparent.

PICASSO: It's a curious thing, isn't it? It was Marie Cuttoli who had the idea for this experiment with gemlike particles. Do you know Jean Crotti, the brother-in-law of Marcel Duchamp and of Jacques Villon? He was the inventor of it. He spent ten years experimenting with methods of superimposing various translucid, colored materials . . .

Someone remarks that these gemmes are not far removed from stained-glass windows.

PICASSO: They are completely different. Nothing to do with panels of glass mounted in lead. It is an amalgam of glass and of color with light. You take a plate of glass, and light it from beneath. Then you arrange on it pieces of colored glass, cut and trimmed to different sizes, shapes, and thicknesses, until you have obtained the forms and colors you want. You can transpose any painting at all into such gemmes, but wouldn't it be more interesting to create original works directly in this process? This translucid material tempts me . . .

As is usual with any new means of expression, Picasso's imagination is stimulated, and he is already itching to try it. He leaves us to go and dress. When he returns, wearing a steel-gray suit, he is holding an envelope in his hand.

PICASSO: People are always asking me for the most incredible things . . . Look what I have just been sent: twelve 1000-franc banknotes, and not stamped for the revaluation of the currency. They're not valid any longer. It was an American girl, Katherine Dudley, who sent them to me. She has been having a lot of trouble. She forgot that these banknotes were in a drawer until it was too late to validate them. Now she is asking if there is some way I can exchange them for her. As if I were the Bank of France! But I have an idea . . . She may be able to get her money back, after all . . .*

Today, July 10, 1945, is a great day for Picasso. Beginning today he will again be able to drive about in his car.

"Marcel is beside himself," he announces. "He has already filled the tank. But before he will take us out, he insists on a trial run on some deserted highway, to revive the motor after five years of enforced sleep."

As we are leaving he says to me:

"I must give you back the manuscript of your *Bistro-Tabac*. I read it and so did Dora. It's very interesting. You have a gift for capturing the essence of a conversation . . . By the way, did you find my name in the guest book at your exhibition? I stopped by the other day. But you weren't there—too bad!"

Then, to Marina:

"Come back to see me again. I'll look for the slippers. And I'll explain to you how you should fasten your waistband."

I go to lunch with Marina.

"Well, are you satisfied?"

"Delighted! How kind he was to me."

"He is like that. There are some people he adopts at first sight;

* Some days later Picasso waved these banknotes at me and said, "Look, I have revalued them." He had cut out a little woodblock and imprinted it on the face of each of the notes, thus "revaluing" them beyond their original worth.

Almost twenty years later, in 1962, I asked Katherine Dudley if Picasso had returned them to her. "Never," she said, laughing. "Don't be silly! Every time I see him, he waves his arms in the air and says, 'Yes, Katherine, I did revalue your notes, and I must give them back to you.' But he will never do it, never . . ."

others, never. Now, you can go to see him whenever you like. You will always be welcome."

"It's curious," Marina says, "I saw him for the first time, and yet I have the feeling of having known him forever. And just between ourselves, he was much better in his shorts than in that gray suit. When he is dressed he becomes too much the proper gentleman, and a tie does not become him at all. But in his shorts, he was incredible."

### *Thursday, August 2, 1945*

The World War is drawing to a close. The newspapers have announced the end of the Potsdam Conference.

At the Deux-Magots, Jacques Prévert, spanking new from head to toe: gray suit, gray hat, red tie, red pocket handkerchief, and two blue-green eyes, like two tropical fish against a glowing background of rose coral. He has just returned from London. We discuss *Les Portes de la Nuit,* a film that Marcel Carné wants to make from the ballet of *Rendez-vous.* Kosma will write the music, and Marlene Dietrich and Jean Gabin are to be the stars. But Jacques is worn out with the trials of the cinema profession.

PRÉVERT: A single day in Paris, and you are finished! Contracts, discussions, appointments, all kinds of crap. Everything connected with a film is so demoralizing, so tiresome . . . I just met Gabin, and he told me: "For someone like me, with a kisser as well known as mine, the Métro is like the road to Calvary. Everywhere around me, all I can hear is things like: 'Look, it's Gabin! God, he's getting old!' or even: 'Is that really Jean Gabin, that old man with the white hair? It's not possible!'

A devoted friend, René Bertelé, has gathered together all of Prévert's scattered poems, and they are soon to be published in one volume entitled *Paroles.*

PRÉVERT: By the way, the jacket you did for *Paroles,* with the graffiti, is going to be very handsome. And look what I have received—an album of my poems. Some high school students in Rheims had the idea of collecting them from magazines, and made this mimeographed book. There is only one copy of it in existence, and they offered it to me. No gift, ever, has given me so much pleasure as that gesture of these unknown boys and their teacher.*

* A few days after this, Marcel Carné, Jacques Prévert, the decorator Trauner, Joseph Kosma, and myself met at Les Vieilles on the rue Dauphine, to discuss *Les Portes de la Nuit.* Carné wanted to re-create in the sets the atmosphere of my early book *Paris by Night.* Marlene Dietrich was supposed to come, with Gabin, but only the actor joined us. Kosma opened his briefcase and took out a few sheets of music. He sat down at the old, out-of-tune piano. Then Prévert said to Gabin: "This is the song you are going to sing with Marlene in the film." Kosma took up the melody, and Gabin, hunched over the music propped on the piano, began to sing, in an uncertain voice:

*Les feuilles mortes se ramassent à la pelle*
*Et le vent du nord les emporte*
*dans la nuit froide de l'oubli . . .*

Thus, we were present at the birth of *Autumn Leaves,* the great postwar love song which later conquered the entire world. In the end, Marlene Dietrich, having paid no attention to the song, although it was written for her, refused her part in the film, on the grounds that it presented too black a picture of France. And Jean Gabin did the same thing. They were replaced by Nathalie Nattier and a young singer discovered by Edith Piaf: Yves Montand. As for the role of Destiny, it was confided to a young actor who was just beginning to make his mark: Jean Vilar.

*Tuesday, November 26, 1946*

SABARTÉS: Yes, they are back. You'll see, he's in splendid form. Françoise is expecting a child. That makes him young again. He has never been so gay, so happy, so overflowing with energy. And he has already begun to work again—lithography. He goes to the Mourlot brothers' studio almost every morning . . .

Picasso comes in, stripped to the waist, bronzed as some Indian chieftain, skull shaven, face baked and rebaked in the sun, the salt and the sea wind still in his nostrils and on his flesh. This past April he spent a few days at Dora Maar's house at Ménerbes, in the Vaucluse; in June he stayed for a short time at Golfe-Juan; and in August he went back to the Côte d'Azur with Françoise . . . It was his first long stay in the South since the war, since August 1939, when the decree of mobilization had forced him to leave Antibes . . . Seven years ago . . .

Picasso's distaste for the fogs of the North, the humidity, the lowering skies, is something he has felt since childhood, when he was wrenched from the gentle climate of Málaga and transported into the mists and rain of Galicia; and it has never been so pronounced as it was during the years of the occupation, when he was almost a prisoner and could no longer escape from Paris every summer. And the nostalgia for light, for warmth, for the sea, has never been so strong in him as it was just after the liberation. It was in 1919 that he discovered the Côte d'Azur, and exclaimed: "I knew at once that this landscape was mine." For a long time the Pyrénées-Orientales and the Côte d'Azur disputed possession of him. Now, the latter seems to have won.

Relaxed, in wonderful humor, his look more piercing than ever, Picasso embraces me. We have not seen each other in seven months.

MYSELF: Picasso, there are stories that you have repainted the Château Grimaldi.

PICASSO: And they are absolutely true. Do you know that palace, along the road through the old walls of Antibes? It's magnificent, isn't it? That old square tower, that terrace overhanging the sea . . . I worked there like a convict . . .

Did I remember the Château Grimaldi! When I visited it for the first time, about fifteen years ago, it was a dilapidated little provincial museum, presenting an exhibition devoted to contemporary documents on Napoleon's landing at Golfe-Juan on his return from Elba. And what a comical demonstration of human inconsistency it was! Heavily sealed letters addressed to the prefect in Grasse, informing him in veiled terms of the imminence of the "distressing" event, demanding horses and reinforcements to oppose it; posters proclaiming that, "The usurper has dared set foot on the soil of the nation!"—to be replaced the next day with posters proclaiming, "Frenchmen! Our beloved Emperor is with us again!" and signed with the same name. In twenty-four hours the leopard had changed its spots . . . The power of the Emperor inhabited these old walls, and the sea air that ruffled these yellowed papers was the breath of that marvelous, futile epic that was the Hundred Days. And now Picasso has driven Napoleon from the Château Grimaldi and taken his place.

PICASSO: One day on the beach I met the conservator of the palace. Very timidly he asked me for a drawing for the museum. Everywhere I go, people ask me for drawings, you know that. But how could I say no? Whereupon, he went on and said: "Perhaps you could give us a painting instead of a drawing . . ." I thought about it for a while, and then I made him a proposition: "You have a lot of empty walls in the Château Grimaldi. It might be preferable if I painted something there." He was delighted. He offered me the whole upper floor of the museum. "Yes," I said, "but I have no materials for fresco here. And painting directly on the wall is too risky." "Don't worry about that," he answered. First they bought me canvases made of sackcloth—unusable. Then they suggested canvas pasted to the wall, and plywood panels. Finally I decided on large panels of fibrocement. And I painted some frescoes for them. Do you want to see them? I have them here.

Picasso reaches for a large envelope, and extracts a mass of photographs by Sima. First, his mural paintings. Then, himself at work in swimming trunks, standing, sitting, squatting, the white of his eyes sparkling against the Indian bronze of his face. I look at the photos of the paintings: little fawns; extravagant horned centaurs with tridents on their shoulders, playing on the flute and the reed pipe; maenads and nude bacchantes with swelling breasts and plump behinds, their flowing hair falling free to the slender waist—everywhere the body of Françoise Gilot . . . In the background, the sea, with little triangles of sails. An innocent gaiety, a sensual delight, a great pagan happiness animates all of these buoyant figures, these pastoral scenes, drawn as if in filigree against the azure of the Mediterranean . . . I ask about the dimensions of the panels.

PICASSO: They are big, but against those enormous walls they seem rather small. About five feet by ten . . . Some smaller . . . This one I nicknamed "La Joie de Vivre" . . . This other one is Ulysses surrounded by the sirens. I painted it on three panels of fibrocement placed side by side . . . I'll leave all of this right there. They want to make a "Musée Picasso" from it . . . Perhaps I'll give them some other things I've done down there, some bones, some sculpted pebbles . . .

The publisher of our book comes in. We had arranged this appointment with Picasso to discuss final details on the album of his sculptures. Unfortunately there are still quite a few we do not have . . . At least fifteen or twenty. This business has been going on now for three years. Certain of his earliest sculptures are in private collections, and I might be able to photograph them, but each of them would require at least half a day. We open the box which contains all of the photographs I have taken thus far.

PICASSO: It isn't possible! Did *I* do all that? I would never have believed I had done so much sculpture . . .

Since I have several versions of each piece, taken from different angles, we must decide on which one is to be used. We begin sorting them out, and at the same time try to set up a tentative layout for the book. Picasso is in favor of keeping it in chronological order.

PICASSO: And in the past months I have been working for you. Little things . . . I'll show them to you.

He returns with a box filled with pebbles, bones, fragments of plates and pots tossed up by the sea, all of them etched, occasionally somewhat reshaped.

PICASSO: I do these things on the beach. The pebbles are so beautiful that one is tempted to work on all of them. The sea has already done it so well, giving them forms so pure, so complete, that all that is needed is a flick of the finger to make them into works of art. In a round pebble I saw an owl, so I made an owl. Another one, triangular, made me think of the head of a bull or of a goat. Some suggested a fawn or the head of a woman. And this one I didn't dare touch: the nose and orbits hollowed out by the sea are exactly the *tête de mort* I saw in it . . . I could have added nothing.

One after the other, then, he brings forth these little pebbles, modeled and polished by the sea, graven and tooled by his hand. They seem to be the vestiges of some ancient, Picassoan civilization.

PICASSO: Now, of course, they should be cast back into the sea. Think how astonished people would be, finding pebbles marked with symbols like these . . . What riddles they would pose for archaeologists!

The publisher asks if the pebbles are hard to work on, and what instrument he uses.

PICASSO: The stone resists. It's incredibly hard work. I begin them with anything at all, anything I happen to have at hand. Then I finish them with very sharp pointed scissors.

The publisher remarks that the "style" of these pebbles is different from that of the ones he had done before the war.

PICASSO: One is constantly changing. You have only to look at the changes in my signature. These are my different stone ages. All of that should be published in the album. I like things to be complete. The only way to follow the creative act faithfully is to pass through all the variations of the series . . .

32. Picasso's rue des Grands-Augustins studio, May 1944

*The light is wonderful today. It shimmers across the rooftops, the chimneys, the bare walls which are always in Picasso's view while he is painting . . .*

33. (left to right) Robert Marion, Marcel, Picasso's chauffeur, and Sabartés cataloguing Picasso's works for the *Cahiers d'Art*, May 1944

SABARTÉS: *Marcel is a good example of the extent to which Picasso's most revolutionary developments become naturally classical . . . At the beginning, this painting must have baffled him completely. But twenty years of intimate and daily contact with it has taught him how to read a language which is still incomprehensible to many people.*

34. Plaster cast by Picasso

*...the casting of a simple piece of pasteboard, folded and refolded, can give a result as monumental as the Great Wall of China.*

35. Plaster cast by Picasso

*. . . the imprint of a crumpled piece of newspaper can assume the aspect of a rocky mountain.*

36. & 37. Plaster casts by Picasso

*The round bottoms of the pastry or sand molds, the rectangle of boxtops, pierced with two, three, or four holes to serve as eyes, nose, and mouth, then give birth to primitive countenances . . .*

38. Picasso's *Femme aux Feuilles*

*. . . a figure born of a corrugated carton, with a rectangular head and a casting of real leaves in her arms: a goddess of barbaric extravagance emerging from mythology.*

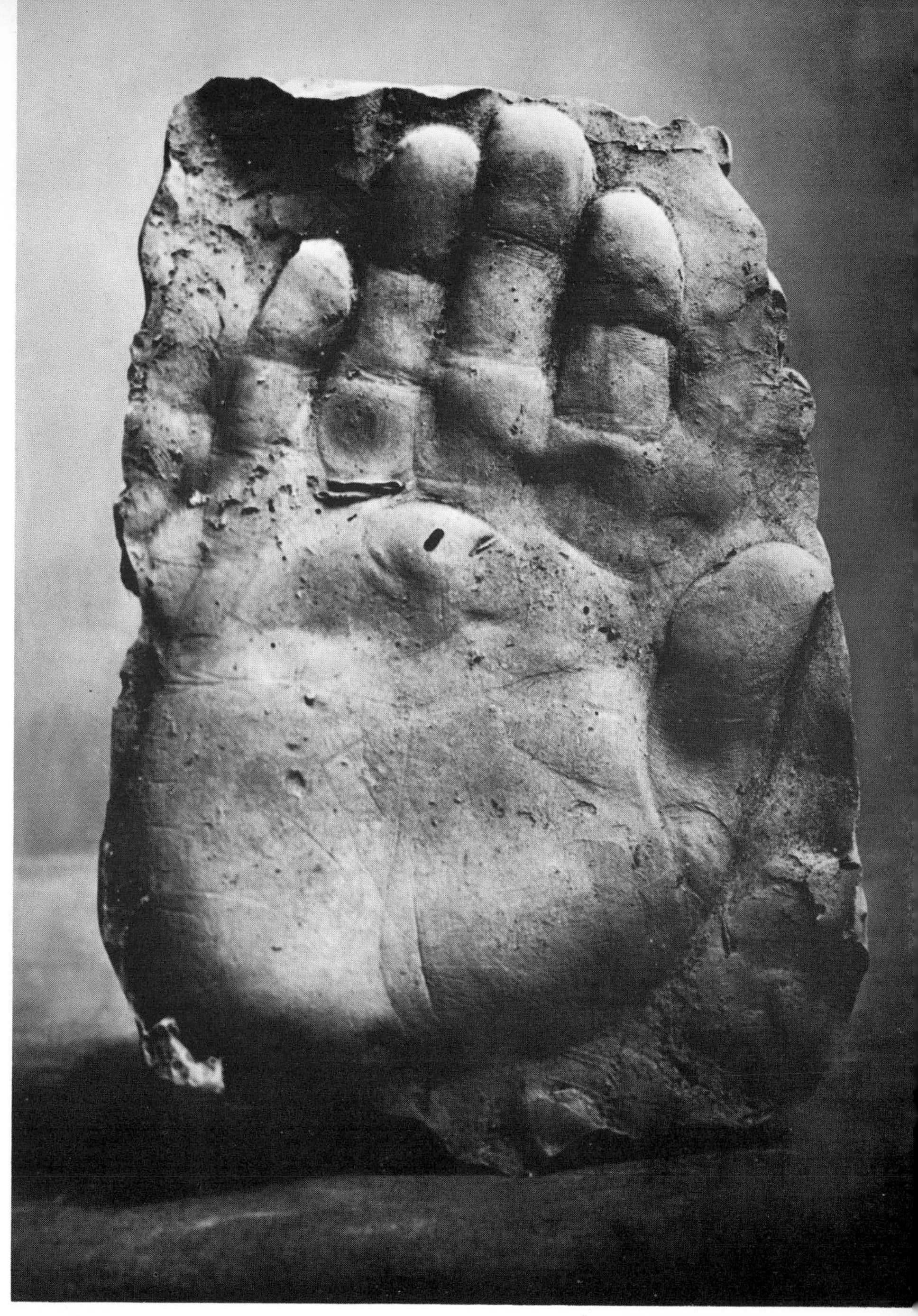

39. Plaster cast of Picasso's right hand

*. . . as if Picasso were then focusing on his hands the attention he had once given to his face.*

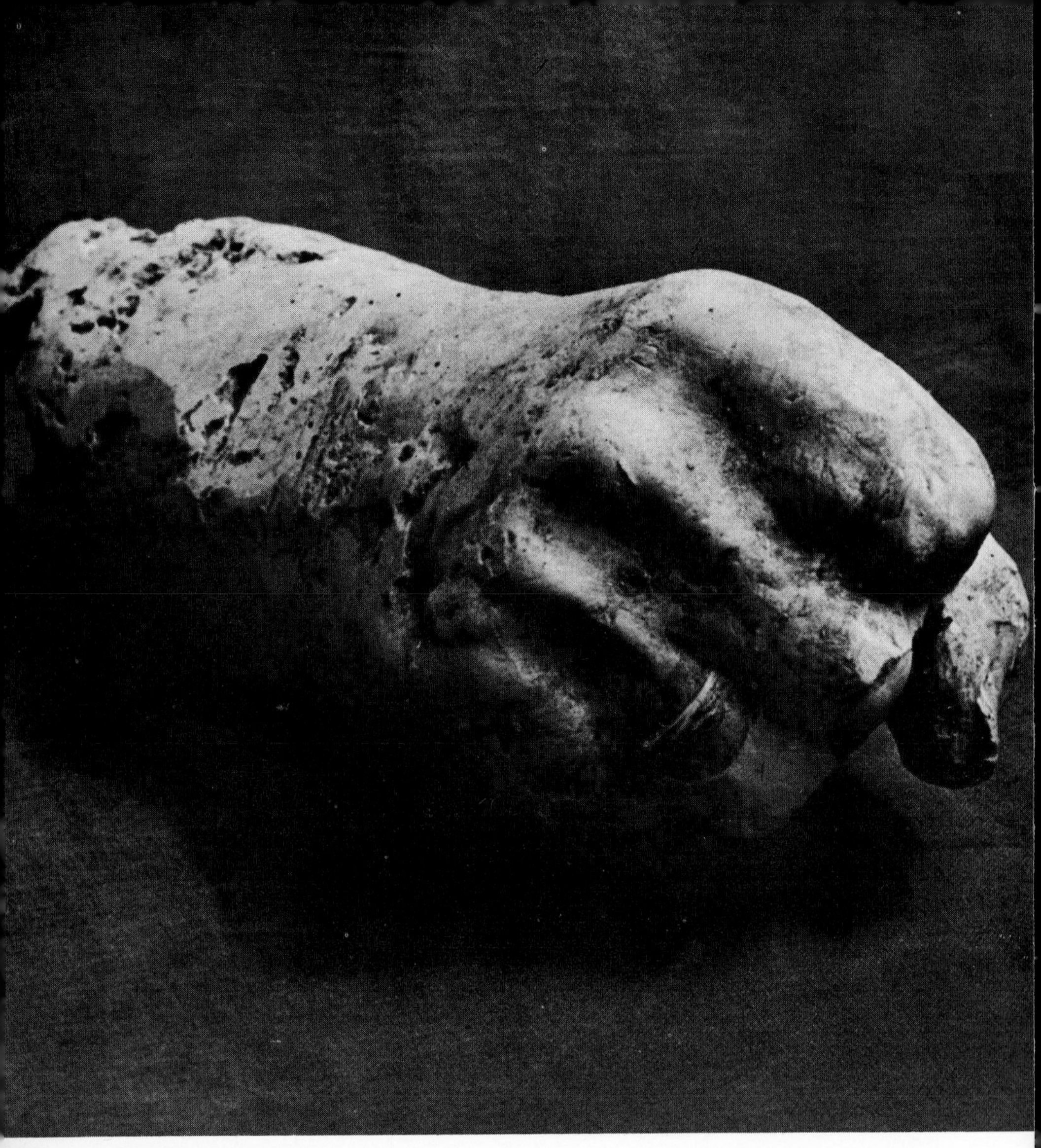

40. *. . . castings of the closed fist and the strong wristbone, as though he wanted to seize all of their concentrated strength.*

41. OPPOSITE PAGE Plaster cast of Picasso's right hand

*. . . a fleshy palm, the hill of Venus bursting with sensuality, a headstrong thumb, fingers so tightly matched against each other that not the smallest ray of light could pass between them.*

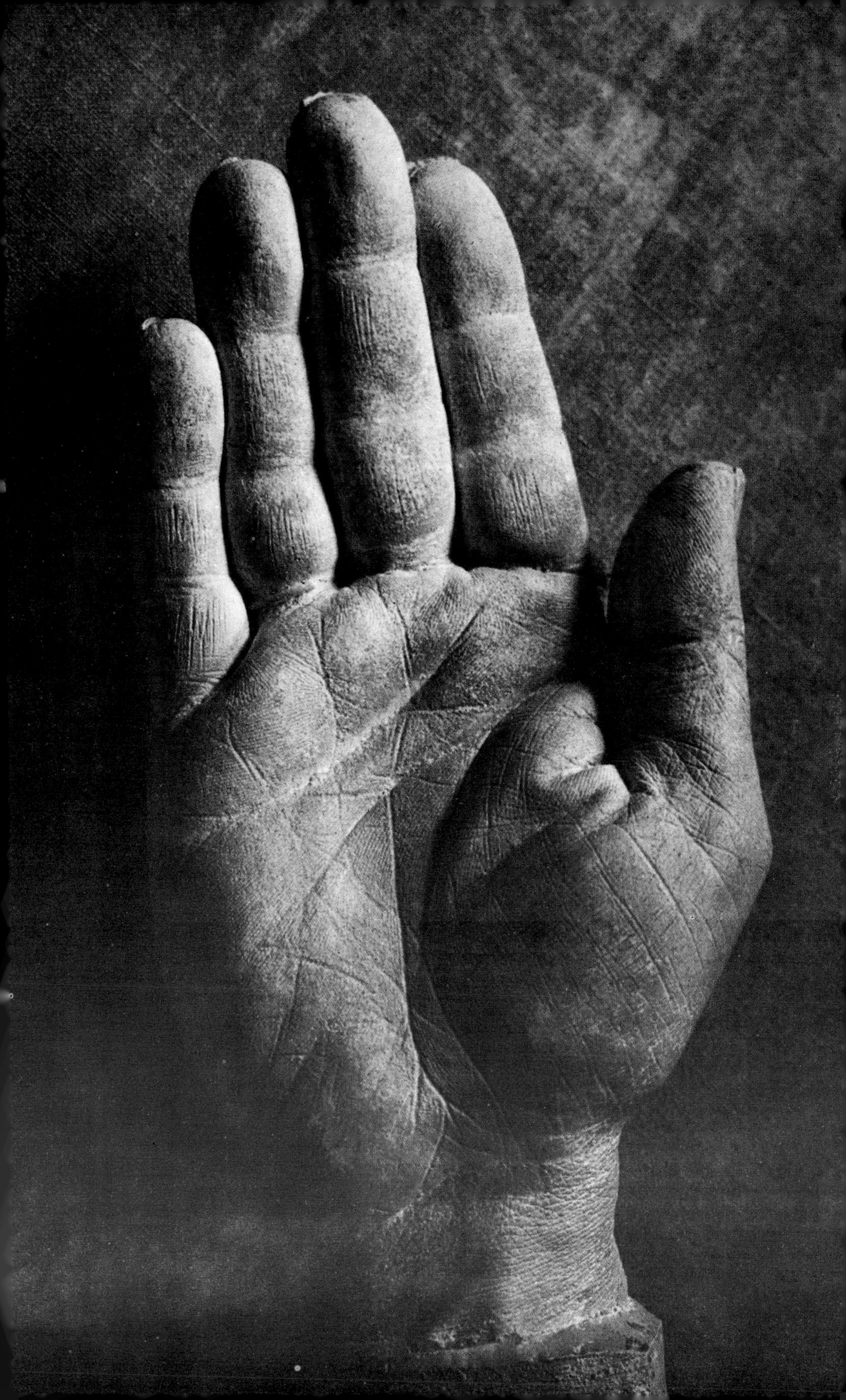

42. Picasso entertains a group of friends who had produced and acted in his play, *Desire Caught by the Tail,* (standing left to right) Doctor Lacan, Cécile Éluard, Pierre Reverdy, Louise Leiris, Zanie de Campan, Picasso, Valentine Hugo, and Simone de Beauvoir, (seated left to right) Jean-Paul Sartre, Albert Camus, Michele Leiris, and Jean Aubrier, June 1944

The publisher mentions his regret that the reproductions of some of the earlier sculptures are so poor.

"Kahnweiler showed them to me," he says, "and I don't like the thought of publishing them in this album."

PICASSO: They are abominable! So far from the objects they are supposed to reproduce, in fact, that they become interesting. They often return to me in black something I did in white. And the color reproductions of my paintings! Sometimes, in place of my colors, I find others, different ones, so foreign to my own that I actually feel a sense of shock. And sometimes it even happens —curious thing, isn't it?—that the worst reproductions, the ones in which there is nothing at all left of my painting, absolutely fascinate me. Yes, it's the truth. The element of surprise gives you something to think about, doesn't it? It's like a new version, a new interpretation of my work. What does a flawless reproduction bring me? I simply find my own painting again. But a bad reproduction gives me ideas, sometimes even opens new horizons . . .

I am left alone with Picasso. As we are talking, his two lovebirds are cooing so loudly that they almost drown out our words. They are in a very handsome cage, made of a reed lattice-work which Picasso often repaints himself.

MYSELF: I took a photograph of them while you were away. One of them was sitting on top of the cage.

PICASSO: As a rule, I leave them free. They often come and sit on my hand, on my head, or on my shoulder.

He opens the cage and the birds instantly fly out, pursuing each other around the room, their wings rustling sharply.

Pigeons have fascinated Picasso ever since early childhood. He has always seen them darting and swooping in the skies around him. His father used to paint them, and often left to his son the task of finishing off their feet. He loves to have them around him, preferably free. Doves, pigeons, lovebirds have become one of the favored themes of his art.

PICASSO: Lovebirds are perhaps the most sensual of all animals. They are constantly playing at love. I would like to know what goes on in their little heads. And the thing that is really odd about my birds is that they are both males. Do you suppose they could be perverts?

Picasso may like or detest men, but he adores all animals—they are as indispensable to him as a feminine presence. At the Bateau-Lavoir he had three Siamese cats, a dog, a monkey, and a turtle, and a domesticated white mouse made its home in a drawer of his table. Frédé's donkey once ate a package of his tobacco, but he loved it nonetheless. He adored the tame crow of the Lapin Agile, and painted it (in the picture called *La Femme au Corbeau*) with Frédé's daughter, the future wife of Pierre MacOrlan. In Vallauris he had a goat; in Cannes, a monkey. And as for dogs, there has not been a day in his life when he has been without their companionship. Even as a young man he painted himself walking with a dog. He has always wanted a cock and a goat somewhere near him, and dreamed of having a tiger. If it had depended only on himself, he would always have lived in the midst of a veritable Noah's Ark.

Knowing how interested he is in the behavior of animals, I tell him a little story:

"I know an old spinster who makes artificial flowers for the great couturiers. She lives in a garret room on the seventh floor of an old building, surrounded by birds. She has a male lovebird, too, and she always leaves him free. And that bird is so much in love with his mistress that when she bought a female as a companion for him the female became violently jealous. As a reward for his devotion the old lady buys him one of those little celluloid dolls every now and then. And the bird plays with the doll so passionately, throws himself down on it so violently that you would think he meant to rape it. I've made a whole series of photographs of the bird and the doll: it's like Leda and the Swan . . . One day I found this same male bird sitting on a porcelain egg. The old lady explained to me that male lovebirds hatch too. And hers, when the mood comes over him, sits on that artificial egg and can't be moved for three weeks . . ."

PICASSO: Have you noticed that animals are extremely sensitive to our amorous behavior? It attracts them, impassions them, sets their blood to boiling . . . especially dogs and cats. I knew a woman who had two enormous Saint Bernards, two males. One day a man came into her life and she fell very much in love with him. Well, the first time they went to bed together, here come the two Saint Bernards, standing at the foot of the bed, gigantic, terrifying . . . They put on such a performance that the lover leaped out of bed and fled from the house in panic.

MYSELF: Speaking of your amorous animals, I know a story about a colonial official who brought two marmosets with him when he returned to Paris from Oceania. He was very proud of them, and was intent on the idea that they should have offspring. But one of his friends, who was a renowned naturalist, told him: "Don't count on it. Marmosets don't reproduce in captivity." Then one day he noticed that one of his little monkeys was obviously pregnant. He invited the naturalist to his home, and said: "Well, what do you have to say now?" The naturalist was skeptical, but in the face of the evidence he was forced to give in. But when he examined the marmosets closely, he exclaimed: "It isn't possible! Both of these animals are females!" The official was both crestfallen and baffled. "Two females? But then where is the male?" The problem seemed insoluble. All night long he racked his brain. Then suddenly he was overcome with a terrible suspicion. Didn't his wife take one or another of the monkeys with her sometimes, when she went out? He hired a private detective, and had his wife followed. And he learned that she was having an affair with a Tahitian who owned a male marmoset. And since monkeys imitate the gestures and actions of humans—and our amorous acts, as you say, set their blood to boiling—the two monkeys had reproduced, even in captivity . . . The man got a divorce and his wife married the Tahitian."

The story amuses Picasso, and he tells me:

"It's astonishing how much you resemble Manolo when you tell a story like that . . ."

I leave him shortly afterward. This is not the first time he has compared me with Manolo. At our first meeting he said, "You remind me of Manolo . . ." But who is this man? For a long time now, I have been trying to clarify "the Manolo mystery." A spanish painter told me one day:

"Manolo? No, you mean Ugue, Manuel Ugue? He was supposedly the son of a general, in much the same way that Apollinaire was the son of a cardinal. In any case, there was absolutely nothing military about him. As a boy he loafed around the streets of Barcelona with all the rest of the urchins. When he was taken into the army, he suddenly came into possession of a horse and all of its harnessings, and a gun. One night, good-bye to Spain! He crossed the Pyrénées, carrying everything he owned with him. In France he sold the horse and all of its equipment, and the gun, and bought a ticket to Paris . . ."

The sculptor Jean Osouf, who was a friend of Manolo's and had lived with him for a time at Céret, told me this:

"Everyone loved Manolo. He could play all kinds of tricks on people, but his delight in life, his spirit, more than compensated for it. He did the most ignominous things with such an air of innocence that no one thought of being angry with him. When I knew him, he had already matured somewhat, but he still delighted in pulling peoples' legs—the instinct was stronger than he was. He could never forgo a witty remark, even if it wounded his best friends. The stories I could tell you . . . One night, at Céret, an orchestra was giving an open-air concert. One of the townspeople—the butcher—was sitting in front of Manolo. He had enormous ears that stood straight out from his head. Manolo leaned over to his neighbor and said, "I can't hear a thing! This character with the donkey's ears is absorbing all the sound." And his neighbor believed him! The next day, he turned up at Ugue's house and said, "I've been thinking about what you said all night, Manolo. Your story doesn't make sense! You can't hide music with your ears, the way you can hide a play with a big hat . . ."

Maurice Raynal asked me to come with him to Montmartre, to take some photographs of the "shrines" of cubism. He is giving a lecture on it, and wants to use some slide projections. This afternoon we climbed the Butte, up the rude slope of the rue Lepic, that teeming, odorous street of food shops. At the corner of the rue Gabrielle, Raynal pointed out a studio perched on the top floor of No. 49 . . .

"That was Picasso's very first studio in Paris! It was up there that he painted *L'Enterrement de Cadagemas.* But did you know that it was a matter of pure chance that Picasso settled in Montmartre, instead of in Montparnasse, when he arrived here from Barcelona? He had practically rented a studio on the rue Campagne-Première when a Catalan artist who was going home offered him his, here on the rue Gabrielle. If it hadn't been for that, the cradle of cubism would probably have been Montparnasse and not Montmartre . . ."

We arrive at that little tree-dotted square which was once the rue Ravignan, and is now the Place Émile-Goudeau. The ramshackle hulk of the Bateau-Lavoir has survived.[49] Raynal tells me that it used to be called "The House of the Trapper." Seen from the outside, it has not changed. The decaying shutters are closed. Raynal explains that the two windows to the left of the entrance, looking out on the square, are those of Juan Gris's old studio. We go into the building, in which the corridors and the studios have all been renovated. Raynal plucks through his memories, calling up pictures of the box mattress with no legs, the round folding table, Picasso's old deal armoire and the rickety, groaning easel he still has with him at the rue des Grands-Augustins. Then he tells me about the day Picasso and Fernande moved from the Bateau-Lavoir to his new studio at No. 11, Boulevard de Clichy, near the Place Pigalle.

MAURICE RAYNAL: I helped them with it. And what a change it was! It was Picasso's first "bourgeois" residence in Paris. A studio with a north light, large and airy; and a sunny apartment, with a southern exposure, looking out on the trees of the Avenue Frochot. The building belonged to a cabinet minister—Delcassé, in fact—and he lived there too. Aside from the canvases, we didn't have very much to move. The few old pieces of furniture scarcely filled the maid's room . . .

We continue our expedition, up to the Place de Tertre. Raynal sniffs about him, like a dog on the hunt, searching out whatever remains of the bars, the bistros, the cafés and the cabarets of those vanished years. Then we make a side trip to the oddly provincial-looking house and garden at No. 12, rue Cortot. It too is one of the shrines of the cubist epoch, and even before that it was occupied at one time or another by Pierre Reverdy, Suzanne Valadon, Utrillo, Van Gogh, and Émile Bernard, the friend of Cézanne and Gauguin. It was in this same street that Picasso rented a separate studio at the end of a garden, about 1908, so that he would have a place to work on his large canvases.

We stop for a "little glass" in a bistro, and I seize the opportunity to question Raynal about Manolo . . .

MAURICE RAYNAL: I was very fond of that man, and Picasso adored him. He was ten years older than young Ruiz, and always called him "little Pablo." It was Manolo who predicted Picasso's future . . . And Picasso listened to him in a way he never listened to anyone else. Ugue was probably the only person he permitted to tease him, criticize him, contradict him.

MYSELF: Everyone is always telling me about his petty swindling. Wasn't he able to live from his sculpture?

MAURICE RAYNAL: He was very gifted, but he squandered his talents. He could never set himself to work in a disciplined manner; he was too high-strung, too unconcerned with his future, his success . . . He preferred to live by expedients, and even by petty larcenies. One morning, when Max Jacob was still in bed, he stole his only pair of pants. And then, a few hours later, he brought them back. It wasn't because of a sudden attack of conscience, as Jacob thought at first—it was because none of the old-clothes dealers would take something that was so badly worn. He did the same thing to Léon-Paul Fargue—"borrowed" a suit of clothes from him, and Fargue never saw it again. And when his good friend, the sculptor Paco Durio, was rash enough to lend him his apartment, he came back from Spain and found the walls stripped bare. Manolo had sold Durio's magnificent Gauguin collection to Vollard. "I was dying of hunger," he told his friend innocently, "I didn't have any choice: it was *my* death or *your* Gauguins. I chose your Gauguins." As it happened, Vollard was afraid of being accused of receiving stolen goods, so he returned the paintings. Manolo was also constantly organizing "lotteries." The prize would be a bust or a statue. He sold tickets on them, but the day of the drawing never arrived. He had sold the first prize somewhere else in the meantime. Sometimes all of the tickets had the same number. "I'm too generous," he would say. "I don't want to make anyone jealous." I had a weakness for Manolo. I even took him with me to my garrison at Toul, near Nancy, during my military service. Curious idea, isn't it—doing your military service in the company of a deserter? But he was a wonderful companion. And in spite of the life he led, he was a model of sobriety. He never drank. When I had my little house on the rue de Rennes, I invited some friends one night for duck I had shot on a hunting trip. About midnight we were all a trifle tipsy, except Manolo. He was behaving like something of a wet blanket. Alfred Jarry, who was completely drunk, suddenly leaped up and shouted at him: "Get out of here! Beat it, or I'll kill you!" Manolo didn't move, and the rest of us all laughed. Then Jarry pulled an old rusty revolver from his pocket and—bang! bang!—fired two shots at him. Fortunately he missed. But Manolo was terrified, and raced out of the house like a frightened rabbit.

MYSELF: But was he a good sculptor? Did he have exhibitions of his work?

MAURICE RAYNAL: Yes, he was a good sculptor! But completely unsympathetic to cubism. And when, by some chance, he actually finished a piece of sculpture he would generally have to exchange it for food or lodging. Several of the cabarets in Montmartre had examples of his work. In Barcelona he was in love with the daughter of a woman who owned a dairy shop, and he used to sculpt figures and animals for the girl, in butter. But in spite of everything, his reputation was beginning to spread. Alfred Stieglitz had heard of him, and arranged his first exhibition in New York. Yes, the photographer Stieglitz. He was also the first person to exhibit Picasso and Matisse in the United States. Then, one day, Manolo met Frank Haviland, the heir to the Limoges porcelain fortune. That was the great turning point of his life! Haviland liked to be surrounded with artists, to dabble in being a patron of the arts. He took Manolo under his wing, and rescued him from his chaotic Parisian existence.

MYSELF: And is that when he went to Céret?

MAURICE RAYNAL: Yes, about 1910, after about ten years in Paris. But before he left Montmartre, he had met Totote, a young and very pretty waitress in a bar in the Latin Quarter, and married her. In spite of his bohemian life here, he had always been filled with a nostalgia for Spain. But since he was a deserter, it was impossible for him to return to his own country. He chose Céret as a place to live because he could scent the odors of Catalonia. Kahnweiler offered him a contract that assured him of a modest income, and he was able to go to work at last.

MYSELF: And when did he go back to Spain?

MAURICE RAYNAL: He was always watching for a political change, a declaration of amnesty. The abdication of Alfonso XIII finally permitted him to return home, after forty years of exile.

MYSELF: And Picasso?

MAURICE RAYNAL: He has remained a very close friend. He spent several summers at Céret with Manolo before the 1914 war, with Fernande at first, and then with Eva. And even now he is always delighted to see him again, with Totote and their daughter, Rosaline.

*Wednesday, November 27, 1946*

I start work on the engraved pebbles this morning. Sabartés counts them for me. He counts and recounts them, for fear of making a mistake.

At noon, I am with Picasso. He takes out a curious plank of wood, engraved by Alfred Jarry.

PICASSO: Jarry left several of these bas-reliefs. What does it represent? It isn't always easy to guess. This one is a man with an owl at his feet. You should take a photograph of it some day. Did you know that Jarry always had a live owl in his home? His owls are the ancestors of mine . . .

I have brought him the latest series of my photographs of graffiti, as he has been asking me to do for a long time.

PICASSO: They are really astonishing. What fantastic invention you sometimes find in them . . . I always stop when I see children drawing in the street, on the sidewalk or on a wall. It's surprising—the things that come from their hands. They often teach me something.

I show him these strange faces, created from two or three hollows in the wall, but so evocative, so expressive. In several of his sculptures Picasso seems to have been inspired by them, or rather to have had a meeting with them.

PICASSO: Look at these eyes. They are deep holes cut into the wall. But some of them seem to be protuberant, as if they were done in relief. What causes that? It's not an optical effect. We can see very clearly that they are holes. Our knowledge influences our vision.*

* This important remark of Picasso's carries us back half a century, to the great turning point of our art. Today it is of little importance whether an eye has been treated as a hollow or as a projection, indicated by a button, a black pebble, or a lump of coal. Located within an oval, this sign will always be identified with the eye. D.-H. Kahnweiler has noted that, in Ouobe masks—and Picasso owns one of these—two long cylinders take the place of the eyes. "Picasso did not, of course, imitate Ouobe art," Kahnweiler says, "but the knowledge he drew from it encouraged him to set in motion a total reshaping of the plastic arts of the West, and to renounce all form of imitation . . . The Ouobe masks testified to this

MYSELF: Do you think that there are different "styles" of graffiti for each country? That's a question that interests me.

PICASSO: I'm sure of it. Italian and Spanish graffiti—I know them very well—do not resemble the Parisian graffiti. The phallic symbols you see on the walls of Rome, for instance, are specifically Italian. Rome is very rich in graffiti, as a matter of fact, and you should find it amusing to photograph them. Making up this collection was a good idea on your part. Unless they are photographed, the graffiti may exist, but it is as if they did not. I've done some things in paper myself, but the only way they can continue to exist is through photography. If you come back tomorrow, early, I'll show them to you. And I want you to photograph them. Otherwise, they will be destroyed without ever having lived.

MYSELF: Even now, most of my graffiti no longer exist on their walls. They have been painted over or demolished.

PICASSO: I would love to help you in your research, and I might be able to give you some "leads." One of these days I must take you to visit the prison at Gisors. It contains some extraordinary graffiti. I used to go there often. Boisgeloup is just next door, and I spent hours looking at them. That prison is unique in the world. One prisoner, who was sentenced to twenty years there, spent all of his time covering the walls with graffiti. It's unbelievable! No matter what anyone may say, people were really more humanitarian in those days. Obviously the prisoner was not free, but in his cell he was completely at home. And he made good use of that. It's a round room, very high. The only light came from windows set high up against the ceiling, so the prisoner took his pocketknife—they had let him keep it —and cut a series of niches into the wall, so that he could climb up to the windows whenever he wanted to. And because of that he was able to cover all of the walls of the cell with

---

character of a "symbol" in all its purity . . . Picasso's reliefs of the period 1912–1914 are spectacular testimony to this new state of mind. Their relationship to Ouobe masks is undoubted. If we consider, for example, the representation of the orifice of a guitar by a steel cylinder or a plastic cone—a solution which transforms a projecting surface into a cavity—the analogy to the cylindrical eyes of Ouobe masks is readily apparent. And there are also instances in which a cavity may signify a projection" (*The Sculptures of Picasso*). It is this same characteristic of the *symbol* which so impressed Picasso in the masks of the graffiti.

absolutely splendid graffiti. You really should photograph them some day. They are little masterpieces!

When I leave, I want to take the photographs of the graffiti with me. He hesitates to return them to me.

PICASSO: Would you leave them with me until tomorrow? I would like to study them again, tonight.

*Thursday, November 28, 1946*

As agreed yesterday, I arrive early this morning.

PICASSO: I'm terribly sorry to have upset your morning, but I have to go out. I have an urgent appointment. Could you come back tomorrow? I really want very much to work on those paper sculptures with you. I was looking at them the other day, against the light of the sun, and it was marvelous. They were as translucid as alabaster . . . (*Picasso goes out, then comes back.*) Where is my béret? Have you seen my béret, Sabartés? It's a very precious object, a béret! I only have one. If I lose it, or misplace it . . . Before the war, it didn't matter, you went into a shop and bought another one. But now? Tell me, Sabartés, can you still find bérets in the shops?

I ask him if the little bronze bust of Dora Maar has been returned from the foundry where it was being cast.

PICASSO, *slightly troubled:* Yes, it came back. But a very annoying accident happened. I wanted to give it a patina, and I completely ruined it. I've been wondering if I can still save it. But Dora has another copy of exactly the same bust. Go to see her. I'll call and tell her you're coming.

This morning, for lack of anything better to do, I photograph the big leather portfolio in which Picasso stores his drawings and washes; the entrance door, with the Kanaka sculpture; the little table, covered with pots and brushes, that serves as his "palette"; and then the old Catalan statue of the Virgin, standing in a corner of the vast studio, haloed by a ray of sunlight. I wonder if it was a gift. This Spanish Madonna, so out of place in this room, seems to be one of the few links which still attach Picasso to the country and the religion of his childhood . . .

An hour later I arrived at Dora Maar's apartment in the rue de Savoie. For some time now, she has been studying and painting, and—a fact that deserves underlining—she has managed to keep herself free of Picasso's formidable influence. Her still lifes—a loaf of bread, a pitcher or jug—are extremely austere and recall nothing of her friend's colors or any of the periods of his work.

Dora possesses a considerable Picasso collection. In addition to his numerous portraits of her, there are several still lifes and a drawer filled with little objects created by Picasso's playful, constantly active and inventive fingers.[50] The other day she took them out for me, infinitely carefully, so that I could photograph them: little birds formed from fragments of tin, or wood, or bone; a splinter transformed into a blackbird; a piece of bone eaten away by the sea and made into the head of an eagle. And bits of deception, *trompes-l'oeil* filled with humor and mischief: a charred piece of wood daubed with maroon to become a cigar; a flat bone changed into a long-toothed comb for dogs . . . Picasso has meticulously drawn in the rows of teeth, and enlivened them with a couple of amorous fleas. The dozens of examples of paper or pasteboard cut out with scissors or torn into silhouettes with the fingers are enchanting. The majority of them are made from paper napkins or cigarette packages. The tail of the Q on a *Celtique* package has become a bow tie around the neck of a little man. There are masks of satyrs, faces of children, death's-heads, a long woman's glove, and among the many animals—fish, fox, goats, vultures—there is an extraordinary series of dogs. There is a story connected with these. Dora had a little white dog, which she adored, and one day she lost it. So, to console the grieving mistress, for the next several days Picasso resurrected the little dog at every meal, using paper napkins.[51] The nose, the eyes and the mouth are usually just holes in the paper, most of them burned out with the top of a cigarette or a match. The fluffy paper of the napkin has become the silky, curling white hair and the long, drooping ears of a little dog, looking out at us from beneath his shaggy bangs . . .

When I mention the patina for the bronze casting of her bust, and the accident, Dora bursts out laughing.

DORA MAAR: You mean you don't know how Picasso gave that bust its patina? Well, I'll tell you then. He urinated on it . . . Several days in a row. He was probably too embarrassed to tell you about it. The bronze has become absolutely horrible to look at.

MYSELF: Not really? I've often heard that story—that urine gives bronze a patina. Maillol used to "water" the big statues in his garden every day. He told me that himself, at Marly-le-Roi.

DORA MAAR: Picasso thought so too, but the result was disastrous. The bronze turned completely green, but a hideous green. And to think that it should have been a bust of me!

I go back to the rue des Grands-Augustins, to leave my equipment. Sabartés is there, and we talk about Manolo.

SABARTÉS: I didn't know him in Barcelona, even though we had the same friends and went to the same cabaret. I didn't meet him until my first trip to Paris, in 1901. I remember our meetings as if it were today. I had an appointment with Picasso, in front of the Luxembourg Museum. He arrived with a Catalan friend—it was Manolo. We became great friends after that, and we used to go together to the cafés and cabarets of Montmartre and the Latin Quarter. At that time he didn't speak a single word of French. And he has never lost his violent Spanish accent. Alas! I've lost track of him since he went to live in Céret. You want to see a photograph of him? I don't have one, but I can show you a self-portrait that was reproduced in a German magazine.

And at last I see Manolo's face—the hollow cheeks, the high forehead and bushy eyebrows that Fernande Olivier described this way: "A little fine-boned Spaniard, with too-dark eyes in a too-dark face under too-dark hair . . ."

As I go down the stairs I meet Inés. I had not known that she lived in the same building, beneath Picasso's studio, that she was married to a metallurgist named Gustave, and had a six-month-old son. I am surprised to discover this little family life, seemingly sheltered under Picasso's wing . . .

"Monsieur Brassaï," Inés inquires politely, "would you like to see my Picasso collection?"

I go into the little apartment, which has almost no light and a ceiling so low that you can touch it with an oustretched hand. The walls are covered with Picassos, accented here and there by indifferent prints. There are portraits of Inés, most of them painted as birthday gifts; a very fine India ink drawing of a bull downing a picador's horse; a first proof of one of the "Buffon" series of etchings, representing a guinea hen; a still life in gouache; and some lithographs . . .*

*Friday, November 29, 1946*

An American journalist has come to see me. He is not the first person to imagine that a word from me is sufficient to be welcomed with open arms by Picasso. The fact is that although I have occasionally introduced friends to him, I have always sent unknowns like this about their business. But this young journalist, Mr. Wallace, is tenacious. He has been preparing for this visit for a year. He has staked his whole future career on it. And now that he has established an impressive list of questions to ask, he is ready, and so determined that he would kill me if I refused. I found that likable, so I gave in. We made an appointment for this morning . . .

Picasso is still alone. We discuss the album of his sculptures, which is now virtually finished. The publisher is due to receive the paper very shortly. What is bothering him now is the text. Who should he ask to do it?

PICASSO: And if you wrote it yourself? I'm sure you could do a good job of it. You know my sculpture very well, and we have talked about it a great deal. You write the text; you'll have my complete approval . . .

In my surprise I object that I am not an art critic and I know too little of his work to put his sculpture in its proper place. He insists I must get to work at it, and he will arrange it with the publisher.

I ask him if we can photograph his "sculptured" papers today.

PICASSO: I should have gone out this morning. But I managed to change that—I'm staying here. So we can go to work. I'm just

* Giving some thought to his numerous families, Picasso later bought several apartments on the rue Gay-Lussac, not far from the Luxembourg garden. One of these apartments is occupied by Françoise Gilot, Picasso's two children Claude and Paloma, and Françoise's husband; another by Inés and her family . . . Inés' son, who is now eighteen, often spends his vacation at Picasso's home in the south of France, in the company of Picasso's children, who are about the same age . . .

going to run over to Dora's for a minute, and then I'll be back. Will you wait for me?

I am left with Sabartés. He tells me that the review, *Le Point*, wants to publish a special number about Picasso, and has asked to have me collaborate on it.

SABARTÉS: Kahnweiler is preparing the number, so it is with him that we will have to make the selection from your photos. The thing has been going on for two years now. And do you know why? The letter that was sent to us by the publishers was put on this table. And of course it was quickly buried. It was just found a few days ago. We planned on giving this special number a more or less personal character. Kahnweiler will include some of his conversations with Picasso, and also some documents—perhaps a sampling from the thousands of letters he receives. And I thought it would be amusing if we made the selection from the insulting ones. We could compile an anthology of those! I was just reading them, and filing them. The worst ones are in this pile. Suppose we just pull one out, as if it were a lottery?

And from the pile of letters, which have come here from every corner of the world, we extract this one:

*A group of painters protests against your work, daubings worthy of a madman, even if there were better paintings than yours in the exhibition by the lunatics at Sainte-Anne.*

*Since all of our efforts to halt your disastrous work, which makes a mockery of France—and especially abroad, as the latest conference of English painters proves—have failed, we have decided on your fate last week at the Club du Faubourg and since the Public Powers leave you free, we are going to act . . .*

*And to conclude, I have to tell you some truths about yourself, I personally. I* know *you, you are an* incompetent *who doesn't know how to* paint *or to* draw.

*Put your garbage beside the works of the great artists; Raphael, Michelangelo, Leonardo da Vinci, and you will see what filth you are!*

*And because you are a failure, an incompetent, you have found the "idiot formula," good for imbeciles!*

*But what a disaster for the country, that young artists should follow you! Poor slobs!*

Signed: *A group of painters, real ones!*
*Paris, June 15, 1946.*

Wallace, the American journalist, arrives, with his lengthy, carefully typed questionnaire. I introduce him to Sabartés, who assumes his air of Grand Inquisitor, and submits to this interrogation. He understands English perfectly. After a time he turns to me:

SABARTÉS: The things the Americans can think of to ask! If I had any hair, it would be standing up on my head. Have you read his list? More than fifty questions, and what questions! The exact speed with which Picasso does a painting, an etching, a drawing; the number of works he creates, by day, by week, by month, by year! How many autographs does he give? The number of his works that have been sold, exhibited, are in museums, in his possession, etc. You would have to have a special kind of brain to ask all that. And how foolish to think that Picasso would answer . . .

In the meantime a dozen or so others—more than that, fifteen or twenty perhaps—have come in, most of them foreigners: Swedes, Dutchmen, a good many Americans. They all want to see and hear Picasso, and they are all left standing, waiting for him; standing in this most inhospitable of all antechambers of glory, where there is never a vacant seat. But they are happy nonetheless, because they can already breathe the atmosphere. There are sculptures and gouaches scattered here and there. They look around them, they hunt out objects of interest, whisper to each other: "Very interesting!" "Very beautiful!" . . . My American is beginning to worry. Picasso's absence disturbs him as much as the presence of all these others. I tell him that these morning receptions at the rue des Grands-Augustins always make me think of those Goethe used to hold in Weimar. Universal renown exercises the same attraction and produces the same phenomena. Arriving from Stockholm, from London, from Paris, and even from New York, the visitors of the "sage of Weimar" waited with the same patience and impatience, the same curiosity and veneration—and doubtless with the same quickening of the pulse—the appearance of His Excellency von Goethe.

"Yes, yes! I understand!" the American says excitedly. "Goethe! Weimar! I'll put it in my paper . . ."

But Picasso is late in coming back. What has happened? It is almost noon. Even if he does return now, we will no longer be able to photograph the paper sculptures. I go into the studio and take a few photographs there, waiting. Goethe . . . Weimar

. . . It would be amusing to write a kind of parallel history: *Goethe and Picasso,* two exceptional destinies in their respective centuries. Paradoxical as it may seem at first, the more I think about it the greater number of affinities I find, in their characters, their nature, their loves, their lives. Great visionaries—but with eyes opened wide to the world around them—and a constant sense of curiosity and astonishment. "I see with an eye that feels; I feel with a hand that sees . . ." (Goethe). An early celebrity; juvenile presumption; authority, and ascendancy over those who surround them. "When I pass in front of him, I am constantly surprised by the mystical force of his presence, and automatically incline my head in a kind of bow . . ." (Sabartés, speaking of the young Picasso). *The Sorrows of Werther,* the blue period—romanticism, then romanticism overcome, denied: "All of that is nothing but sentiment" (Picasso). Cubism. "Little by little, objects lifted me up to their level . . ." (Goethe). Lucidity. The thirst to learn—an innate sense of mimicry: to put oneself in the skin of others; to grasp at all the forms of existence. A stomach and digestive system of cast iron. "The highest form of genius is that which is capable of welcoming everything, of appropriating everything to itself, without being harmed by it in any way . . ." (Goethe). *To give without giving oneself; to take without being taken.* Gertrude Stein and Charlotte von Stein—even the names—educator and source of inspiration, playing almost the same roles of manager, Egeria. The satiric impulse, a taste for farce—the mischievous side of Mephistopheles, more ironic than satanic. Sensuality that is never dormant. Eroticism. The violence of passions. Devotion to love. Ability to shed the skin. Constant rejuvenation, with the appearance of each new feminine countenance: exaltation, an outburst of creative energy, the birth of a new work. Love as a springboard, always subordinate to something else, something that surpasses it. Similarity on an "egocentric" level: "Who is going to take my place, and write what I have in my head?" (Goethe). "Obviously it is only the man who has been most sensitive who can become the coldest and the hardest, since he is forced to clothe himself in a solid armor, for self-protection—and very often that armor becomes a heavy burden . . ." (Goethe). Creative power; technical ability and mastery of tools and talents; capacity for breathing life into all forms of matter. A thirst for the new—Faust, the perpetual malcontent whose thirst is never satisfied. The baffling novelty of each new work. "When they think I am in Weimar, I am already in Erfurt . . ." (Goethe). Incredible activity. Universal, and constantly increasing fame. Never-ending youthfulness. Developing solitude . . .

I hear the chattering of the crowd in the vestibule. I am just photographing one of the big studio windows, with a bronze head in the foreground, when the door opens abruptly and Picasso comes in, accompanied by Dora Maar. He is visibly shaken. He has forced a passage through the horde of visitors without saying a word to anyone.

DORA MAAR, *trying desperately to restrain her tears:* There was absolutely nothing wrong with her. Even this morning she was in wonderful spirits. We talked on the telephone for a long time. We were going to have lunch together . . . She collapsed just like that . . . She lost consciousness . . . And in three hours it was all over. A cerebral hemorrhage . . .

PICASSO, *in a shattered tone:* Nush is gone! Nush Éluard is dead! We loved her so . . .

DORA MAAR: Éluard is in Switzerland. We sent him a telegram . . . Nush was everything in the world to him . . . Everything . . . Everything . . . His wife, his friend, his secretary, his guardian angel . . . A year ago he said to me: "I can't imagine my life without Nush. I can't envisage the thought of losing her. I couldn't get along without her." It's a terrible thing for him . . .

In the vestibule the news has already spread. The visitors are dismayed. They will not see Picasso today . . . the audience is postponed. Poor Wallace folds up the list of his fifty questions.

Everyone has left. Marcel closes the doors. His earthy common sense is the voice of the Greek chorus, commenting on the events: "Ah, what it is to be what we are . . . We are swept away from this earth so swiftly . . ."*

* Nush's sudden, completely unexpected death plunged Éluard into a profound melancholy. In losing her, he also lost his confidence in life, his hope in the world, and even in poetry. The great singer of love, of happiness, of joy in living, fell silent. His friends—Picasso and Dora Maar among them—did everything possible to ease his pain, but they could only stand by, helpless witnesses to his despair. Not until later did the event which had overwhelmed his life burst forth in his poetry, like a sob, a cry of revolt:

*We shall not grow old together.*
*The day is too bright: time overflows.*
*The love I wore so lightly*
*has become the weight of anguish . . .*

*Friday, December 13, 1946*

Yesterday, when I returned home, I found a telephone message from Sabartés: "Brassaï, can you come to see Picasso, as soon as possible?" This morning he called again.

SABARTÉS: Come at once! Picasso has done something surprising . . . He asked me to telephone you . . . What is it? I can't explain it on the telephone . . . You'll see . . . A surprise! Jump into a taxi, right away. He might change his mind . . .

I find Picasso surrounded by a mass of people, most of them foreigners. He is wearing a jacket of thick red wool with big black checks—undoubtedly a gift from an American visitor. I have scarcely said good morning when Sabartés hauls me off to the studio: "Come with me! Leave all of these bores, and come with me! I'll get rid of them in a few minutes. Look!"

And what do I see? *The Artist in His Studio!* There he is, large as life, standing before an enormous canvas, wearing a white smock, holding a palette and a cluster of brushes in his hand. There he is, studying that enigmatic painting which was first called *La Sérénade* and then *L'Aubade:* two women, one of them nude, reclining on a couch, reminiscent of Rousseau's *La Bohémienne Endormie;* the other one fully clothed, seated on a chair, with a mandolin on her knees. Unquestionably the simultaneous presence in his life of two women had played a part in the birth of this picture, and of a series of other canvases with the same theme.*

SABARTÉS, *noting the surprised expression on my face:* What do you think of it? The idea for it came to him on the spur of the moment. And he carried it out at once.

I study the figure of *The Artist*. It is the 1900 mannequin, to which he had added arms and a large bronze head, that Picasso has decked out in this fashion. In his haste to rejoin us, he has dismissed his visitors. His eyes are sparkling with mischief:

"I wanted it as a surprise for you! Quite a character, isn't it? Did you notice the palette? I received it from the United States. They make them of unbreakable glass; Pyrex, I think they call it. As a palette it's worthless. You can't see the colors properly—it's absurd! But just the same, a glass palette is a magical object![52] It was the palette that gave me the idea for this disguise: the 'artist in his studio,' with his luminous, radiant palette!"

I take several photos of the figure. Picasso helps me, enjoying himself as much as a college boy who has played a good trick on a friend. When we have finished, he brings out a few statuettes.

PICASSO: I have located several of them, but, alas, only one of them is intact. I'll have to reglue the others. But when and how? Next week? They are just little figurines of clay . . . I forgot to have them baked. And dried clay is as fragile as it can be; it breaks, chips . . .

I give Picasso the photographs of the graven pebbles, and also some that I have taken of various aspects of his studio.

MYSELF: Canvases photographed in their natural surroundings seem more alive to me than just reproductions of them. You see the picture as it is, in its exact dimensions. Basically nothing is so deceptive as a reproduction! The other day you showed me one of the *Bacchanale* and I took it for a very large canvas. I was surprised to learn that it was actually just a small gouache.

PICASSO *laughs mischievously and extracts the* Bacchanale *from a portfolio:* There it is! I painted it "after Poussin" during the bloody days of the liberation, in the month of August. There was shooting going on everywhere. The tanks going by shook the house.

* Painted in 1942, *L'Aubade* now belongs to the Musée d'Art Moderne in Paris.

I look at the *Bacchanale:* a whirlpool of desire, a confusion of bodies . . . Even in this little gouache, the battle is raging. And although he had based it on Poussin, Picasso had given free rein to his eroticism in those tragic days. Surrounding the bearded faun and the full-bodied nymph with the aggressive breasts, there is a mêlée of other bodies, a hand-to-hand struggle. Hands and legs appear from everywhere, but no one could tell to which body they belong . . .

PICASSO: In the first days after the liberation, an American photographer made a reproduction of it in colors. He was the first American who came to see me . . . I can't think of his name. But you are right to prefer a picture photographed in its own surroundings. I always begged Zervos not to confine himself to simple reproduction. A picture can often be better understood when it is surrounded by its own life . . .

And we return, for the thousandth time, to the subject of these paper sculptures which unforeseen circumstances have thus far prevented us from photographing. I could have done them without Picasso's presence, but he has insisted on being there as I worked, since he thinks that the final touch to the work is of great importance in these fragile, ephemeral objects.

PICASSO: I want to do them with you. We must arrange to have an entire day for it. It takes a long time to find the best angle for the picture, the best lighting . . . But when could we have a whole day, just for that?

### *Tuesday, December 17, 1946*

Great confusion. A truckload of coal has at last been delivered. Laden with heavy sacks, their faces streaked with soot, the delivery men come and go, while Marcel and Inés stuff the fireplaces and stoves. This winter is a hard one . . .

SABARTÉS, *grumbling:* What good will all this coal really do? In this Siberian weather, that enormous studio can never be well heated. Wouldn't it be better to restrict ourselves to a few rooms? The stove swallows the coal as fast as the sacks come up, but it doesn't give out the slightest degree of heat.

Picasso makes only a fleeting appearance. I can photograph only one statuette in terra cotta. He has not had the time to prepare the others. Then I have a conversation with Sabartés. I have just read his recently published book, *Portraits et Souvenirs.* Delightful reading—a disorder which is sometimes baffling but seemingly methodical. Like a faithful dog who romps behind his master, following him always, but darting off on a thousand twists and turns, Sabartés—in the course of a single page—will leap from turn-of-the-century Barcelona to this vestibule swarming with visitors, to the ringing of the telephone, to Marcel announcing someone else, to the letters to be sorted and read and filed . . . It pleases me that this man who has found his god has not devoted himself blindly to his cult, but also criticizes him in his mordant fashion, teases him about his eccentricities . . . He is not embarrassed at the mention of his contradictions, his uncertainties, his pedantry, his fits of temper, all the weaknesses which form his strength . . . With a bitterness he makes no attempt to hide, he even alludes to the quarrel which separated him from his friend for more than a year. This little biography, whose intent is to sketch a portrait of Picasso, also sketches one of Sabartés, as if in filigree: in spite of his extreme discretion, it is almost a self-portrait. It reveals his touchy humility, his prideful modesty, his voluntary self-effacement—the submissive witness who will never permit his personal note to be imposed on Picasso.

I congratulate him on his mercurial, irreplaceable book.

SABARTÉS: So—now you have read the history of my portraits? It was Picasso who urged me to write down these souvenirs. One day in Royan, when I was discouraged and depressed, he advised me to work, to write. It was then that it occurred to me to use the portraits he had painted of me as a connecting thread for my memories. As chance would have it, he had done a portrait of me in each of the periods of my life I shared with him . . . What do you think of the book? Tell me your criticisms.

MYSELF: There is only reproach that I can make to you: you say nothing about Picasso's love affairs . . . nothing about women . . . as if they didn't exist. And by this discretion, you somewhat distort the facts themselves. You have Picasso going off on solitary trips, leaving the reader to feel sorry for him, when in reality he was not alone . . . which changes everything. Why do you never mention the women? You surely recognize their importance in his life, his work? And you are better placed than anyone else to tell about them.

SABARTÉS: Too well placed. My lips are sealed. To me that subject is taboo. And for that matter I don't know what Picasso feels, in his innermost heart, about women and about love. I know that people think he confides everything in me, that I am the repository for his most secret thoughts. Forget it. It simply isn't true. When I am alone with him, we rarely talk. We present a perfect picture of dual solitude. As for his love affairs, the only thing I can testify to is their stimulating effect on his painting, which always follows the graph of his love . . . But is it necessary to talk about women? To count off those who have been important in his life, as if they were so many beads on a rosary? I don't think so. The women pass . . . The work remains . . .

Paulo, Picasso's son, arrives. He is living in Switzerland now. He resembles his mother much more than his father.

*Friday, December 20, 1946*

The other day I had dinner with Gilberte at La Coupole. And among all the diners eagerly consuming shellfish and other *fruits de mer* in this enormous café-restaurant of Montparnasse, I met Henri Matisse. In a splendid mood, with a large-checked cap on his head, he was eating heartily, accompanied by the beautiful Lidia.

MATISSE: We are staying in Paris for another fortnight. I wish you would come to see me—Boulevard Montparnasse—because I have been thinking about you. Before we left the South I said to Lidia: "When he was here in Vence this summer, Brassaï admired that amadou hat that was woven by the Rumanian shepherds. I should take it to him in Paris. Put it in with our things." You tried it on, and it was very becoming to you. Its soft buckskin color sets off the black of your eyes. You should take a photograph of yourself with that extraordinary hat.

Surprised, I thanked him for the thought of me, even though I was sure I had said nothing in Vence about wanting to see myself wearing that bizarre hat. In order not to deceive him, however, I promised to pick it up at his apartment. "I've made my offer," he said as he left us, "now take advantage of it!"

This afternoon I climb the stairs to see him in the building at No. 132, Boulevard Montparnasse. God knows I know this building well! Coincidence: Gilberte lives there . . . From her rooms, the view down to Matisse's apartment occasionally provides the sight of Lidia hanging his still-damp drawings on lengths of wire or cord. Sometimes the entire kitchen is filled with this curious laundry, suspended from clothespins . . . The first time I entered this apartment, about ten years ago, it was to photograph Matisse with his birds, most of which were rare or exotic breeds. He used to amuse himself by offering a selection of woolen threads, chosen from the colors of his palette, to a duo of "workers" who then set to work with their beaks and wove little "Matisse" tapestries in the bars of their cage.

Lidia leads us into the big central room where, at the time of my last visit a few months ago, I had found Matisse in bed, holding great pieces of colored papers and cutting out figures reminiscent of Oceania. As swiftly as he had finished them, Lidia would hang them on the wall . . .

MATISSE: The memories of my trip to Tahiti have only come back to me now, fifteen years later, and in the form of haunting images: madrepore coral, fish, birds, jellyfish, sponges . . . It's curious, isn't it, that all of these enchantments of sea and sky provoked almost no response in me at the time? I came back from the islands with empty hands. I didn't even bring back any photographs, even though I had bought a very expensive camera. But once I arrived there, I hesitated: "If I take photos," I told myself, "of everything I see now in Oceania, in the future I will see only those poor substitutes. And perhaps the photos will prevent my impressions from aging and deepening." I was right, I think. It's more important to absorb things completely than to try and seize them on the run. Now I am cutting out all of these images and elements, and fastening them on the walls, just temporarily. The little lines represent the line of the horizon . . . I don't know yet what will come of it. It may be panels, or wall hangings . . .

All of these images have now disappeared from the walls. I ask him what has become of them.

MATISSE: I made some large panels from them. Then they went to England, and were "published" there: an edition limited to thirty copies, printed on linen, with the motifs in white on a beige background.

In the place of the Tahitian images on the wall, there is now a photographic enlargement of one of Matisse's canvases, on which he has traced several curving lines in charcoal.

MATISSE: I had that photo of my painting made so that I could do a tapestry from it. I'm in the midst of transforming it now. Tapestry is very different from oil painting. It is subject to other laws . . . I'm going to indicate my "color scheme" on a black panel, and that will be all that is needed for the work to be done.

But Matisse, who is always avid for news, is literally trembling with impatience to ask me about Picasso's latest words and actions. For forty years he has been his friend and his rival, his *bête noire* and his comrade-in-arms . . . I remind him of something that happened last year, at the time of their joint exhibition in the Victoria and Albert Museum in London. Matisse had shown me a bulky collection of English articles and reviews of the exhibition, and then had said, with some bitterness, and sadness too: "It's Picasso, not I, who received the majority of the insults. They humor me. Beside him, of course, I always look like a gentle little girl." And that had reminded me of Picasso's joking remark: "Braque is my wife . . ." which he later altered to: "Braque, my *ex*-wife . . ."

He begins his questioning: "How is he? What is he doing? What is happening in his love life?" The smallest of Picasso's actions, the least important of the things he says, the daily events of his life, interest Matisse, fascinate him . . . In Vence he had told me: "Every year I send a case of oranges to Picasso. He displays them in his studio, and tells every one of his visitors: 'Look at those, admire them; they are Matisse's oranges . . .' And no one dares touch them or eat one of them. In exchange Picasso sends me buyers. Recently I had a visit from two men who came on his recommendation. They both had fine old international names. They bought a picture from me, and even paid a very good price for it, in dollars and *in cash*. But . . . the dollars were counterfeit. By the time I found out about it, they were long gone . . . They were crooks . . ."

I tell him the story of Picasso's idea for disguising his mannequin with the bronze head as "the artist in his studio," with a transparent palette in his hand.

MATISSE: Undoubtedly a gift from Paul Rosenberg. I received one too, a palette of Plexiglas . . . What a ridiculous idea! A transparent palette! To see colors properly, it has to be just the reverse, opaque . . . I haven't even tried the one that was sent

43. Drawing by Brassaï

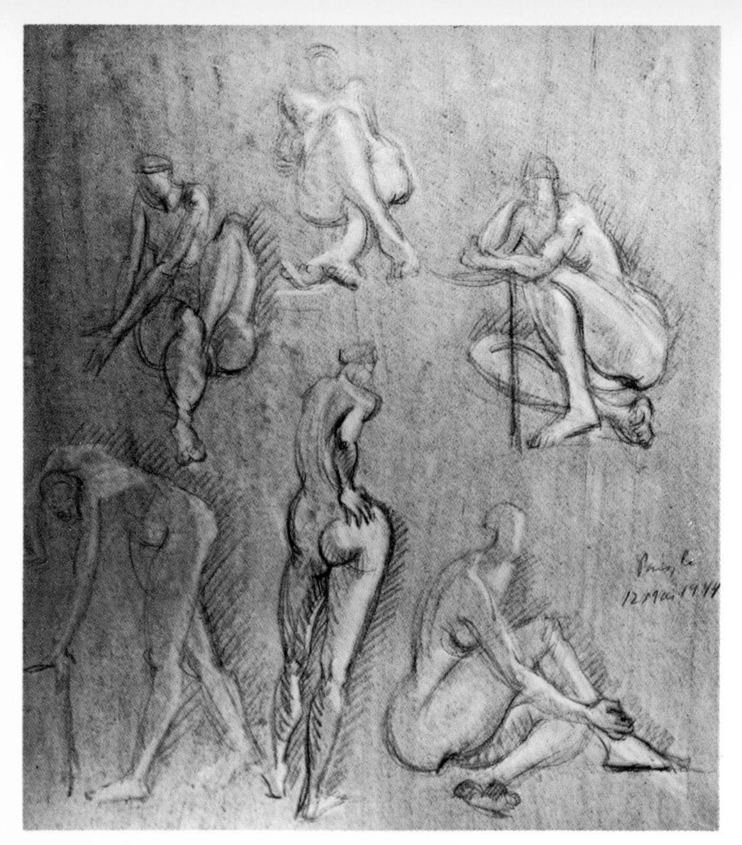

44. 45. & 46. Drawings by Brassaï

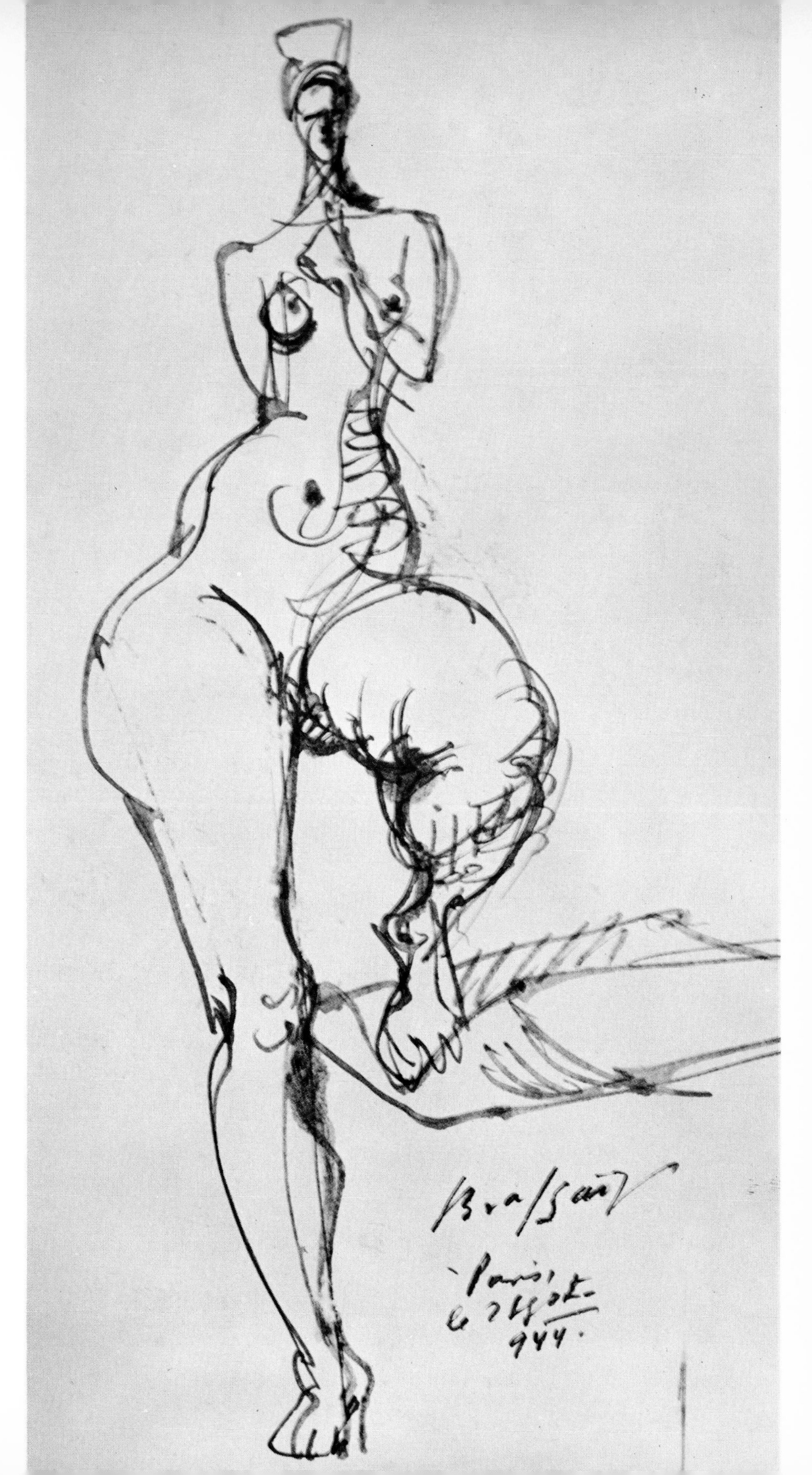

47. Paul Eluard, 1944

*. . . a three-room apartment on the third floor, . . . a chapel of art and poetry in the heart of La Chapelle.*

48. Marina de Berg and Roland Petit in the ballet *Rendez-vous;* first produced on June 15, 1945, written by Jacques Prévert, photographic sets designed by Brassaï, interior curtain by Picasso, costumes by Mayo, and music by Kosma

49. The Bateau-Lavoir, where Picasso and Juan Gris once had studios

50. Paper figures made by Picasso for Dora Maar

*. . . a drawer filled with little objects created by Picasso's playful, constantly active and inventive fingers.*

51. *Dora had a little white dog, which she adored, and one day she lost it. So, to console the grieving mistress, for the next several days Picasso resurrected the little dog at every meal, using paper napkins.*

52. PICASSO: *Did you notice the palette? I received it from the United States . . . Pyrex I think they call it. As a palette it's worthless. You can't see the colors properly—it's absurd! But just the same, a glass palette is a magical object!*

to me: everything you see through glass is difficult. Speaking of that, have you seen my film?

I had seen it, in fact, just a few days before, at a conference devoted to Matisse in the great amphitheater of the Sorbonne. The last time I had seen the artist in Vence, he was still feeling the effects of the filming. "It's a considerable enterprise, being filmed," he had told me, "but I submitted to it willingly. You know yourself better when you have seen your own image on the screen." I had not very much liked the sequences showing the progression of a canvas through the various stages to its definitive state, nor those which showed his hand painting, in slow motion. I found them unconvincing, even labored, and I tell him this. But the appearance of Matisse himself, in his great cape, his hands in white gloves, was impressive. He doubtless wanted to leave this image of himself for posterity.

MATISSE: I was very uncomfortable during the showing of the film. Many things in it embarrassed me. It is indiscreet to reveal your private countenance while you are at work. I understand why Bonnard refused to lend himself to such a display. The same producers also wanted to do a film about him.

MYSELF: I happened to be at Bonnard's house in Le Cannet just at that time. The loss of his wife had afflicted him terribly. "Photograph anything you want," he told me, "except my face . . ." Shortly afterward, knowing that I was primarily interested in doing a portrait of him, he was remorseful and modified his original statement: "You can photograph me, if you want to, but only from the back . . ."

MATISSE: In the middle of the crowd at that showing, I felt naked, as if I had lost my pants. But it was an unforgettable lesson for me. I was completely stunned by the slow motion. What a strange thing it is! Suddenly you see the work of the hand, completely instinctive, surprised by the camera and separated from anything else. This sequence overwhelmed me. I kept asking myself: "But is it really you who is doing that? What the devil could I have been doing at that moment?" And I had absolutely nothing to go by. I didn't recognize either my hand or my canvas. I was really anxious, and asked myself: "Is it going to stop? Is it going on? What direction is it going to take?" I was dumbfounded to see my hand go on and on, until it reached a final point. As a rule, when I start a drawing I have a kind of stagefright, or something even stronger than that. But I have never been so frightened as I was sitting there, watching my poor hand start out on the adventure, in slow motion, as if I had been drawing with my eyes closed . . .

"With my eyes closed . . ." Spontaneity, the obscure power of the hand, removed from control of the eyes and even of the brain, has always preoccupied Matisse. He has wanted to know what it might do if it were abandoned to its fate, as if cut off from the body. It is possible that Picasso's exercises of this kind have played a part in his interest in it. The drawings Picasso did around 1933, in the darkness or with his eyes closed, in which the organs—eyes, nose, ears, lips—no longer occupied their habitual place, were undoubtedly the starting point for the dislocated faces which appeared in his canvases some years later. One day, in 1939, in his studio on the rue des Plantes, Matisse had done a drawing for me with a mask around his eyes. It was a head, drawn with a piece of chalk, almost in a single line. In this very expressive portrait, the eyes, the mouth, the nose, the ears all overlap, as they do in Picasso's deliberately distorted faces.[53] Matisse was so enchanted with it that he asked me to take a photograph of him standing in front of the door on which he had drawn it. There can be little doubt that this particular work of Matisse now exists only in my photograph . . .

MATISSE: And have you seen the film on Fernand Léger? The one that was made in the United States? It's very amusing and unpretentious, although the colors are frightful. The red of Léger's face—awful, awful! You see him making a salad. "Everyone should know how to make a salad!" He puts in salt, pepper, mustard, and adds the oil and vinegar. Then he says: "Everyone should also know how to make a *pot-au-feu!*" Then you see him picking up a ladle and tasting the *pot-au-feu.* And at last you see him in the act of painting, as if painting were the logical sequel to good cooking. "Everyone should also know how to paint . . ." Then he juggles with bits of colored wood. He puts them on the canvas. But he puts on too many of them, everything becomes confused, and you don't understand anything more. His cooking was a good deal more convincing than his painting.

Matisse bursts out laughing, his teeth gleaming behind the silver screen of beard and moustache. I show him some of my graffiti. He studies them with interest, especially those which are concerned with the feminine sex.

MATISSE: Ever since the earliest times, it has been represented in more or less the same fashion: a coffee bean. Do you know the red-light district of Toulon? You will find this symbol everywhere on the walls there. And each of the bordellos carries this coffee bean as its emblem. Sometimes it's painted on the wall, sometimes cut into it . . .

I ask him if he has recovered completely from his illness.

MATISSE: The operation produced a curious shock in me. Before it, I was always very bad at arithmetic. Now, I have almost an infatuation with figures. They run around in my head all the time. The operation must have acted on my numbers bump . . . The effect of shocks is always unpredictable. One of my publishers, after having an operation, could no longer remember anything that had happened before it. It had erased his past life. And once I was cured of a head cold by snuffing tobacco. I sneezed ten times, twenty times, and it was gone . . . The theory of shock is very fashionable at the moment, in fact: electroshock and such things. But perhaps you remember? Picasso himself, when he was suffering so badly from sciatica, about ten years ago, was finally cured by a doctor who applied some kind of electroshock to the base of his nose . . .

When I leave him I speak to Lidia about the famous amadou hat. She tells me:

"Monsieur Matisse is very fond of that hat . . . It's very fragile, and inflammable. If the ash from a cigarette were to fall on it, it would go off like a fuse. And since you are a smoker, Monsieur Matisse would prefer that you didn't take the hat with you and took your portrait in it right here . . ."

## *Friday, December 28, 1946*

At eight o'clock this morning, a violent, continuous ringing of the doorbell awakens me abruptly. Someone is shouting my name in the corridor, pounding at the door. When I open it, I am confronted with a big man wearing snow boots and a black fur hat.

"I want to see Picasso!" he shouts in English. "I want to see Picasso! Now! Now! I am in a hurry!"

He urges me to get dressed, quickly. The taxi is waiting for us downstairs. "I am in a hurry! Now! Now! Take me to Picasso!" Furious at having been awakened in this manner by this madman, I refuse. He explains that he has been sent to me by Carl Holty, and takes a letter from my friend from a pocket. I tell him to send the taxi away. No one can disturb Picasso at this hour in the morning.

"I don't have a minute to lose," he insists. "I just arrived at Orly. I want to hold a Picasso exhibition in New York, the first one since the war . . . And I have to get in ahead of Rosenberg, outdo him completely! It's a question of hours, minutes . . ."

The man's name is Samuel Kootz. He has just opened a gallery near Rosenberg's in New York. He is primarily concerned with American abstract painting. His enormous briefcase is stuffed with gifts . . . He takes out a copy of Sidney Janis' *Picasso,* a book which has just been published in New York. Kootz points out several paintings reproduced in it, and asks me if they are still available. He also asks dozens of other questions: if Picasso has broken with Rosenberg, if he still sells him paintings, etc. . . .

Harriet and Sidney Janis came to see me at the beginning of the year—in February, I think—asking my collaboration on a book in which they planned to reproduce Picasso's work in the period 1939 to 1946; his entire production during the war and occupation, which was still unknown to the American public . . . Thus, the author could announce proudly: "None of the originals of these paintings has yet been seen in our country . . ." I photographed several of Picasso's *motifs* for them: the interior of Dora Maar's apartment, the collection of Madame Cuttoli . . .

Janis was a manufacturer of shirts whose passion for painting had drawn him away from his profession, to the despair of his brother. As early as 1930, he possessed a fine collection of modern paintings, and also of American primitives, on which he had published a very handsome book. Another of his publications was devoted to surrealist and abstract art in the United States . . .

At ten o'clock I arrive at Picasso's with Kootz. I introduce him to Sabartés. And while the art dealer, overjoyed at having arrived at his goal, begins to ferret about in the vestibule, Sabartés takes me aside: "Another American? Where the devil did you fish this one out? I wonder if we will see Picasso today . . . He worked very late last night . . . He is still asleep . . ." Scarcely has he pronounced these words than the sound of steps on the stairway announces Picasso's arrival. He is in a radiant mood. Kootz is lucky. He opens his cumbersome briefcase, like one of the wise men offering his gifts, and proceeds to bring out a box of cigars, some tins of tobacco, cartons of cigarettes, a pipe and cleaners for it, all of them things which are still rare in Paris. Picasso never stops repeating, in English: "Thank you very much! Thank you very much!"

He laughs and turns to me:

"That's the only thing I can say in English. Since the liberation of Paris, the Americans have offered me so much chocolate, tobacco, tea and coffee, so many cigarettes and shirts and hats that the least I could do was learn how to say "thank you" to them . . ."

Kootz also takes out Sidney Janis' book, which Picasso promptly snatches from his hands. I love this curiosity in him, this pawing impatience to gallop straight ahead to the goal. On the cover of the book, there is a reproduction in color of his great 1942 canvas: *Nu Debout et Nu Couché* or *L'Aubade.*

PICASSO, *leafing through the book:* Why, this isn't bad at all! In fact, it's very good! Don't you think so? Of all the books that have been published on my work, it's perhaps the most successful . . . And what a good idea to have supplied some photographs of the *motifs* of my paintings: my window, with the rooftops; Dora; the tip of the island, with the statue of Henri IV; the banks of the Seine; Notre-Dame. I didn't copy anything of all that . . . But the photos prove that I grasped the reality, that the essential is there . . .

Picasso turns and returns the pages: seven years of paintings and sculptures. Sometimes he exclaims abruptly, and laughs his piercing laugh . . .

PICASSO: But this picture that is reproduced here no longer exists! I made another one from it! And this one? Changed, unrecognizable . . . This head that you see here, I erased it completely . . . And in this still life, the pot has become an owl since it was reproduced. I don't know what is happening to me at the moment, but I am possessed with a kind of rage to rework my old paintings. So their reproductions no longer evoke anything but ghosts . . .

Occasionally, also, his features contort in a grimace, because it must be admitted: the color reproductions are frightful . . .

PICASSO: Why do they insist on it, when the color isn't right? I think a black and white reproduction, if it translates the values faithfully, is more complete and gives a more truthful idea of the picture . . .

He is indignant when he comes across the portrait of Dora Maar, in a green blouse striped with red, and a collar of white lace, painted October 9, 1942.

MYSELF: I'm particularly fond of that portrait, especially the blouse . . . It's a beautiful piece of painting . . .

PICASSO: It pleases me that you should have noticed the blouse. I invented it completely, as a matter of fact—Dora never wore it. Whatever people may say or think about my "facility," it happens—even to me—to struggle over a painting for a long time . . . How I sweated over that blouse . . . For months I painted it and then repainted it . . .

MYSELF: Like Cézanne, with Vollard's shirt. He worked on that part of the picture alone more than a hundred times . . .

PICASSO: Yes—he was so strict as a rule, so dissatisfied, but he was content with that shirt . . . And I must confess that I am content with my blouse . . . At first I painted some bars and a jug of water and a loaf of bread in the background of this canvas, but then I took them out . . .

Kootz begins exhibiting a series of reproductions, and commenting on them. Sabartés translates his words for us:

"I have decided to stimulate abstract painting in the United States. The only kind of any importance for the future . . . I am a patron of the arts . . . I finance six painters who are one hundred percent American: William Baziotes, Carl Holty, Glarner, Browne, Gottlieb, Motherwell . . . They all work for me . . ."

I think of Cocteau, who told us the other day: "The poor youngsters in New York! They get a kick in the rump if they dare draw anything recognizable . . . They are trained for the abstract from the minute they leave their cradles . . ."

The American dealer talks about his stable of painters like a horse breeder about his thoroughbreds . . . But he is coming to the purpose of his visit. He explains to Sabartés the idea for this exhibition in New York. There is no need for Picasso to lend him canvases. He wants to buy them, all of them . . . Sabartés, who was suspicious at first, now judges the propositions of the Yankee visitor worthy of interest . . . He urges Picasso to show him his canvases. We go up to the studio. Kootz is in seventh heaven: "Beautiful! Very beautiful!" he repeats. Occasionally he also says, "*Formidable! Formidable!*" the only French word he knows aside from "*Merci*" and "*Je vous aime*" . . . But once in a while, turning to me, he says, "I don't like them very much, they are not abstract enough!" Nothing is abstract enough for him.

Tirelessly Picasso brings out his canvases: still lifes, with jugs and pitchers, with skulls of men and sheep, with mirrors, candlesticks, and leeks. And also the series of portraits of women.

"I think," he says to the American merchant, "that these represent the 'portrait' of the woman of today . . . In the past years I have had occasion to study her at close hand in the Métro . . ."

He reserves the climax of the show for the more recent canvases, painted in Antibes, and invaded by the elements of the sea: still lifes with fish, eels, octopuses, cuttlefish, and especially with sea urchins, whose warm brown color and prickly structure have particularly attracted him . . . But Kootz never ceases shaking his head and murmuring: "It isn't abstract enough! It isn't abstract enough!" Finally, after much beating about the bush, he selects nine canvases: *Jeune Fille au Chapeau, Tête, La Femme Assise, Coq, Tête au Fond Chartreuse, Tête de Femme, Femme avec Tête d'Agneau, Marin, Plante de Tomates.* Then he goes off with Sabartés to discuss the matter of prices . . .

I am left alone with Picasso. He shows me the most recent canvases, with owls.

PICASSO: This is what is running around in my head right now . . . At Antibes I often worked late at night, and the cries of a screech owl, the only inhabitant of the dismantled tower, kept me company . . . Then, one day, when he had been hurt, the author of these cries suddenly appeared. I held him in my hand. He became my friend and companion . . .

And I see the silhouette of the bird, a stocky oval perched on a rustic chair, reappear in several of the paintings.

I show him the photographs of "the artist in his studio," standing before the canvas. Then I remark to him that these photographs remind me a little of some of the pictures he is painting right now . . .

PICASSO: That's perfectly understandable. Although I don't copy anything, my surroundings appear in my canvases in one manner or another . . .

MYSELF: Cézanne never wanted to touch his brushes at night . . .

PICASSO: He had nothing but a kerosene lamp! That light was very yellow, and obviously it falsified colors . . . But with the kind of projectors we have today, giving a light just like that of daylight, we can easily paint at night . . . My own night lighting is magnificent; I even prefer it to natural light. You must come some night to see it. This light that sets off every object, these deep shadows that surround the canvases and project themselves up to the beams—you'll find them in most of my still lifes, because they are almost all painted at night . . . No matter what the setting, it becomes the substance of ourselves, its colors become ours, its forms a reflection of our nature . . .

Picasso then brings me a minuscule canvas representing Paris of this July 14. A little marvel. With a few strokes of the brush he has brought to life the quais, the ranks of Parisian houses, Notre-Dame, the trees, and the flags streaming in the wind. Ever since he has lived in France this festival of Bastille Day has been his greatest delight. He finds in it something of the bustle of the crowd in the streets of Andalusia, the dances in the public squares of Catalonia, the colorful revelry of the *Feria* . . . But the fourteenth of July of the year just passed has caused a very particular emotion in him. This three-day and three-night festival of dancing and gaiety, with its fireworks and its parade, was also a festival of liberated France . . .

PICASSO: We were deprived of this national holiday for five years. This first Bastille Day after the liberation moved me, so I painted it.

The tiny size of the picture makes me think of Hokusai, and of one of his feats.

MYSELF: Did you know that Hokusai once drew two pigeons on a grain of rice? He did it in an inn, as relaxation from the fatigue of the enormous picture—perhaps the largest painting ever done—which he had painted that same day.

PICASSO *pricks up his ears:* I never knew that he also painted large canvases.

MYSELF: The poor man was constantly being told that he was just a painter of little things, and finally he could stand it no longer and decided to demonstrate what he could do. His pupils prepared an enormous frame for him, as large as the façade of a six-story house. They covered it with paper. On the day of the demonstration Hokusai walked up and down across the panel, dragging behind him sacks of rice he had soaked in ink. The crowd that had gathered to watch could make nothing of the sequence of furrows he traced out in this manner. Then he took some brooms he had also soaked in ink, and splattered the panel with these. The crowd still understood nothing, but when the artist gave the order to lift the frame to a vertical position—he had constructed a whole system of cords and pulleys for this—everyone recognized in this gigantic image the features of Dharma, the god of tea . . . The legend of Dharma is magnificent, by the way . . . He was a priest who was overcome by sleep during his prayers, and was so infuriated by his weakness that he tore out his eyes and hurled them away from him. The plant that grew in the spot where they fell to earth is reputed to guard against sleep—tea.

PICASSO: I didn't know that story. I do remember one about Hokusai painting a picture with chickens, but I don't recall the circumstances.

MYSELF: That took place at the palace of a prince who wanted to own a "painting" by Hokusai. The artist ordered a long roll of paper spread out across the floor, and then traced a few waving blue lines across it. After this, he took the chickens, dipped their feet in red ink and let them run across the roll of paper. And everyone immediately recognized the Tatsouta River, whose autumn floods are sprinkled with fallen leaves of maple, looking like the tracks left by the feet of the chickens . . .

If these improvisations of Hokusai fascinate Picasso, it is because he has a great deal in common with him: an intense curiosity about form in all of its aspects; the power of seizing life on the wing and capturing it in a concise and flowing line; a patient attention, followed by a lightning execution . . . Like Picasso, Hokusai experimented with everything, refused nothing. He refused to confine himself to normal pictorial techniques, used whatever tools were available—for example, the tip of an egg, dipped in ink—loved to improvise, to imitate, and did all of these things with humor, with a comic flair, or with tenderness or cruelty . . . For that matter, isn't there something Japanese about Picasso's gift for creating objects from nothing at all? The amusing and marvelous surprises he can extract from a bit of wood, a pebble, a paper napkin—aren't these close to the feats of Hokusai? And this propensity for never relaxing the activity of his hands, for so much as a single day in the course of a long lifetime?

As we are talking, I cannot take my eyes from the little table, strewn with twisted, empty tubes, piles of brushes, stained and crumpled pages of newspaper—resembling the litter of a battlefield on the morning after the battle . . .

PICASSO: My "palette" is very much alive today . . . I painted until late last night. I was too tired . . . I just left it in that disorder . . .

I take a photograph of this table. Picasso announces that he has prepared the famous paper sculptures since we talked about them last . . . They intrigue me enormously, and I ask him to show them to me right away. He takes them from a box. They are very small figures, in thin paper, rolled and modeled by his fingers, as fragile as a butterfly's wing . . .*

Sabartés and Kootz reappear. The financial conference has ended. Now there is a discussion among the three of them about the purchase of the pictures and the exhibition in New York. I leave them alone and go off to look at a sheet of paper on which Picasso has drawn a large bird with a plume. It is not the bird, however, that dominates the drawing, but the date: LE 25 DECEMBRE 46. All around the figure of the bird, in longer and longer lines, as if seized with a fever of exaltation, he has written: LE 25 DECEMBRE 46, LE 25 DECEMBRE 46 . . . It is as though he had wanted to give this Christmas Day just past a place apart in his memory. What could have happened on this twenty-fifth of December 1946? On a stand not far from the drawing, the same bird has already taken its place in a canvas. He is only sketched in, but the work is already signed and dated: December 27, 1946 . . .

* In the end, I was never able to photograph them. I am afraid that they are lost forever.

I leave with Kootz. He is radiant. The affair is in the bag . . . Picasso and Sabartés have asked him to come back tomorrow to settle the details. In his emotion, he has left his snow boots at Picasso's . . .

*Wednesday, January 2, 1947*

When I meet Jaime Sabartés, he has a fat cigar in his mouth, one of those obtained from Kootz's briefcase . . .

SABARTÉS: You gave us one hell of a job with your damned American! I haven't stopped running since the day you brought him here: license applications, waiting rooms, the Préfecture de Police, the customs, the ministries . . . He bought the nine pictures only on the condition that he could take them with him in the plane . . . In three days I've had to go through all that red tape, collect all the authorizations . . .

At the Grand Hotel, Samuel Kootz is packing his bags. *Veni, vidi, vici.* He is content. As a result of countless cables and transatlantic telephone calls, he has organized his Picasso exhibition in New York, ordered posters, catalogues, invitations, and alerted the press. As a final gesture he is even thinking of hiring Louis Armstrong and his orchestra for an evening opening. Paris was of no interest to him whatever. He never had the slightest notion whether he was on the Left Bank or the Right, in Montparnasse or at the Place de l'Opéra. He never saw the Eiffel Tower, or even the Folies-Bergère. He never got out of his taxi long enough to risk a few steps in a Parisian street. I ask him if he has been to the Louvre. "The Louvre? It isn't abstract enough for me," he answers. He had only one thought in mind: Picasso.

# EPILOGUE

*Cannes, Tuesday, May 17, 1960*

Gilberte and I dine with Henry Miller at the Hotel Montfleury. Luis Buñuel is at a nearby table, with his son and a few friends.

MYSELF: I spoke to Picasso on the telephone yesterday. His voice was so youthful that I asked myself: "Is it really him?" And so friendly: "What a surprise to hear from you, Brassaï! Come day after tomorrow, if you are free. We can spend the whole afternoon together. We'll be alone . . . I'll expect you at *La Californie* at two-thirty . . ."

HENRY MILLER: So, tomorrow you will see him again . . .

MYSELF: Henry, you wrote to me and you told me again in Paris that you had agreed to be a member of the jury for the Cannes Festival only in the hope of meeting Picasso.

HENRY MILLER: Yes, I wrote to you, and I asked you to introduce me to him. To me Cannes is indissolubly linked with the name of Picasso. But tomorrow I have a very busy day. The Festival is ending and we are more harassed than ever. There are three showings, instead of two, and the second one begins at three o'clock.

MYSELF: From *La Californie* you could get to the Festival Hall in a taxi in five minutes. And you would have met him . . .

HENRY MILLER: To meet Picasso . . . It's one of my strongest desires, no doubt of that. But I don't like to rush at things. I could go with you to see him, of course, but the very thought of having to leave at a specific time would poison every minute of it. What good would such a hasty meeting do? There should be more time, more calm, to establish any real contact.

MYSELF: I'll introduce you, and then you can go back to see him another day. You're here in Cannes, just a few steps away from him. Soon you'll be back at Big Sur, or in Greece or Japan or God knows where, and Picasso may be at Vauvenargues . . . It will be a lost opportunity.

HENRY MILLER: You're probably right . . . But don't tempt me. We have to let chance play its part. Opportunity may knock another day. I am a fatalist. It's possible that Larry Durrell will take me to Vauvenargues when I go to see him at Nîmes. And if I don't make his acquaintance in this world—I'm sixty-eight and he is eighty—I am sure to meet him later, ten million years from now, I don't know where, because such energies, such strengths are always active . . .

GILBERTE: Do you really believe that? Do you believe in immortality?

HENRY MILLER: Yes, in a sense. Immortality! Hum-hum, ha-ha-ha . . . You know, my dear Gilberte, I am close to being a follower of Krishnamurti, even though I have never met him . . . The Hindu sage, you know him—he lives in Ojai, in California . . . Immortality? As Nietzsche said, at the edge of madness: an eternal return . . . Why not? I'm a philosopher myself, on occasion . . . In any case, tell Picasso how much I love and admire him, how much I would have liked to meet him . . .

*Cannes, Wednesday, May 18, 1960*

At two-thirty in the afternoon, in the hills behind Cannes, standing in front of *La Californie* . . . Picasso's villa is as banal and luxurious as all those surrounding it, dating from the time of the Grand Dukes, the glorious epoch of the Côte d'Azur. But the gardens . . . There must have been a lack of gardeners, because pine, cypress, eucalyptus, mimosa, medlar trees, oleander, and honeysuckle have all grown wild, stifling themselves in their own luxuriant vegetation. Above them can be seen the high crown of the palms, breathing the sea air and questing the blue horizon of the Mediterranean . . . By what chance had it happened that it should be this villa that now offered shelter to Picasso and his treasures, that had even inspired his creation in these last years, adding its name to the list of the Bateau-Lavoir, Boisgeloup, Vallauris, the Château Grimaldi? Picasso's choice could only be explained by his horror of everything that is generally considered "good taste," his affection for the droll, the outlandish, the baroque—the villa seems about to collapse beneath the weight of its ornamentation—his indifference to the places in which he lives, and his penchant for placing himself in the hands of Providence . . . It was because of this that he left to Kahnweiler the task of moving his studio from Montmartre to Montparnasse while he was away on a honeymoon trip with Eva, and later asked Rosenberg to find him a new apartment in Paris while he was in Spain with Olga.

I hunt for a bell to ring, but to my great surprise the gate to the villa is not closed. The wife of the caretaker leads us in. The courtyard is empty. There are several cars in the garage, dominated by a big white Lincoln. To the right of the steps leading up to the house, an old acquaintance: *Le Cerf*, from the park at Boisgeloup; to the left, a strange metallic flower with shattered petals, the forms of an exploded mechanism for sowing death.

Picasso appears on the landing at the top of the steps, seeming very small beneath the high glass awning. He kisses me on both cheeks. He has not changed. His torso molded into a woolen sweater, his face bronzed by the wind and sun, he is solid as a rock and his eyes have lost nothing of their fire. He takes us into his "studio": three enormous rooms, one after the other, bathed in light from great glass bays opening onto the park.

Actually nothing has changed since the day I first met him on the rue La Boétie, except for the greater space, and the things that have accumulated around him. I am so happy to see him again. Unfortunately I will not see Jacqueline Roque, the young companion whom he met at Vallauris and who has shared his life for six years. She has just had an operation. But Picasso is now reassured. She is much better, and has been brought back to *La Californie*.

PICASSO: I often think of you . . . You had an exhibition of drawings and sculptures recently, didn't you? I heard about it.

I still know everything that goes on . . . How long has it been that we haven't seen each other?

MYSELF: Since 1947, I think. Thirteen years . . .

PICASSO: Is it possible? Thirteen years? But why haven't you come to see me?

How many times have I been tempted to call on him? And the temptation was never so strong as it was at the time of the Cannes Festival of 1956, when my film *Tant qu'il y aura des bêtes* was being shown, and another entry was *Le Mystère Picasso* . . .

MYSELF: I come to the Côte d'Azur quite often. I have a house in Eze. In my thoughts I have often been with you. But to telephone you—you . . .

PICASSO: You were wrong. I no longer want to see new faces. Why should I? But I am always here to my friends . . . And their visits are that much more precious to me because I live in seclusion, like a prisoner. I would not wish my celebrity on anyone, not even my worst enemies. I suffer from it, physically. I protect myself as best I can. I barricade myself behind doors that are kept double locked night and day . . .

MYSELF: But the gate was open.

PICASSO: If you found it open, it was because I was expecting you and gave instructions that it should be opened for you at two-thirty.

MYSELF: If I understand you correctly, we are in a besieged castle. We let down the drawbridge for friends . . .

PICASSO: Alas! That's almost it.

MYSELF: And Vauvenargues? Aren't you better protected there?

PICASSO: It's worse. There are always crowds of curious people. They spy on you with binoculars. They watch everything you do. Perhaps at this very moment people are watching us from the Îles de Lérins, with telescopes . . . If I really wanted to be safe from all of this indiscreet prying, I would have to draw the curtains on all these windows. But then I would be deprived of the view of the park and the landscape, and I need that . . .

It's frightful . . . And that's not all. There is another danger that threatens me here: an enormous building of I don't know how many floors is going to be put up in the garden just next to mine. Not only will it hide the view of the Îles de Lérins, but all of the tenants will be able to watch us from their balconies. It will probably force me to leave here . . . But what are you doing on the Coast?

MYSELF: I'm spending three weeks in Cannes with Henry Miller. He's a member of the jury for the Festival. He is always very busy during the day, but we spend the evenings together . . . He's frightened of celebrity too; he's afraid that, if his books are published in the United States, he would lose all peace of mind.

PICASSO: I understand him. What good does it do to have even more money, when you have enough money? You can't eat four luncheons or four dinners just because you are richer. And whether I am rich or poor, I will never smoke any cigarettes but Gauloises. They are the only ones I like. And by the way, could you offer me a Gauloise? I don't have one in the house!

MYSELF: I wanted to introduce Henry Miller to you. He would like so much to meet you. But today was a bad day. He had a showing at three o'clock. And he didn't want to see you that way, just for a minute.

PICASSO: I have a great admiration for Henry Miller. Perhaps you could come back with him after the Festival?

As we talk, Picasso is studying Gilberte, looking very springlike in a green print dress . . .

PICASSO: What part of the country do you come from?

GILBERTE, *laughing:* I'm partially Catalan.

PICASSO, *his eyes sparkling with warmth:* Catalan? I saw right away that your eyes were not from here, but from *down there.* One is always a reflection of his own country. But where, exactly?

GILBERTE: I doubt that you know the little village in the Pyrénées-Orientales that my father came from.

PICASSO: Tell me, just the same. I know the country very well.

GILBERTE: A tiny little village, with a ridiculous name: Caudiès-de-Fenouillèdes.

PICASSO: But I know Fenouillèdes very well. It's in the Roussillon, very high, near the Spanish frontier. And do you speak Catalan?

GILBERTE: A few words . . . *Boutifares* . . .

Picasso laughs, and asks her a question in Catalan, which she does not understand.

PICASSO: I see . . . You are not a very good Catalan . . .

MYSELF: That may be, but she adores that country. She is mad about the music of the *sardane* . . .

Picasso lifts his arms, begins to whistle a *sardane* . . . It is a young and alert Catalan who is dancing now, his feet, shod in curious buckskin moccasins, marking the cadence on the parquet floor. His features are radiant, he has left us, gone somewhere else—somewhere in Catalonia. Is he in Gozol, overlooking the valley of Andorra, free, happy, drinking, hunting with the peasants, dancing with the girls, joking with the smugglers, jogging about on muleback, as once he had? Or at Céret, in the Pyrénées-Orientales, where he passed so many of his youthful summers with his friends Braque and Manolo? He was dancing the *sardane*. He was down there. Yes, one is always a reflection of his own country.

MYSELF: When I arrived in Barcelona one Sunday afternoon, I had quite a shock. That harsh, bitter music . . . that great square filled with young girls and young men . . . handbags and jackets placed in a pile on the walk, and around each pile a circle of dancers weaving back and forth . . . It was so unexpected. And the expressions on their faces—serious, tense, almost desperate. No sound of laughter, not even a smile. All of them so solemn . . . I had the feeling I was taking part in a religious ceremony.

PICASSO: But it's a very serious thing, the *sardane*! And difficult! Each step must be counted. In every group, there is one person who does this for all of the others. This dance is a communion of souls . . . It abolishes all distinction of class. Rich and poor, young and old dance it together: the postman with the bank director, and the servants hand in hand with the masters . . .

I show him the album of my graffiti which has just been published in Germany. In order to look through it together, we all sit down around a little table . . .

I am trying here to transcribe faithfully the words and ideas exchanged, but removed from their context some of their vital breath is lacking, just as it is to a fish removed from water. Picasso's studios, wherever they may be, of whatever kind they may be, invariably provoke commotion. Only the frequency of my visits to the rue des Grands-Augustins had immunized me to some extent against the violence of the shock. But now I have not seen Picasso for thirteen years. The majority of his work and the objects that surround me here are unknown. There is nothing to protect me any longer . . . I have occasionally been assaulted and almost overwhelmed: in the port of Tangiers by the mob of Arab porters, screaming, gesticulating, clutching at the lapels of my jacket while one snatched my overcoat and another my suitcase; in Istanbul, on a deserted plain at Pera, by a tribe of gypsies who encircled me with an unbreakable ring; at Bahia de Todos os Santos, in Brazil, by an army of Negro children in a frenzy of excitement at the sight of my camera, dancing a sarabande around their prisoner . . . But never in my life have my emotions been so brutally assaulted as they were in that villa of *La Californie*. Art and nature, creation and myth, chivalry and tauromachy, folk imagery, Olympus and Walpurgisnacht all vie for your attention . . . The voices all rise at once, outbidding each other, dragging you from left to right, knocking you down, flaying you, leaving the nerve ends raw and quivering . . .

Even as I talk with him, *Les Demoiselles d'Avignon* are staring down at me from a wall at the end of these enormous rooms. What are they looking for here? Haven't they gone to live in the Museum of Modern Art in New York? And what is the meaning of their strange new colors? And these bronze heads of bulls? Are they recent? I have never yet seen them reproduced . . . And what is that great sun shining on the wall, pale as the sun of winter, disquietingly beautiful? Where does it come from? From Mexico? Could it be Picasso's work? And these silver cups? It is at this moment that I drop my cigarette holder and, before I can move, Picasso has picked it up and is holding it out to me. At the age of eighty his muscles are as supple, his reflexes as quick as they have always been . . . I can't help wondering about the curious, horizontally striped cloth of his trousers. Raw silk? Unbleached, hand-woven linen? Where does it come from? I study his face, I make an inventory of the furrows of his profile: starting at the corner of the eye, they spread out like a fan, some toward the forehead, some toward the ear, and some toward the cheek. When he laughs, there are twelve blades to the fan etched in his profile . . . And what is all this movement around us? These sudden splotches of black, white, and chestnut color? This one must be a basset . . . And the one behind him, a dalmatian? Another one, a third, a boxer? . . . I half expect to see dozens, hundreds of other dogs appear, from every nook and cranny of the studio: the two mastiffs from Montrouge, his first Parisian fox terrier, all the Frikas, the Elfts, the Kazbeks . . . All those Picasso has owned in his lifetime, or would have liked to own . . . I listen to what he is saying, but at the same time my eyes and mind are distracted, monopolized, by all of these objects made by him, gathered together by him, or having found their way here through some mysterious paths of their own: *La Femme Enceinte,* with her swollen belly and projecting breasts, still in plaster; the screech owl in ceramic; and a crane . . . I try to decipher the secret of the outcast objects from which this bird is formed. The tail is undoubtedly a shovel, but is the long neck a length of cable? And the tufted plume, an old gas faucet? But the delicate foot? And the carafes, the bottles, the bronze fruits, brothers and sisters of the *Verre d'Absinthe,* and, like it, repainted in oils? Are they recent? And those three enormous projectors focused on the easel? I have already seen them somewhere . . . But of course! They figured in the series of paintings he did of this studio . . . This ordeal of the senses is augmented by my emotion at seeing Picasso again after so many years, hearing his voice, which has become graver, more settled, submitting to the dark fire of his eyes . . . And suddenly the whole host of memories is shaken up—thirteen years to be recaptured, a thousand questions to be asked . . . My thoughts are as confused as bees swarming around a hive, or ants when their hill has been disturbed.

How can I set down in all of its intensity this gathering of sensations, images, words; the emotions they provoked, the rushing flood of memories? I am accustomed to an abstract, instantaneous vision of things, and the forcibly arbitrary order imposed by an attempt to describe them baffles me . . . It is as though an orchestra leader were forced to have the instruments play a symphony, not together, but one after the other, in a fortuitous, haphazard sequence . . . Only a form of writing conceived in the manner of a musical score, disposed on as many different levels as there are simultaneous impressions and emotions to convey, could render with some accuracy moments such as this—they are too rich, too highly charged. It would be no more than an artifice, and outside the "rules of the game" of language, but how else would it be possible to replace in their proper context the words and ideas I am reporting, so that they might have some accent of truth?

We are seated around a little table, and Picasso is leafing through my book *Graffiti* . . . I tell him that I have included in it some of his remarks about graffiti . . . "In what bank did you do that graffiti you told me about?" I ask.

PICASSO: The B.N.C.I. Ask Sabartés about it . . . He knows everything . . . How is he? Fine. Faithful to his post, as always . . . At the rue des Grands-Augustins every morning. Sometimes he comes to see me here at Cannes or at Vauvenargues, because I never go to Paris anymore . . .

Picasso comes to the chapter in the album titled "The Language of Walls." He is surprised by the great brushstrokes of paint, effacing the inscriptions on the wall.

PICASSO: You did well to photograph that . . . because it's a good demonstration of the nature and limits of abstract art. These brushstrokes are very beautiful . . . but it is a natural beauty. A few strokes of a brush that have no meaning will never make a picture. I do this sort of thing myself, and occasionally you might even say it was an abstract. But my brushstrokes always signify something: a bull, an arena, the sea, the mountains, the crowd . . . To arrive at abstraction, it is always necessary to begin with a concrete reality . . .

He comes to the chapter on "The Birth of the Face," in which I have grouped faces done from two or three holes in a wall.

PICASSO: I have often done faces like this myself. The people who scratch them out like this naturally gravitate to symbols.[55] Art is a language of symbols. When I pronounce the word "man," I call up a picture of man; the word has become the symbol of man. It does not represent him as photography could. Two holes—that's the symbol for the face, enough to evoke it without representing it . . . But isn't it strange that it can be done through such simple means? Two holes; that's abstract enough if you consider the complexity of man . . . Whatever is most abstract may perhaps be the summit of reality . . .

At the chapter on "Masks and Faces" he exclaims: "This is a Rouault!" or "That one is a Klee!" . . . At the chapter on "Animals" he hesitates for a long time over a bird I have labeled a pigeon . . .

PICASSO: A pigeon? Isn't it more likely that it's a swallow? I say that because the wings intersect like the arms of a scissors . . . But it probably isn't either a pigeon or a swallow, but a Bird, the idea of a Bird . . .

We come to the chapter on "Love." Two hearts immediately attract his attention: superimposed on each other, the sharp tip of one piercing the top of the other, as if in a kind of secret embrace.

PICASSO: But that's stupendous! I've seen thousands of hearts on walls, but never in a constellation like this . . .

At the chapter on "Primitive Images," an "Aztec" head makes him pause abruptly, and then he cries:

"That is as rich as the façade of a cathedral! . . . Your book links art with the primitive arts . . . And it also shows—and this is important—that abstract art is not far removed from the random brushstrokes or carvings in a wall. No matter what anyone thinks or says, we always imitate something, even when we don't know we are doing it. And when we abandon nude models hired at so many francs an hour, we 'pose' all sorts of other things. Don't you agree? You might be happy to learn that right now I myself am making graffiti. But they are engraved in cement, instead of on a wall . . . The invention of a Norwegian artist . . . My graffiti are enlarged, and cut out with electric chisels . . . They are being done for a building in Barcelona, and each of them will be two to three stories high. I'd like to show you the model . . ."

And Picasso picks his way through the extraordinary jumble of his studio, without hesitation but not without difficulty clearing a path through the cliffs of paper toward one specific pile, from which he draws out an envelope of the photographs he is looking for. The building with the giant graffiti is outlined against those four incredible towers of the Sagrada Familia.

MYSELF: You'll be going into competition with Gaudí . . . When I was photographing his architecture in Barcelona, Pratz sent me to see your sister and the Vilato family, at the Paseo de Gracia,

53. Henri Matisse, 1939

*Matisse had done a drawing for me with a mask around his eyes . . . the eyes, the mouth, the nose, the ears all overlap, as they do in Picasso's deliberately distorted faces.*

54. Matisse at work in his studio, 1939

55. Graffiti found scratched on a wall in Paris

PICASSO: *I have often done faces like this myself. The people who scratch them out like this naturally gravitate to symbols.*

56. Daniel-Henry Kahnweiler answers his mail in front of an immense Picasso in his office at the Louise Leiris gallery, October 1962

57. D.-H. Kahnweiler with Picasso's *L'Ange*, reinforced concrete, in Kahnweiler's "Priory" at Saint-Hilaire, October 1962

and also to see the Junyers . . . I was surprised to see how many examples of your work there still are in Barcelona . . . With the ones the museum there owns, they could start a separate "Picasso Museum."

PICASSO: There has been some talk of it. The municipality wants to acquire an old palace for it. We'll see . . .

I ask him the origin of the great sun on the wall.

PICASSO: Barcelona, as it happens. It's a slice from the trunk of a palm tree. They are carried as "suns" in the processions on Palm Sunday . . . Marvelous, isn't it? Once upon a time, I did paintings with palm leaves . . .

GILBERTE: Do you know those objects they sell in front of the churches in Nice, at Easter? The palm leaves are slashed, folded and refolded. Sometimes they are very beautiful.

PICASSO: That sort of thing is typically Mediterranean. Look at the delicacy of the tones in my sun. As the wood dries, it becomes clearer, more luminous. It really is joy and sunlight, isn't it?

Shortly afterward, he reveals to me the secret of *Les Demoiselles d'Avignon* which dominates the studio.

PICASSO: Come over here and look at them closely. It's a tapestry. An old chap in Toulon took it into his head to do it, copying it from an ordinary postcard. A lot of my visitors think it's horrible and talk about sacrilege . . . It's the change in colors that shocks them . . . but it's precisely that that fascinates me. The colors of the original were completely different, even in the reproduction, and then the Sunday painter who did this invented still others . . . It's almost another picture, even though it reminds you of *Les Demoiselles d'Avignon.*

We go on with our tour of the premises. He points out an extraordinary mahogany armoire, equipped with a large number of shallow drawers.

PICASSO: It belonged to Matisse, and since I had often admired it when I went to see him his family made me a gift of it after his death. He had it made for his own use, specifying that it should be very high and have at least forty drawers to hold his drawings. Isn't it beautifully proportioned? Whenever I look at it, I think of Matisse; it's a perfect reflection of the man . . .

MYSELF: And this magnificent totem from the New Hebrides?

PICASSO: Another gift from Matisse.

Not far from where the totem stands, there is a rich glitter of gold braid from the suit of a toreador.

PICASSO: That's a sad story. The suit of lights you see there belonged to the matador Chicuelo II. He sent it to me himself . . . But he died in a tragic manner. If only he had been killed by a bull! But no, he died in a stupid airplane accident . . . Nowadays matadors are constantly on the move, always in a hurry. Many more of them are killed in automobile and airplane accidents than on the horns of a bull. By the time this costume reached me, he was already dead. It was like a last message of friendship.

I ask him if he still follows the bullfights as assiduously as he has in the past.

PICASSO: Yes, it's a passion with me. But sometimes I can't do it, there are things that prevent me. Then my thoughts will be in the arena, I hear the paso doble, I see the crowd, the entrance of the cuadrilla, the first bull as he charges the picadors . . . One day I was so upset at having missed a corrida that I set to work on a series that would evoke all the phases of it. For the past few months I have done several drawings in India ink every afternoon . . .

We talk about the large exhibition of his work at the Tate Gallery, organized by Roland Penrose. I ask him if he has considered going to London to see it himself.

PICASSO: Why should I waste my time going to see my paintings again? I have a good memory, and I remember all of them. I loaned a great many of my own canvases to the exhibition, and that gave me quite enough trouble. They are only going to exhibit paintings, and very few of my recent works. But there will be the big curtain for *Parade*. Exhibitions don't mean a great deal to me anymore. My old paintings no longer interest me. I'm much more curious about those I haven't yet done . . .

One of the rooms contains a grouping of his new sculptures, including some bronzes which were originally ceramics—Picasso explains to me that he has had this done because the form of some of these terra cottas seemed to lend itself to casting—and one of his masterpieces, *La Chevre,* made from a wicker basket, palm branches and terra-cotta jars. At the sight of all those new works I cannot refrain from saying:

"No one could ever publish an album of your work that would be really complete. It would no sooner have appeared than you would have made it obsolete. After four years' work we thought we had collected photographs of all of your sculptures. But since then, I have seen others that are not in the book. Just recently a curious wooden sculpture of yours, resembling an African fetish, was sold at auction at the Hôtel Drouot in Paris. I have never seen it reproduced anywhere. I only knew three of your sculptures from the cubist period: the two *Femmes Nues* and *L'Homme à la Tête Carrée.* I didn't know that this little figure existed . . .

PICASSO: I had forgotten it myself. Do you know what it was? I'll tell you the story of it. The little daughter of my cleaning woman wanted a doll. I was still living in Montmartre and I was fairly broke at the time. So, to take the place of a doll, I carved her that little "cubist" statuette. I don't remember now whether the child appreciated it! And I have no idea of how it came to be in an auction at the Hôtel Drouot.

MYSELF: Kahnweiler wants to edit a new collection of your sculptures, "brought up to date" . . . To be done, apparently, by a publisher in Stuttgart . . . He asked me to photograph the things you have done since 1947 . . .

PICASSO: Whenever you like. You can break them too. I'm joking, but photographers really are terrible, and the most terrible of all was Man Ray . . . The statues of mine he broke! Even the unbreakable ones . . .

At this moment we arrive at a collection of silver plates.

PICASSO: François Hugo made these for me . . . Jean Hugo's brother, a marvelous craftsman . . . I did some drawings for him . . . All of these objects are in silver. It's impressive, isn't it? And yet it actually doesn't cost much more than bronze. He's also going to do some jewelry for me, in gold . . .

The three dogs reappear on the scene. The one I had thought to be a basset is a *teckel.* His name is Loump. Yan, the boxer, is blind. But Picasso tells us that his blindness does not prevent him from going wherever he pleases, and coming when he is called.

The third, black and white, is a magnificent dalmatian. "He has appeared in several of my paintings," Picasso remarks.

In a silver tray on a sideboard, there is half of a cake, its sides veined with grottoes, like the walls of a cliff eaten away by the sea . . .

PICASSO: It's an Italian bread, with raisins. It's called a *panettone*. We ate a part of it about . . . oh, about two years ago. Then I forgot it . . . Quite a feast for my mice, isn't it? They began nibbling at it, and eventually drilled a labyrinth into it. So I left it to them. Now that it is completely dried out, it's as hard as iron. But I keep it. Petrified, it's as beautiful as the rocks at Les Baux . . . Don't you think so?

Night has begun to fall on *La Californie*. We have been with Picasso for many hours, talking unceasingly, and he is still eager to ask questions, to show us this or that, to guide us through the detours of his labyrinth. I have brought with me a parcel of manuscripts. A few months ago, when I was trying to get things in order, I came across a box on which I had written: "Conversations with Picasso." I reread them, and I wanted to show them to Picasso. He is not surprised to learn that it is a record of our conversations. Years ago he read and liked my *Histoire de Marie*, and also the ideas and reflections I had written down in *Bistro-Tabac*, during the occupation.

PICASSO: You wrote down all of this? But this is fascinating! Let's sit down, and you can read me a few pages . . .

I read aloud to him then, from several of my "visits," picked at random from the pile. I read him twenty pages, thirty . . . He asks me to go on . . . And he listens, attentive, thoughtful, amused, interrupting me occasionally to point out a detail or complete a story. For example, when I read the account of my visit with the dancer Marina de Berg, he stops me.

PICASSO: As it turned out, I never was able to tell her how to fasten the waistband, was I? Well, you do it with a coin! Olga used to use one of those fifty-centime pieces that had a hole in the center. You roll it into the cloth and then the waistband holds. Every profession has its own little secrets, and no one else can invent them. It was that little trick I wanted to tell her about. By the way, what has become of her? She was such a mischievous girl, so gay, Marina . . .

MYSELF: She gave up dancing and went into a convent.

I am forced to interrupt the reading. Henry Miller will be waiting for us at the Festival Hall at seven o'clock. We get up to leave. Picasso places a hand on the parcel of manuscript and says:

"This is just as true, as authentic, as your graffiti. It should be published . . ."

As we drive off, I think of the three or four gouaches or India ink drawings that will never see the light of day, that no collector and no museum will ever possess, because instead of working through this afternoon of Wednesday, May 18, 1960, Picasso has given his time to his friends . . .

# POSTSCRIPT

*Thursday, September 22, 1960*

Madame Georges Duthuit—Marguerite Matisse—came to see me today. I have not seen her now for many years. She has not changed, but the little rainbow-colored cloche she wore did not entirely conceal her white hairs . . .

MARGUERITE DUTHUIT: I have taken on an enormous task; I am trying to make up a definitive catalogue of Matisse's paintings. So, I am going to need your photos. They can provide me with very valuable information on individual pictures. I have all of my father's documents, but even so it's a very difficult business . . . All these forgeries . . .

MYSELF: Forgeries?

MARGUERITE DUTHUIT: It's incredible! I have just been working on this since June, and I have already come across several of them . . . And you wouldn't believe the really diabolical skill of the forgers. They borrow elements from several different canvases and put them together to form an entirely new one. Sometimes it's very difficult to distinguish them from the real thing . . .

MYSELF: And the experts on your father's work . . .

MARGUERITE DUTHUIT: The few people who knew his work almost from day to day are dead. And Bernheim too. As for myself, I lived away from my father a large part of the time. It was only during the last three years of his life that I was with him all the time.

MYSELF: If I remember correctly, Matisse always had reproductions made of his paintings.

MARGUERITE DUTHUIT: Only in certain periods.

MYSELF: Do you still have much of his work?

MARGUERITE DUTHUIT: Not very much. My father didn't leave many paintings, and the three of us shared the few there were equally. Since I have very little room at home, there are none of them hanging; they are all packed away . . .

MYSELF: And Picasso?

MARGUERITE DUTHUIT: Picasso . . . I remember as if it were yesterday the day the Steins took my father and me to the rue Ravignan. That's where we met him for the first time. He had a big St. Bernard dog then . . . They were amusing people, the Steins! Leo, Michael, and Gertrude. They had all had a Germanic education. The family was very rich; their father owned a streetcar company in San Francisco. After we left Picasso, we walked down from Montmartre to the rue de Fleurus, where the Steins lived then. We could have taken the old double-deck Batignolles-Clichy-Odéon bus, or the one that went from the Place Pigalle to the Halle-aux-Vins, but we preferred to walk. And we did not go unnoticed! On the avenue de l'Opéra, everyone turned around and stared at us. The Steins were rather oddly dressed, to say the least, especially Gertrude, who was a big woman anyway, very masculine-looking. She always wore dresses of heavy corduroy velvet and paid no attention to styles. And all three of them wore leather thong sandals on their bare feet, like the Romans, or like Isadora Duncan and her brother . . .

MYSELF: Do you see very much of Picasso now?

MARGUERITE DUTHUIT: Very seldom. But when I do chance to see him, he is the soul of kindness. He chides me for neglecting him: "Marguerite, but why don't you ever come to see me any more? We are all in the same boat now, we are all getting old . . ." But if I do telephone him or want to see him, I come up against a barrage of obstacles . . .

MYSELF: Pierre Reverdy was staying on the coast for a short time, not long ago, and since he didn't want to go through that experience, which can be humiliating, he let Picasso know that he would like very much to see him, but only on condition that Picasso came to him. And Picasso went. But if he were to do that with everyone, he would have no time left for painting.

MARGUERITE DUTHUIT: I know. And I understand it. He does what he can, but his fame has become a terrible burden. His attitude is sometimes very puzzling though. When Matisse died, we let him know at once. Their relationship was very friendly, intimate in fact. You would have thought he would have come to the telephone and spoken to us, at least to say how sorry he was. After a long wait we were told: "Monsieur Picasso is having lunch and cannot be disturbed." We kept expecting a telegram, a telephone call. Nothing. Thinking that perhaps he had not been given the message, we telephoned again. It was the same thing. When we tried to speak to him for a third time, we were told: "Monseiur Picasso has nothing to say on the subject of Matisse, since he is dead." Could he really have said that? Or did someone else answer for him, without his knowledge, thinking to spare him?

MYSELF: Picasso does not like anyone to mention death and he has an absolute horror of emotional display. But I am certain that this news was terrible for him. It was because he was afraid of revealing himself that he took refuge in work and silence.* He liked Matisse, very much, and he was always a champion of his painting. He bought many of his canvases. He had quite a collection of them.

MARGUERITE DUTHUIT: No one knows exactly how many Matisses he owns. Some very old landscapes, painted in Switzerland, before the fauve period, and some later works. About 1939 they made an exchange of canvases. Picasso selected a painting of my father's that he wanted, but he didn't permit Matisse to make his own choice from his. He gave him a rather terrifying portrait of Dora Maar. My father admired it, but he never liked it too much.

* Every time Picasso lost a friend, the entire world waited to hear "what he thinks." He was literally besieged when Braque died, and he had to flee from his own house at the time of Jean Cocteau's death.

MYSELF: He also had the big *Nature morte aux Oranges et aux Bananes* of 1914. Picasso loved that picture and was vehement in his praise of it.

MARGUERITE DUTHUIT: He also has a portrait of me, from 1907, in his collection. I had long hair then, and that was the way my father painted me. A year later, after their first meeting, they exchanged canvases and Picasso chose my portrait, because he liked the extreme simplicity of it.

MYSELF: To my way of thinking, Picasso and Matisse did not have a great deal in common. It was their fame that drew them together. Their friendship was more or less like that of rivals who form an alliance so that they can spy on each other. Their natures were so different . . .

MARGUERITE DUTHUIT: My father didn't need to surround himself with a circle of friends, as Picasso does. He was more reserved, more solitary. He often said to me: "Conversation with other people does nothing for me. It just steals my time, and leaves me empty." And he always categorically refused invitations to social functions. How many times I heard him say: "One must make a choice in life; either paint or go out in the world. But one cannot do both things at the same time."

MYSELF: He was very sociable, though. Much more so than either Braque or Bonnard. I always had the impression that he enjoyed my visits. When he insisted that I come to see him, it always seemed to me that he wasn't just being polite.

MARGUERITE DUTHUIT: You were one of the people he really liked, one of those whom he felt gave him something . . .

MYSELF: And what about his famous Cézanne? Do you still have it?

MARGUERITE DUTHUIT: My father made a gift of it to the Petit Palais before his death. He bought it from Vollard, along with a canvas of a woman's head by Gauguin. It cost him a fabulous sum for that time: a thousand five hundred francs! He even had to pawn my mother's ring to get the money together. His friends told him: "You are mad to pay a fortune for such a piece of rubbish. Take it back to Vollard and ask him to let you return it, even if you lose a few hundred francs." But my father answered: "I am not mad. I don't know what I will get out of life myself, whether my painting will bring in some money one day or not. All that I know is that this painting is a masterpiece and will be worth a great deal some day. Could I make a better investment for my children than to buy it for them?"

MYSELF: I understand very well why he wanted that painting. What astonishes me is the fact that he was able to keep it. He was often in need of money, and must have been tempted to sell it.

MARGUERITE DUTHUIT: There was no lack of temptations. We were often actually on the borderline of destitution. No money, no prospects, and not the slightest possibility of getting away from Paris. I remember once, when he had gone for several years without being able to take a day of vacation, my father suddenly cried out: "I can't go on! I am stifling! Air, air! I must see the country again, the sea, the sky! We absolutely must get away . . ." Obviously, the sale of the Cézanne would have made it possible for us to take a trip occasionally, to go to stay in the country and lead a more comfortable life. But my father would never consider it, even in the worst moments. One day, through some miracle—I don't remember just what—we did get away at last and went to Saint-Tropez. Matisse had rented a little place there, a kind of half-ruined dovecot on the grounds of an estate. Aristide Maillol lived not far away. He was expecting a visit from Bernheim. Seeing the state we were in, he said to my father: "Sell your Cézanne. Bernheim will give you a good price. I can talk to him about it. How much do you want for it?" The offer was very tempting. My father didn't want to upset Maillol, so he gave him a price, but a price so large that it was certain to wreck any possibility of a sale: ten thousand francs! And it did work out that way; Bernheim did not want to pay such a sum, even for the Cézanne . . .

MYSELF: I admire his strength of character. But wasn't it just stubbornness, too? After all, it was his own work that suffered . . .

MARGUERITE DUTHUIT: Stubborn, he certainly was. When he had made up his mind about something, he never gave in. Friends such as Camoin and Bonnard were already beginning to find buyers for their paintings. But he sold nothing, because he refused to bargain about the price. When the *Femme au Chapeau* was first shown at the Salon d'Automne, he had not sold a single canvas in three years. That painting was completely baffling to most people, but he had set its price at five hundred francs, which was a considerable sum at that time. How did he expect to find a buyer for it? Then, on the day before the Salon was to close—you probably know the story—there was a message from the secretariat, saying that someone had offered three hundred francs for the *Femme au Chapeau.* I remember it as if it were yesterday. The concierge had just distributed the mail. My father was still in his pajamas, and took the letter and went over to a window to read it. As usual, my mother was watching his face. She knew all of his expressions: good news, bad news, anger, sorrow, dismay . . . But that day she didn't know what had happened. As he read the letter, my father's expression was one of such complete anguish, and he blinked his eyes so rapidly—that was always a sign of some painful emotion with him—that my mother was terrified. "What's the matter?" she demanded. "Are you ill? Say something!" My father did not seem to realize how much his strange expression had upset my mother, and he just said: "There is nothing to be worried about . . . But this letter was a terrible blow to me!" Then he held it out to her: "Someone has offered three hundred francs for my painting." My mother, as always, rose to the occasion: "I hope that you're not going to let it go for that price!" she said. Later, when we became friends with Gertrude Stein, she told us that she had said to her brother: "This canvas is certainly worth five hundred francs. The man who painted it made no concessions to public taste, and he will not come down on the price . . ." When someone told her brother later that Matisse had stuck to his price, she felt really triumphant . . .

MYSELF: Is your mother still living? I met her in that wonderful, sunny apartment your father used to have in Nice, just behind the Quai des États-Unis.

MARGUERITE DUTHUIT: She died eighteen months ago. She went to sleep one night and did not wake up again. It's an end to be dreamed of, isn't it? She had a prodigious memory, recalled everything, everything, the slightest event, the least important date . . .

We looked through all of the photos I took of Matisse, of his various apartments and studios, the Boulevard Montparnasse, the rue des Plantes, at the Villa des Rêves in Vence, at the Salon d'Automne.

MYSELF: He loved being photographed or filmed. Whenever I made any portraits of him, he was always impatient to see them.

On the morning after one photographing session in his studio on the rue des Plantes, in 1939, he came to my apartment and demanded, point-blank: "Have you developed the photographs? Are you satisfied with them? What do I look like in them?" He was always preoccupied with "what he looked like." He often said to me: "I am really a very gay man . . . but I have a sullen expression. I am always being taken for some gloomy professor. I look like an old bore . . ." And it was true. Matisse was a jovial man, but laughter was not becoming to him. It disfigured him. He was constantly trying to find an accurate reflection of himself in his portraits, but very seldom succeeded; if they were severe, they belied his real nature; if they were laughing, they caricatured him. Just a hint of a smile on his face was best . . .

MARGUERITE DUTHUIT: You are right. I detest the protraits where he is laughing. They give the impression of a man who is not in full possession of his faculties. And, in spite of his age and his physical deterioration, Matisse retained all of his intelligence, all of his lucidity, until the very end. Just before his death, he reworked his big collage panel completely. As a matter of fact, it's curious how, as he grew older, he came to resemble his father more and more. I don't know whether you knew it, but his father was an important grain dealer in the north.

I mentioned something about the fact that Matisse had had a religious funeral.

MARGUERITE DUTHUIT: When my parents were married, it was my father who wanted the marriage blessed by a priest. It was he who insisted that his children must be baptized. It was probably not so much a matter of religious conviction as respect for the family tradition of his parents and grandparents. It was for this reason that we decided that he should have a religious funeral . . .

*Gisors, February 14, 1961*

A real spring day, bright and sunny. It is much warmer in Paris than it is on the Côte d'Azur, probably as warm as it is in Tamanrasset. We are going to Gisors to see the "Prisoner's Tower" and its graffiti, which Picasso has been telling me about for twenty years.

We follow the same route I took with him when we went to

Boisgeloup. That was at almost this same time of year, thirty years ago. Since that time, the Parisian suburbs have spread out as far as Pontoise. Now, one must travel a good thirty-five kilometers from Paris before the real country begins, the broad expanse of fields, the horses grazing and at work, the peasants harrowing in the fields. When we come to the junction where the roadside marker saying "Hamlet of Boisgeloup" still stands, I can not resist the temptation to catch another glimpse of the place that was one of the landmarks of Picasso's existence. And I would like to show it to Gilberte. I recognize the little chapel, with its weather vane in the familiar form of the Gallic cock, and the gate to the château. A boxer dog is frolicking on the lawn. I can make out the silhouette of a young man standing in the courtyard. The present owner of Boisgeloup, undoubtedly. And then Fuego, my mad two-year-old griffon, sees the boxer and leaps out of the car. I follow him, calling for him to come back and trying to apologize for this intrusion. It is only then that I realize that this young man is Paulo, Picasso's son.

He must be about forty now, but in this heavily lined, almost piratical face, there is little resemblance to the fragile countenance of the young Paulo which inspired so many of his father's Pierrots.

MYSELF: I thought that the château had been sold a long time ago.

PAULO: No, my father never wanted to sell it. He always keeps everything.

MYSELF: But he did sell the apartments on the rue La Boétie.

PAULO: Because he was forced to: they were requisitioned. Otherwise he would still have them, you can be sure of that.

MYSELF: And now he is also leaving *La Californie* . . .

PAULO: Yes, because of the apartment building they put up just next door. He is going to settle in Mougins, where he has just bought another property. But he will not sell *La Californie* either; I will be living there . . . And he is going to keep Vauvenargues.

MYSELF: But he isn't really very fond of that.

PAULO: Vauvenargues is too far from the coast. The thing that's odd about it is that my father isn't mad about the Côte d'Azur at all. He much prefers the Pyrénées-Orientales, Banyuls or Collioure. At one point, he was even thinking of settling permanently there. The old fortified château of Collioure was for sale. He learned about it to late. And since he doesn't like to waste time looking for a new place to live, he stayed in Cannes.

MYSELF: In Collioure, of course, he would be at home, in Catalan country . . . But there must be a great many things that still attach him to the coast: Antibes, Vallauris, friends.

PAULO: No, you are mistaken. There is nothing to keep him there. And friends even less than memories. Friends and visitors follow him everywhere . . .

While we are talking, the two dogs are racing up and down the green and sunny lawn, and Fuego is paying tumultuous court to Paulo's young female boxer.

MYSELF: You were eleven years old when I spent an entire day here photographing your father's sculptures. Do you remember it?

PAULO: It was for *Minotaure,* wasn't it? I remember it very well. My wife and I take care of Boisgeloup now. We often come here from Paris for a few days at a time. But everything had been permitted to run down terribly here. There wasn't even a caretaker. Would you like to make a tour of it?

My eyes had automatically been drawn to the old stables, facing the château across the courtyard; I was sure that the walls had been completely covered with ivy. Now, they are naked. I mention this to Paulo.

PAULO: Yes, everything was covered with ivy, even the roofs. The chapel could no longer be seen, not even the walls or the steeple. The ivy was so thick in places that it was more like the trunks of trees, so I had it all cut down.

We walk around the grounds for a few minutes. The courtyard has considerable charm in this state of abandon. The flowerbeds have all disappeared and the handsome square enclosure of the poultry yard has become a wasteland, strewn with piles of rotting beams. But what still interests me primarily, of course, is the stable where Picasso created all of those great statues.

PAULO: It's still there, but it is completely empty now. And just as damp as it ever was . . .

A nearby barn had been the garage. On the door, in big black letters, it still bears the painted legend: HISPANO-SUIZA. We return to the house, and find Gilberte with Paulo's wife in the kitchen. She has gray eyes, almost transparent, and a delicate profile, very pretty.

PAULO: For the time being, this is where we live. The kitchen is big and we can keep it warm. But some of the other rooms are being repaired. Would you like to see them?

We go into a large, dilapidated room, filled with piles of firewood and kindling, apparently just a storage place now. It is only with difficulty that I recognize the salon and the fireplace which I photographed with Picasso and Olga in 1932.

PAULO: This room was too badly damaged. I am not doing anything about it for the moment. The soldiers were billeted in here.

We go up to the second floor, where the ceilings of the rooms are pitched to the angle of the mansard roof. In the right wing, there are two charming and well-heated rooms.

PAULO: This is our little apartment. And this is where my father used to paint. He left spots and streaks of color all over the floors. He was very fond of these rooms. The view from up here is the best in the house.

Beyond the little chapel and the gate, we look out on the hill and the staggered rooftops of the hamlet, stretching away toward the green curtain that marks the entrance to the forest of Boisgeloup.

On a wall of one of the rooms, three little amateur snapshots: Picasso, with Olga and Paulo at the age of five. The photos date from 1925 or 1926. Picasso looks ill at ease, stiffly erect in a tight-fitting suit and hard collar.

Paulo and his wife suggest that we have a glass of wine in the kitchen. Two large bullfight posters on the walls bear witness to the fact that we are in the home of an *aficionado*. At his father's instigation, in fact, Paulo and Paquito Muñoz had organized the first bullfights in Vallauris. I ask Paulo if he is still interested in organizing the *corridas* in the South . . .

PAULO: It fascinates me. Unfortunately the Spanish version in which the bull is actually killed is prohibited on the coast, and we can only put on the sort of thing they do in the Camargue. And now Paquito Muñoz, our great impresario down there, is dead. He had a heart attack. It is a great loss. I miss him very much . . .

MYSELF: But you go into the arena yourself, don't you? What is it like for you?

PAULO: I am afraid. But not all of the time. When the bull brushes by you, you don't have the time to be afraid. But when he is charging at you from a distance, that is a terrifying moment. That great black object, growing larger every second, and the horns . . .

There is a little transistor radio on the table, and Madame Picasso tells me that she heard me speak last Sunday. I ask them if they saw the telecast in which I appeared with Kahnweiler.

PAULO: No, because we have no television set. But Picasso undoubtedly saw you. He is mad about television these days. He has had a set at *La Californie* for the past year and a half. At first he was inclined to be contemptuous of it: "All of those faces mean nothing to me," he would say. Then he saw a telecast of his exhibition in London and also the wedding of Princess Margaret, and that conquered him. He has a weakness for Princess Margaret. He even had a dream about her, and told me: "If I had had that dream in the reign of Elizabeth I, I would certainly have been decapitated!" Think of Picasso at Buckingham Palace!

We are preparing to leave when their eighteen-month-old son awakens from a nap in his carriage. This is Bernard, Picasso's only grandson. I ask if he knows his grandfather.

PAULO: Yes. And when he was even smaller, my father made a whole series of drawings of him.

The young Picasso couple accompanies us to our car. Suddenly a swarm of children surges out of nowhere. They are wearing extraordinary masks, long flowered skirts, multicolored blouses, straw hats woven with ribbons. The scene abruptly resembles Mexico or Peru. And they all hurl themselves toward us, holding out collection boxes improvised from tin cans. We had completely forgotten that today is Mardi Gras.

*June 6, 1962*

A crowd of people in the gallery of Louise Leiris on the rue Monceau, where there is an exhibition of the very latest harvest of work of the octogenarian artist. After Velázquez' *Las Meninas,* Picasso has focused on *Le Déjeuner sur l'Herbe* of Manet, and presented us with a series of dazzling variations on this theme. The unexpected and, at the time, scandalous nudity of the woman, in a group of fully dressed men, has undoubtedly attracted him strongly. He takes up this figure of the nude over and over again, moving it about in the group and casting it in attitudes which are sometimes delightfully comical . . .

In the midst of the crowd, I catch a glimpse of a man's back, a bald skull, stooped figure, face glued against one of the canvases as though he wanted to taste of it physically, to savor the colors. It's Sabartés! He has recovered very well from his partial paralysis. The fact that one of his legs still drags slightly and one of his arms is still paralyzed is scarcely noticeable. He stares at me for a moment, recognizes me.

SABARTÉS: Well, so there you are! Good news! Good news! The Picasso Museum in Barcelona will be opening shortly. And the man who is addressing you now is the honorary curator. It was the town council of Barcelona that decided that! What do you think of it? There will be thirty-five rooms: on the ground floor, the ceramics and the sculptures; on the second, the paintings and the pastels; on the third, Picasso's graphic work . . . There will be a research center, a library, and even a photo library . . .

MYSELF: That's marvelous! I congratulate you! And what about all of the things that were in the Municipal Museum of Barcelona?

SABARTÉS: They will also come to the museum: twenty canvases, fifty engravings, and thirty lithographs, everything that Picasso has given the city of Barcelona since 1917 . . . And *Las Meninas,* of course; he has been keeping that for this museum. And some day, perhaps, *Guernica* . . .

In spite of his serious illness, this Sabartés who stands before me is a man transformed, happy . . . This Picasso Museum in

Barcelona is the result of his devotion, the official crowning of his life's work, his apotheosis. He talks as though he were consumed by a strange fever . . .

SABARTÉS: One day Picasso said to me: "By the way, my friend, what are you planning to do with all of my paintings and books in your collection?" I told him that I hoped to establish a Picasso Museum in Málaga. "In Málaga?" he asked. "It is my native city, of course, but I have very few links with Málaga . . . If this museum were to be in Barcelona?" The negotiations went on for three years. I could not say a word about it to anyone. Now I can tell you: it was Jean Ainauv, the director of the museums of Barcelona, who managed everything. Little by little, all of the difficulties were overcome. José de Porcioles, the mayor of Barcelona, then proposed a choice of one of two magnificent fourteenth-century palaces that belonged to the city. He sent photographs and models of both of these two palaces to Mougins. In the end, Picasso decided on the Aguilar palace. It is splendid. I will soon be going to Barcelona.

MYSELF: And Picasso? Will he return to Spain for this occasion?

SABARTÉS: He would certainly like to go, to see Barcelona again. But you know very well that in 1939, on the day the treaty of Burgos was signed, he swore that he would not set foot in Spain so long as the Franco régime remained in power. So, in spite of his desire to go, he still refuses. But he was completely in agreement with the idea of the museum. In fact, he was fascinated with it. He supervised the plans and the whole conception very closely . . .

Sabartés was silent for a moment, and then, quite suddenly, he said: "How did it happen that the mice in the studio at the Grands-Augustins nibbled up your drawings and spared Picasso's?"

This question leaves me perplexed. Picasso's mice did not "nibble up" my drawings. This man has not changed at all. He invents things out of whole cloth and presents them as if they were perfectly serious matters.

As I am leaving him, he remarks: "Do you know that we are neighbors again? I had to give up my old apartment, because of the stairs, and now I live quite near you, at No. 124 Boulevard Auguste-Blanqui. Come to see me there . . ."

*Wednesday, October 17, 1962*

At Daniel-Henry Kahnweiler's, 47, rue Monceau. I have known him for a long time. Still astonishingly lively and alert, he welcomes me in his vast office. What a contrast between his tiny gallery on the rue Vignon and this almost sumptuous installation. Picasso has said: "Without him, I would never have attained the goals of my career." Kahnweiler was, in fact, so overcome by the daring of *Les Demoiselles d'Avignon* that he decided, in 1907, to buy all of Picasso's future production, with the exception of five paintings per year which the artist would keep for himself. Picasso was then twenty-seven, and Kahnweiler twenty-three. They have been linked thus closely for almost sixty-five years! Only the catastrophe of two world wars caused a temporary break in their agreement: in 1914, since he was still a German citizen, Kahnweiler was forced to flee France; in 1940, although he had become a French citizen, he was forced to flee Paris again, because he was a Jew. Twice in his life, he was separated from Picasso, only to be reunited with him after the cataclysm had passed. This man made it possible for the artist to subsist in the early, difficult years, and ever since then he has received a commission on the sale of all of his paintings, varying according to the individual canvas and often as much as half of the selling price.

Kahnweiler is in the midst of examining with a magnifying glass a portrait by Juan Gris that he has just acquired. After this, he goes through his mail and writes his letters, seated in front of an enormous Picasso: a woman lying on the ground beneath a pine tree, the whole composition done in facets, as though it were carved in the rock.[56] Before going into his office I had lingered in the gallery, fascinated by Picasso's new linoleum prints: faces of women, and still lifes bursting with color.

D.-H. KAHNWEILER: They are stupendous, aren't they? Picasso has made innovations even in this field, just as he has in so many others. Five years ago, he began by cutting out in linoleum a Cranach portrait of a woman. Then he had the idea of recutting this single plate, instead of making a separate plate for each color. In seeking for his own means of expression, he innovates audaciously in every medium and brings it to perfection. At first he was satisfied with three or four colors; now he is doing prints with as many as twelve colors, using the same plate! It's like witchcraft! He must be able to foresee the effect of each color exactly, because there is no way of correcting or altering here! I don't even know what name to give to that kind of mental operation . . .

MYSELF: Prophecy.

D.-H. KAHNWEILER: Yes, it is a kind of prophecy. I would call it "pictorial premonition." I was at his home a few days ago and I saw him working. Even at the moment when he begins work on the linoleum, he foresees or divines the final result . . .

MYSELF: But how did he happen to begin working with linoleum?

D.-H. KAHNWEILER: By chance, as usual. Do you remember the time, about 1945, when he began going to Mourlot and working in lithography? It was still cold in his studio then, and he preferred working in a well-heated place. It was for that purely material reason that he interested himself in lithography. It's somewhat the same thing with the linoleum. In the south, where he can't see his proofs immediately, he has no interest in etching or lithography. He has to send a plate or the stone to Paris, to get a proof of each state. It's too complicated and it bores him. He has done very little of that kind of work since he has been living down there. For the linoleum, however, he has found the man he needs, in Vallauris: a young printer who brings him in the morning a proof of the plate he cut the night before. It's this speed in seeing results that stimulates him. And that explains all of these marvelous plates he has been making recently . . .

Studying the linoleum prints again, I remark that the brilliance of their colors reminds me a little of Matisse's cutout paper arrangements.

D.-H. KAHNWEILER: Oh, no, I do not agree with you there! Picasso has used colors just as bold as these at several periods of his life, even as far back as the cubist period. And do you remember the canvases he did about 1932–1933?

MYSELF: The period of the *Femme au Miroir,* about 1932?

D.-H. KAHNWEILER: Yes. And all of those canvases where the forms are set off by heavy black lines? They had the same sort of brilliance of color as stained glass windows. But Matisse has nothing to do with it! I don't mean by that that Picasso wasn't very fond of him though. Did you know that, one day when Matisse was confined to bed, Picasso heard that he had mentioned being unhappy because he could not go to see his latest work, so he loaded a whole collection of his most recent paintings into his automobile and took them to the Hotel Regina in Nice, to show them to Matisse himself? He thought that it would please him, and that was what he wanted to do. Yes, Picasso liked Matisse, and admired his painting . . .

I tell Kahnweiler the story of the El Greco that was for sale during the war, and how Picasso, having compared it with his Matisse, had declared: "Decidedly, I prefer my Matisse!"

D.-H. KAHNWEILER: Picasso's passion for El Greco is not quite so great as it once was. There can be no denying Greco's influence on him, but as he matured he tended to draw away from him and become closer and closer to Velázquez, who is now, undoubtedly, the painter he appreciates most. He still likes some of Greco's portraits, but he no longer has such great admiration for his compositions. As for myself, my great passion is still Rembrandt. I place him above either El Greco or Velázquez. In addition to his qualities as a painter, there is a radiant, incomparable human warmth to his work. And no matter what people may think today, this is an essential quality to me. Picasso has it too . . .

I tell him that Sabartés does not share Picasso's admiration for Matisse.

D.-H. KAHNWEILER: There is a very simple reason for that. To Sabartés, there is not now, there never has been, and there never will be any painter but Picasso: this is not the greatest painter of all time, but the only one, the unique. The case of Sabartés is unique in itself . . . How is he? He has recovered quite rapidly and quite well from that paralytic stroke, which can be very dangerous at his age. Of course, a part of his body is still somewhat paralyzed, but his morale is good and he is back at work. I had dinner with him at his home the other day. He had just come back from a trip to Barcelona. He is completely absorbed in the Picasso Museum there . . .

While I am taking my photographs, Kahnweiler scans the newspapers and suddenly cries out:

"The philosopher Gaston Bachelard has just died. He was seventy-eight, the same age as myself. And we were born on almost the same day: I was born on June 25, 1884, and he was born on June 27 . . ."

When I leave him, Kahnweiler gives me directions for driving to his country home at Saint-Hilaire, near Châlo-Saint-Mars. We have been invited for lunch, next Sunday. "Zette and Michel (Louise Leris and her husband) were very sorry that they could not be there. They have gone to Africa, for an ethnographic conference. You will see them when they return . . ."

## *Sunday, October 21, 1962*

We leave for Daniel-Henry Kahnweiler's quite early in the morning. The weather has been gray and unpleasant for several days, and I was afraid that it was going to remain that way. Today, however, the sky is cloudless and a warm southern sun floods the countryside. Kahnweiler's property, "The Priory" of Saint-Hilaire, is magnificently situated on a hill overlooking the valley and a long lane of poplars. The outer courtyard, adjoining the ruins of an ivy-covered Benedictine chapel, provides us with our first surprise. An enormous statue stands here, eighteen to twenty feet in height and resembling a giant insect having just emerged from its chrysalis. The pieces of its wooden framework are still lying around it on the lawn. It is undoubtedly Picasso's work. Since the sun will soon be turning, I take a few photos of it at once. As I am doing so, Daniel-Henry Kahnweiler comes out to meet us through a little door in the wall which separates this courtyard from the garden surrounding the house.[57] He looks pink and cheerful but is somewhat disturbed by the presence of our dog, Fuego; his own dog, a boxer, is not very friendly with other dogs.

D.-H. KAHNWEILER: This statue was originally intended for the Salon d'Automne. Then we changed our minds. I had it set up here, and here it will stay. The work required more than a month, and was just finished about two weeks ago. Wooden frameworks had to be made first, for each of the different planes: it's a kind of architecture in reinforced concrete. It weighs several tons, so it also had to have a solid foundation. It's a Norwegian sculptor, Carl Nesjar, who invented the technique and also this material, a mixture of gray gravel and cement. The original forms have a smooth surface. But the gravel content can be exposed by blasting it with a kind of pistol that fires sand, and the bluish, grainy surfaces that result provide a contrast to the surfaces which are left clear and smooth. You should see this Norwegian at work with his strange weapon, wearing a helmet that makes him look like a Martian . . . The statue is called *L'Ange,* and Douglas Cooper wants to set up another one, just like it, on his property at Uzès.

MYSELF: Picasso told me about this Norwegian sculptor and showed me models of a house in Barcelona with great cement surfaces on which he was planning to carve out some graffiti.

D.-H. KAHNWEILER: It is finished now, done in the same process as this. It's a curved surface, about twelve feet high and covering the whole corner of the building. The effect is really striking . . .

Guided by Kahnweiler, we make a tour of the ruins of the Benedictine chapel, which was demolished during the revolution. A few of the twelfth-century cornices are almost all that remains. Sheltered beneath the great trees around the chapel, there are two isolated columns, linked by an arch and covered with ivy.

D.-H. KAHNWEILER: Henri Laurens made them for Jacques Doucet, the collector. The capitals are cubist in form. He also sculpted a fountain for Doucet, who kept all of these works in his country house. He wanted to reconcile an old house in the country with modern works of art. Picasso's *Les Demoiselles d'Avignon* was imbedded in the wall of the staircase. After Doucet's death, I bought the Laurens' sculptures, and *Les Demoiselles d'Avignon* went to the Museum of Modern Art in New York. You will see the fountain in the garden, down below. I also have *La Sirène,* by Laurens; it's in front of the house. In this part of the Île-de-France, the terra cotta is as weatherproof as stone and takes on a very good patina. Its handsome rose color is already turning to green in some places . . .

The Priory is a beautiful house, built during the First Empire. Kahnweiler bought it about ten years ago. I ask him if Picasso has ever come here.

D.-H. KAHNWEILER: Only once, eight or nine years ago, before he went to live permanently in the south. He has not come back to Paris at all, since the spring of 1955. He is still very much interested in everything that happens there, keeps himself very well informed, wants to see all of the photographs of his exhibitions, but without displaying the slightest desire to be present at them or to leave the south. Obviously, he has not seen The Priory as it is now. The house had to be almost entirely rebuilt and the garden replanted. I had seen some gardens in Germany that I liked very much, done by a landscape architect. So I brought him here. It was he who planted everything you see, all of those perennial plants which are rather rare in France but very common and very well liked in Germany because they keep their green foliage. But there are others, too. These young bushes are Judas trees . . .

MYSELF: I saw them along the Bosphorus in the spring, laden with purple flowers. They were magnificent . . .

D.-H. KAHNWEILER: Mine have white blossoms. They flowered this year. And can you see the apple trees, and the pear trees on the espaliers? They bore a great deal of fruit, except for those that were placed too close to the wall. I am having them transplanted.

My host also shows me the kitchen garden, with its rows of cabbages, tomatoes, and greens. A trifle surprised by the lively interest in trees, flowers, and fruits displayed by this man who has spent his life in the commercial world of art dealers, I ask him if he really likes the country.

D.-H. KAHNWEILER: I am primarily a city man myself. Without Zette, I would never have thought of having a house in the country. It was she who looked for it and found it. And we were fortunate to have found The Priory. Saint-Hilaire is the last village which is still completely surrounded by trees and parks. We are just at the frontier of Beauce, which stretches from Étampes to the forest of Orléans. Beyond that, there are just wheat fields, a monotonous plain . . . As you know, my gallery is open on Saturday, but only during the morning. We leave every Saturday afternoon for Saint-Hilaire, and stay here until Monday afternoon.

We have an apéritif on the terrace. Kahnweiler introduces us to his two sisters-in-law. Berthe is the wife of the artist Lascaux, who is also here today. Their daughter married the artist Vilato, Picasso's nephew. I ask Kahnweiler for news of Picasso.

D.-H. KAHNWEILER: Michel and Zette saw him two weeks ago and found him in excellent form. He is continuing his series of linoleum prints. Now he is doing some heads of bearded men, very beautiful it seems. I spoke to him on the phone just yesterday, as a matter of fact. He told me himself that he was satisfied with them. When I telephoned him, he was just about to leave for the beach in Cannes, with Jacqueline. They go for a swim every day. The end of October and he is eighty-two years old, isn't it wonderful? And he has always been so concerned about his health! In his youth he thought that he was tubercular. He was afraid of having every imaginable disease. In reality, he has never been seriously ill. Basically, he had nothing but neuroses. And do you know how he took care of himself? With cat skins! Several times I went to see him and found him in bed, with his shoulders covered with cat fur. The enormous amount of work he turns out gives the impression that he must overwork. Not at all: he watches over himself and takes care of himself very carefully. Even now he has himself examined frequently by his doctor; the same doctor, as a matter of fact, who took care of Matisse. Whenever he feels a need to rest and regain his strength, he simply stays in bed for two or three days . . .

MYSELF: Has he settled permanently in his new property at Mougins?

D.-H. KAHNWEILER: Permanently? No one would venture to say that. There is never anything permanent with him. In any case, he is happy there, for the moment at least. It's a beautiful house—it's called Notre-Dame de Vie—equipped with several bathrooms, very pleasant, very comfortable. Picasso has added an annex to serve as a studio. And he himself told me very proudly one day that there is a *white* telephone in every room. The modern aspect of his newest installation is apparent the minute you reach the entrance gate: visitors have to announce themselves by speaking into a microphone in the wall. And there are high walls all around it, to protect Picasso from indiscreet intruders . . .

MYSELF: And *La Californie*?

D.-H. KAHNWEILER: Almost all of his possessions are still there. He goes back every now and then to pick up something he might want. And if he decides to spend a night there, he can do it, because even the beds are still in place.

MYSELF: And Vauvenargues?

D.-H. KAHNWEILER: It is a magnificent place, but too vast, too severe. Even the landscape is so sad. When I went there for the first time, I mentioned it to him. He answered: "Too vast? I will fill it up. Too severe? You are forgetting that I am a Spaniard and that I enjoy sadness." Nevertheless, he never liked Vauvenargues enough to live there. As for Jacqueline, she is actually afraid in that isolated, mournful château.

MYSELF: Picasso wanted to have his own Escorial.

D.-H. KAHNWEILER: That's about it . . . a whim. He stays there sometimes, when he goes to the bullfights in Arles or in Nîmes. Aix-en-Provence is on the way . . .

I tell Kahnweiler of my surprise at having found Paulo's family at Boisgeloup.

D.-H. KAHNWEILER: After the war, about 1946, Picasso wanted to go back to Boisgeloup himself. I accompanied him. We found the property in a state of total abandon. The grass had grown wild everywhere; it was waist deep in places. That was when he first thought of giving it to Paulo. He is a nice, frank young man. I like him and I also like his young wife.

I ask my host to tell me what he knows about Manolo.

D.-H. KAHNWEILER: In his youth, Manolo lived in frightful poverty. So, in order to live, he became a kind of amateur pickpocket. Unfortunately this became "his legend," and it did a great deal of harm to his career as an artist. On another level, Erik Satie was also the victim of a legend. He acquired the habit of giving fantastic, farfetched titles to his compositions. This gave rise to the belief that his music itself was fantastic and farfetched. The fact is that Satie was a very great composer, and his music is nothing if not serious. But the public is just beginning to recognize it today. Manolo was a good sculptor. Of course, he understood nothing of cubism, but his statues have strength, a kind of robust, peasant force. You undoubtedly know some of the stories of his petty thievery. I can tell you one of them, because I myself was the victim of it. After he left Paris and went to Céret, and then to Calda se Monbury in Spain, I sent him some money every month. One day he wrote to me that he was working on a "very large sculpture," and that because of this I must double the amount of my monthly remittance, which I did for several months. When he finally sent me this "very large sculpture," it turned out to be a little statue, about sixteen inches tall. I demanded an explanation, and do you know what he wrote to me? "If my statue seems small, it is because the woman is in a crouching position. If she were to stand up, she would be very, very large." But I was not angry with him. No one, in fact, was very angry with him. Manolo was a person who was full of charm and spirit. His nerve and vitality were inexhaustible.

We talked for a time about Sabartés' recent trip to Catalonia. I asked Kahnweiler about the Picasso Museum in Barcelona.

D.-H. KAHNWEILER: It is a magnificent fourteenth-century residence of the nobility, the Aguilar palace on the Calle Montcada. But, like the majority of that kind of building in Paris, it was completely run-down, and had been turned into a warehouse. It has since been very well restored, and they have even discovered some sixteenth-century frescoes on the walls. Picasso gave the museum his series of *Las Meninas,* along with all of the preparatory drawings. Theoretically, there was to have been a formal inaugural ceremony for the museum this autumn. Sabartés and I were scheduled to be present for it. But, because of the floods in Catalonia—and primarily for political reasons, I'm sure of that—it was opened without any ceremony at all . . .

MYSELF: And what about the Picasso Museum in Málaga?

D.-H. KAHNWEILER: It exists, but without even a sample of Picasso's work! It is really odd! I visited it some time ago. Do you know what you can see there? All sorts of stereotyped paintings by Málagan artists, friends of Don Ruiz, Picasso's father . . . As it turns out, Sabartés is only going to give the Málaga museum his collection of Picasso's graphic work . . . But that is of very great value.

MYSELF: And the Vilato family? Will they give the Barcelona museum the canvases they have? Picasso's relatives showed me their collection one day, and I saw some of his earliest canvases, such as *La Science et la Charité,* and also some of his more recent works.

D.-H. KAHNWEILER: The Vilatos are not rich. They could not give their collection to the museum, though I am sure they would like to sell it. But that would depend on the price the museum could afford to pay . . .

Luncheon is served in the sun-filled dining room. On one wall, there is a Picasso still life and some drawings of Henri Laurens. An abstract fresco in the bright colors of Fernand Léger covers all of another wall.

D.-H. KAHNWEILER: It is probably his last work. He painted it here, directly on the wall, scarcely two weeks before his death. Do you see that little place where the paint has run? Léger intended to come back here and go over it. It is still there, and I scarcely notice it anymore . . . Léger really had a great gift for large mural decorations. But he did very few of them, for lack of commissions. The state turned a deaf ear to any such projects. It must be admitted that, in France, only the Catholic Church has provided any real stimulus for the great contemporary artists: Matisse, Léger, Rouault, Le Corbusier. You have to go to Vence, to Ronchamp, to Sancellemoz, to Rocquencourt, if you want to see any real synthesis of contemporary art. Father Couturier deserves a great deal of credit for having obtained acceptance of his views from a clergy that was often reticent and sometimes actively hostile. It was not an easy task. The objection was made, and not without reason, that the majority of "his artists" were nonbelievers. In spite of that, however, the most beautiful work Léger ever did is certainly the windows for Rocquencourt. I find it quite extraordinary that this religious work, by a painter who was both a communist and an atheist, does not in any way clash with religious sentiment. Léger simply utilized the elements of the Crucifixion best suited to his art: the hammer, the nails, the sponge, the dice, the ladder, etc. . . . In other words, all of the objects he normally employed . . .

MYSELF: He did almost the same thing in the church on the plateau of Assy. The whole façade is a mosaic representing the attributes of the Virgin: the throne, the crown, etc. . . . And Picasso? Do you think that he would have done many more large frescoes if he had had commissions for them?

D.-H. KAHNWEILER: Picasso is another matter. He doesn't like the idea of commissions very much. Even *Guernica* and *War and Peace* were created spontaneously. And it was almost against his will that he accepted the commission for the UNESCO panel. He gave in at last only because of the insistence of Georges Salles. And to tell the truth, he was not rewarded for his effort. None of his other works have been so poorly received.

MYSELF: Through the fault of the architects! They offered him a very large surface, but it is one that cannot be seen from a suitable distance. That is what is really shocking. As soon as one moves back a little, the view of the panel is cut off by a footbridge. And do you know what that footbridge serves for? As a passageway between the two auditoriums for the electrician who handles the projectors.

D.-H. KAHNWEILER: That footbridge surprised me, too. I asked the architect, Breuer, the reason for it. He answered me: "I put it there to create a rupture."

MYSELF: It's that "rupture" which prevents anyone from seeing Picasso's fresco properly . . .

D.-H. KAHNWEILER: But you did a panel for UNESCO too, didn't you?

MYSELF: *The Reeds,* twenty-two feet by ten feet. And I have no complaints. It is well located. As the author of that panel, I was invited to the dinner that was given for all of the artists who took part in the decorations for the UNESCO Building. We were all there, except for Picasso and Miró. And what a collection of architects! Le Corbusier, Nervi, Breuer, Gropius, Zehrfuss. At the conclusion of the dinner, Evans, the director of UNESCO, stood up to propose a toast. He had had his share of whiskey and good wine, and brought his fist down on the table with a thump that made us jump: "It's done! It exists! And we are the ones who did it!" Then he added, with a very sly expression: "And now, our friend Georges Salles will tell us in all sincerity what he thinks of Picasso's panel." Georges Salles started to stand up, seeming a trifle surprised, but Le Corbusier was already on his feet: "All that I can say—and I think you can trust my experience and my judgment—is that this panel of Picasso's is a masterpiece. It's of no importance what anyone thinks about it today. Its beauty will be clearly evident in ten years, twenty years . . ." And he suggested that a telegram of congratulations be sent to Picasso, signed by everyone present. And that's what was done.

We took our places around the dining room table.

D.-H. KAHNWEILER: This caviar is fresh. It just arrived, directly from Moscow. Nadia Léger brought it back, and the bottles of vodka too. She spent several weeks there, making preparations for the big Fernand Léger exhibition that is to be held in December. It will be the largest Léger exhibition that has ever been put together, as a matter of fact. Everything that is now in the Léger Museum will be hung there, and many other canvases as well. I loaned them some myself. I think—and I hope—that it may prove a turning point in the artistic life of the Soviet Union, which shares with East Germany the distinction of being the most backward of any of the countries behind the Iron Curtain. By comparison, Czechoslovakia is positively avant-garde, followed by Poland and Hungary. I am going to Russia myself for the opening of this exhibition. Michel and Zette will accompany me. Nadia Léger has asked for all of our head sizes, so that she can order fur hats for us. In the month of December, it may be very cold in Moscow . . .

Kahnweiler, who will soon be eighty, still has a splendid appetite. He serves himself repeatedly with heaping spoonfuls of caviar and empties several glasses of vodka. The main course is a delicious duck à l'orange, followed by cheeses and a *tarte au chocolat.* We begin talking about art collectors.

MYSELF: I recently saw the collection of Madame Jeanne Walter. It is much richer than I had imagined it. They are making alterations in the Orangerie to house it. It seems that Paul Guillaume's widow stipulated that the paintings must be exhibited just as they are in her home, with the furniture, the rugs, the hangings, the chandeliers . . . That was an express condition of her gift.

D.-H. KAHNWEILER: We should always be grateful to collectors who bequeath their collections to the State. But I reproach them for just this matter of posing conditions. It is stupid to demand that a collection should be exhibited as a collection. What sense does that make? It does nothing but prevent the works from being exhibited in a more logical order: all of the Renoirs, all of the Cézannes, all of the Picassos, together, or possibly a grouping by school or by period. This is the only form of presentation that is really worth while. The ensemble of such and such a collector, no matter how praiseworthy it may be, is of only very relative interest. It is much more logical to break up these collections, but of course the name of the donor should be shown on each painting . . .

MYSELF: Camondo was another one who stipulated this same condition when he bequeathed his collection to the State.

D.-H. KAHNWEILER: Yes, and for a long time there was a Camondo collection in the Louvre. But since it was a ridiculous thing, the authorities were eventually forced to disperse it.

I asked him what has become of the collection of Roger Dutilleul.

D.-H. KAHNWEILER: Since his death, his nephew, Jean Masurel, has the collection in his home in Roubaix. He loves painting himself and would undoubtedly have gone on with his uncle's admirable collection, but unfortunately his wife does not appreciate paintings as much as he. Roger Dutilleul, there was a great collector! And what a delightful man! Did you know that he was one of my first, if not my very first client? I was also very fond of Wilhelm Uhde, such a cultivated man, so spiritual . . . He played a very important part in the evolution of modern art. And he has not been given the place he deserves. He lived in Paris from the very beginning of the century and knew Picasso before I did. It was he, in fact, who told me about a strange canvas called *Les Demoiselles d'Avignon*, and urged me to go to see it. Uhde was a German citizen, as I was myself, and he lost his beautiful collection after the 1914 war. It was when he returned to France that he began collecting the naïve painters. He was one of the first to discover and love the Douanier Rousseau . . .

After this, we discussed some of the Spanish painters, friends of Picasso's.

MYSELF: Oscar Dominguez had an astounding facility, a kind of mimicry, which enabled him to assimilate all kinds of techniques. During the occupation, when he came to Picasso's studio almost every day, he appropriated Picasso's palette to such an extent that there were times when it was difficult to distinguish his work.

D.-H. KAHNWEILER, *with an ironic smile:* He carried his mimicry a little too far . . . But Picasso has always been very indulgent toward anyone who was inspired by his work, even though some of them have actually painted fake Picassos. A clever painter who has not been able to make a name for himself will always be tempted to turn out forgeries. One day I spoke to Picasso about the forgeries in his name, and told him that something must be done. Do you know what he answered? "How can you expect me to lodge a complaint against forgers? I would be certain to find myself, standing in front of a judge, face to face with a group of handcuffed Spanish artists—my friends. So . . ." One day, to help out a painter from South America, Picasso gave him one of his pastels. This painter came to see me and offered to sell it. I bought it from him. A few days later, Pierre Loeb came to see me, in a state of panic. He told me: "I have just bought this pastel by Picasso. And now I have been told that it is identical with one which you already own!" We compared the two pastels. His was a copy. This same artist had made three or four of them and sold them all. How did Picasso react? Believe it or not, he was thoroughly amused. And he reimbursed his friend's victims from his own pocket. It seems that the painter had committed these frauds because he wanted to return to his own country and could not afford a ticket. As soon as he did get home, he sent a telegram to Picasso, saying: "Pablo, I am a bandit . . ."

When we have finished lunch, Kahnweiler takes us on a tour of his house. There are four or five canvases in every room including many Picassos, especially the recent works. Perhaps the most curious of these is a slightly lascivious nude with a protuberant belly and a very clearly indicated cleft in the pubis, offering her feminine charms from a place on the wall just above the bed. But there are also some still lifes of Juan Gris, several paintings by André Masson, and examples of Kermadec, Rouvre, Beaudin, and Lascaux. On one wall, there is the very handsome portrait of Madame Kahnweiler painted by Derain, which I had known only through reproductions. A beautiful faïence table by Picasso especially delights me. The library contains a large Picasso painting of a goat, done in varying shades of green. The preparatory drawings for it are hung along the stairway. Kahnweiler takes a tiny goat from a display case and demonstrates the movement of the legs, which are made from copper wire. It too is by Picasso. In this same display case, I see a curious mask by Juan Gris, made for a costume ball. All of the drawings and paintings Picasso has given to Kahnweiler are signed: "For D.H.K., his friend Picasso," or: "For his friend D.H.K., Picasso."

Night is falling as we leave The Priory.

*Thursday, November 27, 1962*

At the apartment of Louise and Michel Leiris, 52 *bis* Quai des Grands-Augustins. A noiseless glass cage carries us up and deposits us on the fifth floor. The five rooms of the apartment are set one beside another and all look out over the Seine. Through the curtain of plane trees and poplars, already denuded by the autumn, one can see the Palais de Justice, the Quai des Orfèvres, the Sainte-Chapelle, the Pont Neuf, and the Vert-Galant, one of the most beautiful landscapes of Paris. Alas, it too is invaded by the ever-increasing swarm of automobiles, disfiguring it like some insidious disease of the skin.

Michel Leiris receives us in the "music room," where Picasso's *Desire Caught by the Tail* was played for the first time, during the occupation. The pictures on the walls are all very handsome—Juan Gris, Braque, André Masson, some Légers of the cubist period, and especially Picasso. But it is the rugs and the chairs which give this apartment its particular stamp. One walks and sits on works of arts. One of the rugs—the most beautiful one, in tones of beige, chestnut, and gray—is by Henri Laurens; another, in brighter colors, is by Miró. The chairs in the dining room, lined up around the table, are all by Juan Gris, woven in Aubusson tapestry from his designs.

Kahnweiler has just returned from his gallery and offers us an apéritif. He talks of his recent visit to London, where he had gone for an important sale.

D.-H. KAHNWEILER: When I was young, I lived in London, and in later years I stayed there often. My brother and sister still live there. I find it extraordinary that this country, which considers itself superior to others, which was and still is in some fields, should permit itself to be left so far behind. They are deluding themselves with illusions now. Simply in the matter of comfort, London has become the least comfortable city in the world. Central heating has spread through the entire world, but in London it exists only in a few rare and very expensive apartment buildings and hotels.

Kahnweiler takes us to see his own apartment, which is more or less separate from the central rooms. Near the bed, I notice the splendid portrait Picasso did of him in charcoal, and of which there is also a lithograph. The large portrait of Madame Kahnweiler, one of the best-known works of André Derain, is in this room too. The other walls are hung with some paintings of Fernand Léger and a small Van Dongen.

D.-H. KAHNWEILER: I am not a collector, but an art dealer. So I keep only those paintings which I really love and which my walls will permit me to hang. My collection is primarily sentimental. But once I have made a decision, nothing in the world could separate me from my paintings. Zette unearthed this apartment during the occupation. I was hiding in the south with my wife at that time. Our old apartment was in Boulogne, but the rural charm of that area could not stand up against the growth of an industrial city. It became uninhabitable. My sister-in-law managed to bring all of our things here. When we returned to Paris after the liberation, we had the pleasant surprise of finding our own apartment again, on the Quai des Grands-Augustins now, a stone's throw from Picasso and exactly as it was in Boulogne . . .

In the library, whose shelves are crammed with books from floor to ceiling, a very beautiful wooden fireplace is being dismantled.

D.-H. KAHNWEILER: I am very upset about sacrificing my fireplace. But I need the room it takes up to store my art books. It will be replaced by more shelves . . .

Everywhere I go these days, an avalanche of books has flooded the rooms, blocked the corridors . . . The "book problem" in apartments is almost as crucial as the "traffic problem" in the streets. Everyone I know is plagued by it. The time is not so far off when one will not be able to go out in the street because of the automobiles or return home because of the clutter of books.

MYSELF: What about Picasso? What does he do with his books? I have never seen any on shelves. He has never had a library. But he must have a great many books . . .

D.-H. KAHNWEILER: Ever since I have know him, his books have always been packed away. From time to time, when he has to make room, he has them stored in cases. He has cases of books everywhere, in Paris, in Cannes, Vauvenargues . . . Picasso maintains that he knows everything that is in these cases, that it is easy for him to find any book or object he may want. Until his stroke, it was Sabartés who was delegated to rule this particular kingdom. Now, it is up to Zette and myself to find whatever he asks for. Little by little, everything he left in Paris has been sent to the south. I couldn't tell you how many trucks it required. I doubt that there is very much left, even at the rue des Grands-Augustins. And, in spite of Picasso's lists, his prodigious memory and his absentee supervision, there are some things that simply cannot be found. For instance, it has been impossible for us to put our hands on a series of engravings done about 1930, very richly colored. But Picasso maintains that he put them in one of those cases . . .

## INDEX

H41